D1482764

The Sunflower Forest

The publisher gratefully acknowledges the
generous contribution to this book
provided by Sally Lilienthal
as a member of the Literati Circle
of the University of California Press Associates.

The Sunflower Forest

Ecological Restoration and the New
Communion with Nature

William R. Jordan III

UNIVERSITY OF CALIFORNIA PRESS
Berkeley / Los Angeles / London

University of California Press
Berkeley and Los Angeles, California

University of California Press, Ltd.
London, England

Library of Congress Cataloguing-in-Publication Data

Jordan, William R., 1944–.
    The sunflower forest: ecological restoration and the new communion
with nature / William R. Jordan III.
        p.   cm.
    Includes bibliographical references and index.
    ISBN 0-520-23320-4 (cloth : alk. paper).
    1. Restoration ecology.   I. Title.

QH541.15.R45 J67   2003
333.95′153—dc21   2002005538

Manufactured in Canada

11   10   09   08   07   06   05   04   03
10   9   8   7   6   5   4   3   2   1

For Buffy

and in memory of
Kate and Bill
and
Florence and John

Contents

Introduction   1

1. Weeding Key Biscayne   10

2. The Challenge of Reinhabitation   28

3. Paradigms of Community   54

4. Awareness: Restoration as a Way of Seeing, and as
   Work and Play   74

5. The Exchange: Restoration as Repayment, and the
   Gift of Ecological Immortality   96

6. Value and Make-Believe: A Primer on Performance   137

7. Sacrifice and Celebration: Restoration as a
   Performing Art   160

8. Conservation and Community: Restoration, the
   Environment, and Environmentalism   195

Notes   205

Selected Readings   237

Index   239

Introduction

Not long ago a friend came to me with a complaint. She had just come from a meeting of her professional society at which a colleague of mine had given an address. His topic had been the conservation of natural areas, a subject on which he is expert and speaks eloquently. Yet my friend, a thoughtful, well-educated woman who takes a serious interest in environmental issues and is well informed about goings-on in the scientific community, was dismayed.

"He just had nothing to say that offered any prospect for saving these places," she told me. "After the talk we asked him questions—what can we do about this? But the response was the same. He just didn't have anything to say that provided a basis for any kind of hope."

This book is in a way a response to my friend's dismay, and my answer to the question she and her colleagues were raising. It is a summary of reflections, reading, and conversations on the act of ecological restoration, carried out over twenty-two years in the course of my work at the University of Wisconsin Arboretum in Madison, where I was in charge of publications and public outreach from 1977 to 1999. When I began this work I had no idea it would ever have any relevance to questions such as those my friend raised about the future of natural landscapes. I was simply trying to make sense of the restoration effort that had been undertaken at the Arboretum during the 1930s when a handful of faculty, including the pioneering conservationist Aldo Leopold, decided to recreate a collection of historic—or "native"—ecological communities on several hundred acres of university-owned land on the outskirts of Madison.

Their effort was remarkably successful and resulted in the restoration, or partial restoration, of a half-dozen major ecological community types covering roughly 300 acres. But as a model of conservation, it had proved curiously sterile. Leopold himself had lost much of his confidence in the prospects for environmental management by the 1940s, and his skepticism set the tone for the environmental movement that took shape a generation later. In the late 1970s, when I showed up at the Arboretum, no one anywhere, with the exception of the occasional landscape architect and a handful of people involved in work such as the reclamation of land disturbed by mining, had any interest in restoration. Environmentalists almost universally ignored it, seeing it at best as a distraction from the serious work of preservation, and at worst as a threat—a false promise that could be used to undermine arguments for preservation.

Yet restoration had more to offer environmentalism than environmentalists realized. A major concern of the environmentalism that took shape in the 1960s and 1970s, for example, was the conservation of natural landscapes and ecosystems. Arguing for the protection of natural areas, environmentalists stressed their vulnerability, often insisting that they were not only "fragile" or susceptible to human or "outside" influences but were actually "irreplaceable." Though understandable, this sort of rhetoric and the thinking it represented had devastating implications for conservation. It implied that conservation is a one-way street, essentially nothing more than a delaying action, that might slow the inevitable decline of natural landscapes toward eventual extinction but can never reverse it. It also conveyed the idea, often expressed quite explicitly by environmentalists, that the influence of human beings on natural landscapes is invariably negative and destructive: though we may take from such a landscape, we can never give anything back to it.

Such thinking and rhetoric may at times project a superficial optimism, celebrating the gains achieved by an agency such as the National Park Service or an organization like the Nature Conservancy in acquiring natural lands for preservation. But at bottom it is deeply pessimistic. And it was this pessimism, clearly evident in my colleague's presentation, that my friend found so discouraging.

Restoration is important, I gradually realized, not because it offers a neat way of solving the problem of habitat loss in all situations, but because it offers the *possibility* of actively reversing environmental damage, at least in some situations. Introducing a positive factor into the conservation equation, restoration complicates it but also rescues environmentalists from an unrelieved negativity about the future of natural landscapes. In addition, since restoration is an active process—in fact, a kind of gardening—it offers something that has eluded environmentalists for the better part of a century—a way to "use" classic landscapes such as prairies and forests, actually participating in their ecology, without changing their character or using them up. Granted, the Arboretum planners had achieved this result on a modest, one might even say symbolic, scale. Even so, the fact that restoration was possible at all opened up the prospect of a positive relationship with natural landscapes that environmentalists had overlooked.

Equally important, I eventually realized, were the limitations of restoration, and the troubling questions it raised about natural landscapes, our relationship with them, and our proper role in them. These included questions about our right to assume authority over other species, the feasibility of restoration on an environmentally significant scale, and the nature or authenticity of restored—or "artificial"—natural ecosystems. Such difficult, in some ways painful, questions are easy to overlook in a "preserved" landscape where we maintain the pretense of a "pristine" landscape unaffected by "outside" (human) influences. But they are impossible to overlook in a restored landscape where both the defects in the restored system and the ongoing process of restoration itself constantly bring them to our attention.

Reflecting on these questions, I wound up exploring ways other cultures have found for answering them, drawing mainly on the record of anthropology and religious experience. This eventually led to some ideas that carried me beyond the mere optimism suggested by the possibility of restoration to the basis for hope my friend was looking for—and not finding—in environmental thinking.

By the early 1980s I had come to believe that the work that had been going on at the Arboretum for the previous half century had a crucial contribution to make to environmentalism. Basically, it combined the best elements of two forms of environmentalism—the conservationist's willingness to participate in the ecology of a natural landscape, and the environmentalist's insistence on the inherent value of that landscape, independent of its value to humans—into a single act that linked engagement with total respect. This act, it seemed to me, provided the basis for a new kind of environmentalism—actually a new environmental paradigm—that might remedy the shortcomings of these earlier paradigms, neither of which—who would dispute the point?—has proved adequate to the task of ensuring the survival of the world's natural landscapes or of providing the basis for a healthy relationship with them.

Certainly the practice of restoration raises questions that challenge various assumptions of the environmentalism of the past generation—that was why the conservationists who invented it had overlooked most of its value, and why the environmentalists of a later generation had ignored and resisted it. At the same time restoration itself is not a new idea, and in recent years it has gained wide acceptance as a conservation strategy. As this has happened, practitioners have begun to learn how to make the most of this work, both as a way of repairing damaged ecosystems and as a way of raising questions about them and forming relationships with them. During the past decade in particular, restoration has matured rapidly, not only as a technology, as a discipline, and as a conservation strategy, but also as a form of play and a context for negotiating the relationship between our own species and the rest of nature. All this provides a basis for a measure of optimism, and ultimately of hope for the future of the natural landscape.

Discussions about the environment and environmental problems often rely on ethical formulations and invoke virtues such as restraint, humility, respect, foresight, simplicity, thrift, and so forth in our dealings with other species and with the rest of nature generally. Doubtless this is good advice, but it is not what I am concerned with here. What I propose is not so much an ethic as a way *to* an ethic, a process by which we might create the values on which any system of ethics is based while giving those values a hold on the consciences of individuals or groups of people—a way, as anthropologist Victor Turner said, of making the obligatory desirable. This process begins, I suggest, in an impulse of regard for nature or the "other"—reflecting perhaps the innate tendency to affiliate with life that biologist E. O. Wilson has called "biophilia"—expressed in a gesture of respect, or perhaps in a feeling of shame or guilt that seeks some means of expression or resolution. Both respect and shame, I believe, happen more or less spontaneously when we reach out and engage nature reflexively and self-consciously through any kind of deliberate action. Such acts, made more reflexive through the psychological and spiritual technologies of performance and ritual, then become contexts for the creation of values such as community, beauty, and meaning, which in turn provide the foundation on which a system of ethics may be built. The point is that without this first, emotionally demanding process of value creation, talk of ethics will always be just that—talk, and talk that has little hold on either the imagination or the conscience because it takes values for granted and fails to provide ways of coming to terms with the most problematic aspects of the experience underlying the process of value creation. I also propose that when we don't do this work for ourselves in a deliberate and self-conscious way, we do it unself-consciously or carelessly, or we leave it for others to do. In either case we become the victims rather than the beneficiaries of these powerful technologies. In any event, my concern here is not with ethical principles, but with what might be called the technology of value creation, on which the formulation of ethical systems and the formation of conscience both depend. If there is any prescription here at all, it has to do with the idea that these technologies have, like any technology, certain basic elements of form, structure, and grammar that must be respected if they are to be effective. This is a prescription, but it is a content-free prescription, at least so far as end results are concerned. I offer it in the expectation that if it were followed the resulting values and ethical systems would reflect the peculiarities of region and group but would also converge toward basic, more or less universal values that I believe emerge from reflexive interaction with others.

I am aware that many readers will find this emphasis on performance and ritual puzzling, since we have learned to regard performance as of marginal or secondary importance, and ritual, which I understand to be a form of performance, as prescriptive—an intrinsically conservative social and psychological technology that serves mainly to perpetuate and impose conventional or officially sanctioned values. My thinking, however, is based on a very different idea of the nature of performance, which I have taken from the work of anthropologists Victor and Edith Turner, their son, literary critic Frederick Turner, and other scholars in anthropology, psychology, criticism, and comparative religion. In this understanding, ritual, though formulaic, is not essentially or purely prescriptive and, though it may have an important conservative function, is fundamentally creative. At the deepest level, ritual offers the only means we have of transcending, criticizing, or revising a morality or ethical formulation prescribed by authority or handed down by tradition. Most fundamentally, it is the means by which humans generate, recreate, and renew transcendent values such as community, meaning, beauty, love, and the sacred, on which both ethics and morality depend. In the absence of both a well grounded ritual sensibility and a repertory of rituals adequate to the various tasks at hand, the lower values of economics or power or top-down appeals to ethics and other prescriptive systems erode and override these higher values in the ongoing struggle to define what is valuable and how people should behave. Both failings, I believe, are characteristic of environmentalism and of modern Western societies generally. We in the United States are seeing this now, for example, in medicine, where, in the absence of means to create and renew the higher values associated with the work of healing, what was once a priestly or shamanistic vocation is in the process of being reduced to a mere technology and even to a merely commercial enterprise. The problem is that, as our grasp of the means of creating and renewing value weakens, we wind up living on the spiritual capital of the past. And so we find environmentalists constantly appealing to the higher values, and to ethical systems based on them, but offering no way to create these values or even gain access to them.

Finally, a comment on the environmental crisis and its role in this book. Discussions about the environment commonly focus on an environmental crisis of one kind or another, whether an external crisis of supply, as it were, or the internal one of attitude, value, and relationship. These discussions commonly reflect the assumption that this situation is unique—a peculiarity of modern or industrial or agricultural or, perhaps, patriarchal cultures.

My perspective on this is quite different. To begin with, though I am certainly prepared to take seriously the predictions of experts regarding matters such as overpopulation, acid rain, global warming, habitat destruction, or species extinctions, I am not willing to build my case on them. For one thing, the projections are always open to debate, if not over whether then at least over when catastrophe will occur, and there is always a danger of overstatement on both sides. More important, I am not willing to accept the idea that the prospect of a crisis is our best, most effective motive for action. I believe that positive goals are more effective in the long run, and I also believe that the challenge we face is ultimately a positive one—not of losing a species of plant that offers a cure for cancer, or of someday seeing water cover New York City, but the more important matter of learning to live graciously on this planet. This is not a novel problem, unique to modern or technically advanced cultures, but rather a problem that has challenged all people at all times. Solving it is one of the perennial tasks of culture, and I have become convinced over the years that the act of ecological restoration has a crucial role to play in carrying it out. Drawing attention to that role is my primary purpose in writing this book.

In writing about the act of restoration, I have drawn from the work of scholars in a number of disciplines. I suspect that many readers who are familiar with the environmental thinking and writing of the past few decades will be surprised at the sources of the ideas I bring together here. Many of them are either old books, or books that lie at or beyond the margins of environmental thinking. Others are not books at all, but conversations I have had with restorationists and scholars in various fields.

There are two reasons for this rather unsystematic procedure. First, much of the pioneering work on restoration has been done by practitioners outside the academy in the context of what amounts to an oral culture. Even now, with two journals devoted entirely to restoration, much of the best thinking in this area is not well represented in the formal literature, and with a few notable exceptions much of what has been written deals only with the technical aspects of the work and has proved to be of little use in helping me think through its value in a critical and constructive way.

Second, the environmental thinkers of the past generation, though reflecting a variety of perspectives, have had little to say about restoration and have uniformly failed to come to grips with the more problematic aspects of restoration specifically, or of our relationship with the rest of nature generally. This being the case, in my attempt to make sense of what has always seemed to me an interesting and beautiful, yet certainly problematic way of interacting with the landscape, I have had to proceed pretty much on my own. Basically, I have observed the process of restoration at the Arboretum and elsewhere, occasionally participating in it myself in a modest way, and I have kept this experience and the questions it raises in mind in the course of my reading and conversations.

In this way, I came across many ideas and connections that have proved useful. An important insight (at least for me) was the realization that since our relationships with other creatures have spiritual, psychological, and political as well as purely ecological dimensions, many of the ideas and institutions that make up and maintain the human community—liberalism, for example, or gift-exchange or sacrifice or initiation—are also relevant to the task of achieving community with the rest of nature. Other insights came about more or less by chance, as small, sometimes unintended, gifts from others. For example, a casual remark by a participant at a conference in 1988 first drew my attention to the notion that restoration had an interesting relation to ideas about rebirth and redemption. And my son, after taking a course in anthropology, introduced me to the practice of world-renewal rituals in traditional societies by performing a maintenance ceremony for a typewriter, complete with bell and returns, one evening in our living room. Still others suggested readings. Friends and colleagues introduced me to Leo Marx's writings on pastoral literature; to Mircea Eliade's books on world renewal, initiation, and other ritual traditions; to Marcel Mauss's work *The Gift;* and to R. W. B. Lewis's book on nineteenth-century American literature, which forms the basis for chapter 3. Other connections and ideas came in the course of my own reading, often in books I came across more or less by chance. I first encountered the writing of Fred Turner in *Harper's Magazine.* That led to a fruitful association with him, and eventually to an exploration of his parents' work, both of which inform many of the ideas I discuss here.

In short, this was less a scholarly enterprise than a purposeful browsing around looking for material that might prove useful in the task of making sense of the act of restoration. The result is a rather unusual juxtaposition of ideas and a new perspective on restoration and on environmentalism generally. Proceeding in this way, I am aware that I must have passed by many interesting and useful leads; and many of the ideas I explore will benefit from further development. I only hope that readers will keep in mind the kind of work this is—an attempt to make sense of a form of environmental management that gradually developed into an outline, certainly more ambitious than I intended at the outset, of a new way of thinking about and interacting with natural landscapes.

Insofar as the book is a critique of environmentalism from the perspective provided by the act of ecological restoration, it is a friendly critique, intended to strengthen environmentalism, not to question its importance or its objectives regarding conservation of the classic landscapes that are my primary concern. Though I consider myself an environmentalist and have devoted my career to work on behalf of the environment, for many years I have felt that our various environmentalisms, diverse as they are, share serious weaknesses, perhaps most evident in their inability to provide the basis for a satisfactory relationship between culture and nature as it is represented by classic landscapes. In my view, what might now be called the restoration movement offers a way to correct this weakness.

I am indebted to scholars and colleagues in an unusually wide range of disciplines for help in putting together and developing the ideas outlined in this book. Since the conversation has gone on for so long, I cannot acknowledge everyone who has contributed to it. Those to whom I owe a special debt of gratitude include John Aber, Kat Anderson, Peter Bowler, Sue Bratton, John Cairns, J. Baird Callicott, Andy Clewell, Ed Collins, Steve Davis, Dave Egan, Ron Engel, Peter Fabian, Cheryl Foster, Virginia Gibson, Mike Gilpin, Paul Gobster, Ron Grimes, Matthias Grosz, Gene Hargrove, George James, Anne Jordan, Barbara Jordan, William Jordan IV, Jay Knight, John Leonard, Andrew Light, Dave Mahler, Suzanne Malec, Dave McCloskey, Curt Meine, Mike Miller, Bill Morgan, Chris Norden, Judy Nystrom, Steve Packard, Roy Rappaport, Walter Rosen, Tom Simpson, Alex Turner, Fred Turner, Keith Wendt, and Neil Whitehead. I am also indebted to the National Science Foundation's program in Science, Technology, and Society (Award Number 9496144) for support for a year of study at the University of North Texas from 1993 to 1994, where I engaged in many helpful conversations and where I wrote the first draft of this book. I would also like to express my appreciation to Baird Callicott, Gene Hargrove, Dave McCloskey, Fred Turner, and Max Oelschlaeger for their helpful comments on early drafts of this book.

CHAPTER I

Weeding Key Biscayne

Good Friday 1977. The burning of Curtis Prairie that year, my first year at the Arboretum, was held on a bright day early in April. It was a clean burn, fast and hot, and a good introduction to this quintessential prairie event. At its climax, when the crew let the fire go to run with the wind, it burned over some 20 acres in the center of the prairie in about a minute, and for that minute it seemed that the fire was no longer just a tool but a wild force, an orange plasma that rushed through the tall grass, clearing the ground and blasting the heat of last summer's sunshine back into the mild spring air.

For that minute the crew, who had tended the fire carefully in its early stages, could only watch as the lines of fire rushed together behind a thickening column of smoke. Then the fire died abruptly, the sound of water pumps, the voices of the crew, and the murmur of the traffic on the nearby Beltline Highway reemerging as its eager clatter and roar died away.

Fire and prairie, which when they kiss consume.

Another scene—Central Park in New York City. Restorationists there, looking for a way to minimize trampling, have learned how to avoid walking on the piece of ground they are replanting. Occupying the site, they take up positions within reach of each other. Tools, plants, plant markers, and buckets of water are then handed from person to person, and the work takes on the quality of a dance—a choreography arising naturally out of the work and expressive of its rhythm and quality, of the workers' cooperation, restraint, and respect for a patch of ground.

A Sunday morning in February, hot under a brilliant sun on Key Biscayne, recently mauled by Hurricane Andrew. Here the objective is to remove exotic

10

plants springing up in the clear-cut left by the storm in order to give native species a chance to recapture the island. Today the principal targets are Burma-reed, a tall, coarse grass growing in clumps as much as a yard across, and spindly seedlings of Australian pine, offspring of mature trees that had covered large areas on the island before the storm. The plan is to help the island recover, not to its ecologically degraded condition prior to the hurricane but—the common goal of restorationists in North America—to its condition at the time of European contact.

We work in pairs, tugging and sweating in the sun while big pleasure boats plow back and forth through the turquoise water a few yards offshore. Small plants come out of the loose sand easily, but the big clumps of Burma-reed are a challenge. While one of us pulls, the other gets in underneath with a shovel and pries. Clumps of a satisfyingly large size come out and we leave them behind, tipped over on the sand.

Joining the group late, I realize that my partner, wiry and acclimated, will quickly outwork me in the heat. I recall Levin in Anna Karenina, *playing at agriculture, struggling to keep up with his peasants in the mowing field. Soon I am seeing spots in front of my eyes and am looking for a place to sit down. The others break for water, then go on down the beach, wrestling out Burma-reed. Weeding Key Biscayne.*

Ecological restoration is the attempt, sometimes breathtakingly successful, sometimes less so, to make nature whole. To do this the restorationist does everything possible to heal the scars and erase the signs of disturbance or disruption. He or—just as often—she removes exotic plants and animals that have invaded an area. He reintroduces species that have been eliminated. In some cases—in grasslands, for example—this may mean replanting hundreds of species. In others, such as some kinds of wetlands, it means planting just one or two, by hand, rice-paddy fashion, at densities of many thousands per acre. To restore seagrass beds in the shallow water along coastlines, restorationists go underwater, hovering over the ocean floor with scuba equipment, setting plants and fastening them in place with metal staples. When they can, they enlist the help of the natural forces they seek to reinstate. Restorationists working in arid ecosystems in the West have relied on kangaroo rats to collect and disperse seed; others, working on landfills in New Jersey, have set up perches to attract starlings and robins, counting on the seed they deposit in their droppings to help establish a new plant community. When necessary, restorationists rehabilitate soil, recontouring it, adding nutrients to promote growth of native plants, or in some cases finding ways to remove nutrients in order to discourage the growth of fast-growing, weedy species. They reintroduce natural drainage patterns and seasonal patterns of flood and drought, closing ditches, putting the bends back into channelized streams, probing soil with metal rods to find—and then remove or break—drainage tiles put in place generations earlier, in order to nudge a mowing meadow back toward wet prairie, or a field that had been producing soybeans back toward bottomland forest. Working on creeks and rivers, they go upstream to eliminate or abate sources of stress: road salt; toxic chemicals; acid draining from a mine; or altered drainage patterns. When appropriate, as on the prairies, they reintroduce fire, insects, bison, rocks. Restorationists working on Curtis Prairie at the University of Wisconsin-Madison Arboretum in the 1930s disassembled stone fences, rescattering the stones where glaciers had left them ten thousand years earlier, before replanting prairie around them. In some cases restorationists have recontoured entire landscapes at sites disturbed by mining or other forms of land remodeling. For the past decade the Army Corps of Engineers has been putting the meanders back into a stretch of the Kissimmee River in southern Florida, replumbing the landscape to specifications provided by nature and history.

On a smaller scale, restorationist Ed Collins is supervising a project to do the same thing on Nippersink Creek in northern Illinois. There a series of kames, or "gumdrop" hills left by glaciers, were mined decades ago for material that was used to channelize the creek. Collins is taking this "filler" out again, restoring the old meanders and using the recovered glacial till to rebuild the kames. Today, the view from the top of one of Ed's new kames is beginning to resemble that of two hundred years ago. Farm fields are gone, and a program is underway to begin easing out exotic species and replace them with species that once made up the prairies and savannas of the area. As in all restoration projects, the idea—or ideal—is ultimately to replace everything, not just trees, flowers, and free-flowing rivers. If rattlesnakes, mosquitoes, poison ivy, fire, or flood belong in the system, they are brought in too or are encouraged to return. The outcome, when all this is successful, is paradoxical. The aim of the restorationist is to erase the mark of his own kind from the landscape. Yet through the process of restoration he enters into a peculiarly profound and intimate relationship with it.

Restoration is not a new idea. In a general sense humans have been rehabilitating ecosystems altered or degraded by activities such as agriculture or tree cutting for millennia, through practices such as tree planting and the fallowing of land. And projects that were restoration efforts in the fully modern sense—that is, active attempts to recreate whole, eco-logically accurate examples of historic landscapes or ecosystems—were undertaken in the United States as early as the 1920s.[1] These were an ini-tiative of conservationists that in certain respects anticipated concerns of the environmentalists of more recent generations. Yet, while restoration has been available, both as an idea and as a practice for most of the past century, until very recently its role in conservation has been negligible. Only since the mid or late 1980s have environmentalists and conservation practitioners begun to take restoration seriously as a conservation strat-egy.

Today thousands of projects are underway in virtually every kind of ecosystem, from tallgrass prairies and alpine meadows to the coral reefs and tropical forests that have traditionally served as tropes for the irre-placeability of natural ecosystems. Canadian restorationists have done ex-tensive work to restore vegetation on cliff faces of the Niagara Escarp-ment damaged by climbers, and at least one project has been undertaken to restore the ecosystem inside a cave. Others are working on the resto-ration of woodland in downtown Manhattan. Restoration projects range in scale from backyard projects of a few square yards to projects like the multi-billion dollar CalFed program being carried out in the watershed of the Sacramento River in California, or the restoration of Everglades National Park, a project that will eventually encompass tens of thousands of acres. Some of these projects have been planned and are being carried out entirely by professionals, though most involve amateurs, participat-ing as volunteers. Many, especially in major cities like Chicago, San Fran-cisco, Seattle, and New York, have been carried out almost entirely by volunteers. Some have been remarkably successful, summoning back bits and pieces of historic landscapes in places where, surrounded by suburbs, shopping malls, or cornfields, they have reappeared as biological Rip Van Winkles, visitors from the past and rare islands of biological diversity. Others have been less successful. For many, perhaps most, the outcome is not yet clear. In a basic sense, all are works in progress and always will be—a circumstance that many find unsettling.

For generations environmentalists have assumed that the loss or degradation of areas generally described as "natural" is an irreversible process—that we can only subtract from or degrade the natural land-scape, never add to or improve it. Yet the best work of restorationists shows that this is not always true. It is possible to recreate reasonably ac-curate versions of some landscapes or ecosystems. Besides this—and even more important—restoration, properly understood, turns out to be the key to the survival—or preservation—of *all* natural landscapes, not just those that have obviously been degraded or abused.

Whatever we may prefer to think, indulging fantasies of untrammeled wilderness or Edenic landscapes unviolated by human influence, the hard logic of ecology—the principle that everything interacts with (and therefore influences) everything else—makes the conclusion unavoidable: preservation in the strict sense is impossible. Protection from damage or "outside" influence may be a crucial step in the conservation of a classic landscape, but it is only a first step because it is never complete. However high the wall we put around a preserve, we cannot protect it from all novel or outside influences. And since an ecosystem will always respond to these influences, however subtle or indirect, in the long run, which is the only run that counts in natural-area conservation, the best natural— or "classic"—ecosystems will not be those that have been "preserved" from human influences but those that have been subject to management aimed at identifying those influences that do exist and then compensating for them in an ecologically effective way—that is, in an ongoing program of restoration.[2]

While the intensity of restoration will of course vary enormously, reflecting the coefficient of interaction between a particular classic landscape and the novel ecologies created by humans, some kind of restoration is always necessary to keep a classic landscape on its historical course because the coefficient of interaction is never zero. In any event, however small it is, we must never ignore it. As the ecological term in the equation defining our relationship with the landscape, it must be the basis for any program of management, any idea of our relationship with the classic landscape, and any philosophy of nature grounded in ecology. For this reason we are not free to "neglect" it, as a mathematician may drop a small term from an equation to make it easier—or possible—to solve. And if that makes the equation troublingly complex, or even impossible to solve, there is a lesson in that: our relationship with the rest of nature, as with anything, is not really an equation or a problem to be solved. It is a mystery.

So far as wilderness areas are concerned, we will, as environmental managers have long insisted, want to make them as large and as remote as possible, to reduce "outside" influences on them, and to maximize their self-organizing abilities. And we will naturally take pains to minimize our own influence on them. But we must never regard or treat them simply as *preserves,* since to do that is merely to abandon them to drift in the variable breezes of ecological influence toward a future shaped as much by "outside" influences as by the "internal" forces of succession and natural selection. Of course we may chose to allow this on rare occasions, as a kind of experiment. But the landscapes that result from this kind of neglect will not be "preserves" in the old sense, but zones of sacrifice, entailing changes in ecological character and historic quality, and justified not by their effects on the landscape, but by the information they produce or the feelings they generate.

To say this is not to deny the value of wilderness or the importance of preservation as a conservation goal. It is, rather, to acknowledge that restoration, understood in this way, is simply the best way we have of reaching that goal. Understood not merely as an emergency measure, to be deployed in response to dramatic or acute insults to ecosystems such as oil spills or surface mining, but as an ongoing process of ecological compensation, restoration quite simply defines the terms of our relationship with natural landscapes, and the terms on which they will survive through the twenty-first century and beyond.

Americans first learned this lesson on the tallgrass prairies of the Midwest during the early decades of the twentieth century as conservationists sought ways to reverse what was by then the near extinction of this once vast ecosystem. But that lesson has implications for every kind of ecosystem influenced by humans, which is to say, ultimately, for every ecosystem on the planet. It is relevant, for example, to riparian and arid areas in the West, altered by decades of grazing, alterations of hydrological cycles, and introduction of exotic species such as tamarisk. It is relevant to wetlands affected by filling, alterations in hydrology, or the introduction of exotic species. It is relevant to the forests of the Northeast, where in many areas forests have recovered fairly well from clearing during the colonial period but often lack "minor" species such as ants or salamanders or the spring flowers that lend these forests so much of their charm, and which in many instances do not reappear unless reintroduced.

More dramatically, it is urgently needed in the ponderosa pine forests of the Southwest, where years of fire suppression have resulted in accumulations of fuel and closing of canopies that have made thousands of square miles dangerously combustible. This is bad enough, as the fires of 2002 dramatically illustrated. What makes it worse is that, in contrast to fires in other, moister forests farther north, crown fires in ponderosa pine forests are ecologically terminal events. Sterilizing the landscape, they are followed on steep slopes by catastrophic erosion, not only killing the ecological community but destroying the infrastructure of soil and seed that sustains it. Once burned, many such areas are left a moonscape where vegetation of any kind will not recover for centuries.

The situation here is dramatically different from that on the prairies, which die if deprived of fire, but die quietly, leaving the ecosystem intact as the prairie is gradually replaced by another kind of community, often oak forest. The ponderosa pine forests, in contrast, die violently, striking back viciously and self-destructively, demonstrating in a way the prairies do not the worst consequences of human neglect. If it was on the prairies that conservation learned the value of restoration, it may be in the ponderosa pine forests that the rest of us will at last learn its importance.

Importance for the landscape, but also—and inseparable from that—for our relationship with it, since restoration provides, as other paradigms of relationship between our own species and the rest of nature do not, a basis for a relationship that is active, positive, and, in a psychological sense, comprehensive. And this, of course, brings us to the root of our problem. Ultimately, the future of a natural ecosystem depends not on protection from humans but on its relationship with the people who inhabit it or share the landscape with it. This relationship must not only be respectful, it must also be ecologically robust, economically productive, and psychologically rewarding. This being the case, the central task of natural-area conservation is to provide a role for people inside the old, "natural" system that is not only both active and constructive, but that engages and challenges all the human interests and abilities, including those for manipulation and invention as well as for observation, description, and caretaking. Even more challenging, it must provide a way of confronting and coming to terms with the negative and troubling, as well as the more attractive, positive aspects of nature and our relationship with it.

And so far as the classic landscape is concerned, restoration provides the only way of doing this. In effect creating an ecologically and psychologically satisfactory niche for humans in that landscape, it actually solves the "dilemma of use" that has troubled environmentalism for more than a century. Besides this, as projects in cities, suburbs, and rural and wilderness areas are showing, restoration offers a way to bring the human community together and to strengthen the relationship between human and nonhuman nature, on which the fate of the classic landscape ultimately depends.

Despite this, environmentalism has been extremely slow to accept restoration or take it seriously as a conservation strategy, and I have come to believe that the reasons for this have as much to do with the ideas and values of environmentalism as they have to do with the nature and short-comings of restoration. There are many reasons for skepticism about restoration. Some are political and reflect the concern that the promise of restoration might be used—as in fact it has been used—to undermine arguments for the preservation of existing historic landscapes. Others are economic, restoration being, in many cases, a costly and uncertain process that is often seen as a kind of fool tax—the pound of cure that is demanded of those who neglect the ounce of prevention. Still others are conceptual. Sixty years ago conservationists took little interest in restoration because the restorationist's emphasis on historical accuracy and ecological completeness seemed silly and self-indulgent—a kind of boutique conservation. More recently, environmentalists have seen it as presumptuous. Many have been uneasy with restoration because it violates in a particularly troubling way the categories of "nature" and "culture" that play so large a role in environmental thinking and rhetoric. Overall, restoration, with all its complexity and uncertainty, is simply not the way we have expected a healthy relationship with nature to *feel*.

Only recently has that expectation begun to change as environmentalists and managers have begun to discover the value of restoration as a strategy for conserving classic landscapes and developing a vital, satisfying relationship with them. As this has happened it has become clear that the neglect of restoration has been a mistake—indeed, one of the defining mistakes of twentieth-century environmentalism.

When I first started thinking seriously about restoration in connection with my work at the UW-Madison Arboretum, restoration was simply not a topic of conservation in environmental circles. Activities such as mine reclamation or land rehabilitation were carried out on the margins of environmentalism and in any event generally fell far short of the restorationists' ecologically ambitious goals. The few projects that aimed at actual restoration were for the most part the work of dedicated amateurs. Most were small in scale. Their quality varied considerably, and few believed that they had any important implications for conservation. Even at the Arboretum, which I eventually took to describing as the "Kitty Hawk" of restoration, consciousness of the restoration effort had faded into the background. The staff did not think of the Arboretum primarily as a restoration project or present it to the public in that way. The director generally referred to the site and its several hundred acres of meticulously restored ecological communities as a "preserve." And when, early on, I pointed out that what was going on at the Arboretum had more to do with an enterprise like mine reclamation than with natural-area preservation, the observation met with a mixture of disapproval and indignation.[3]

Despite this, I found the restoration story intriguing, in part because it was the single most distinctive feature of the Arboretum, and I thought we ought to have something to say about it. Being a gardener myself, restoration struck me as an interesting kind of gardening—interesting in a technical sense, certainly, but also in a more philosophical sense. I was struck, somehow, by the figure of the restorationist in the landscape, working hard to disappear into it.

I found myself spending quite a lot of time thinking about restoration and discussing it with Keith Wendt, the Arboretum ranger who, unlike me, had a good background in ecology. At first we talked mostly about the Arboretum's restored ecological communities, which included an array of prairie and forest types—some three dozen in all when broken down into the ecologist's types and subtypes. We discussed their value for research and teaching—their official purpose, since the Arboretum serves as an outdoor laboratory and classroom for the university—but we also discussed their value as features in the local environment and for conservation generally.

Oddly, since I had no experience in this area, it was our talk about the research program that led to my first idea about the value of restoration. Both Keith and I felt that the Arboretum was underused as a research facility, in part because the restored communities were small and, even after some forty years of effort, incompletely restored. All of them were missing some species. All of them harbored exotic or otherwise ecologically inappropriate species. And all were growing on disturbed soils and were in various stages of completion, which made it hard for an ecologist to know what to make of them. If a plant ecologist wanted to study a tallgrass prairie, for example, all he or she had to do was drive an hour in almost any direction to find a reasonably good remnant of "real" prairie. That remnant might be small. It might be contaminated by exotic, weedy plants. And it would certainly not include bison or antelope. But at least it would be "real" in the sense that it had once been part of the old, or "original" prairie, and it would not be necessary to apologize for it in writing up the results of a research project.

Quite soon, however, it occurred to me that, while the defects in the Arboretum's restored communities might be a disadvantage from the point of view of an ecologist interested in doing descriptive research in a "real" ecosystem, from another point of view these defects were the most interesting thing about the restored communities. Since each defect pointed to features of the system that the restorationists had not fully understood and had not gotten quite right, each of them represented an unanswered question, and an opportunity for research. In other words, if you stopped thinking about the restored communities as defective representatives of their "natural" counterparts and started thinking about them as experiments in progress, you realized that they offered remarkable opportunities for research that actually could not be undertaken in an undisturbed, "natural" system. The classic example of this at the Arboretum was early work on the ecology of fire on prairies, which was a direct result of the failure of early attempts to restore prairie without fire. As soon as Keith and I started thinking about this, examples proliferated, and we realized that virtually all the most important research carried out in the Arboretum over the previous four decades had been carried out, not in spite of, but because of the shortcomings of the restoration efforts.

I coined the term synthetic—or restoration—ecology to draw attention to the value of this approach to basic ecological research. Later I realized that, if restoration had great value as a technique for basic research, it also provided an excellent context for learning in more informal ways, and I eventually worked with Arboretum ranger Brock Woods to develop an educational program at the Arboretum based on the practice of restoration. Keith left the Arboretum in 1980, but I continued my reflections and gradually developed a number of ideas about the value of restoration. Exploring it first as a process, a way of creating a product and studying the ecology of the ecosystems being restored, I later began to see its value as an experience, the subjective side of process, and ultimately as a performance, an expressive act and a context for the creation of higher values such as meaning, beauty and community.

As my list of values grew, extending into these several dimensions, I gradually realized how limited a perspective environmentalism had offered on this interesting, challenging, certainly worthwhile, and obviously very beautiful work. Seeing nature as an environment—a collection of objects that surrounds but does not fully include us—environmentalists had seen restoration strictly from the point of view of its product, the restored ecosystem regarded as an object in the landscape. And in the spirit of the preservationism that was especially pronounced in environmental circles in the 1970s, they had seen even that in negative terms, as ecologically defective and "unnatural"—basically, a second-rate substitute for the real thing.

They had completely overlooked the other dimensions of value, and as I became aware of this I realized that in order to think about these values I had more or less unconsciously made a series of right-angle turns, so to speak, each of which was discouraged by the liberal, academic culture in which I was working. The first of these was simply the turn from product to process. Stepping back to think not only about the object being studied, but also about the way in which it was being studied, I eventually realized, was something that most scientists simply don't do. My next turn, from objective process to subjective experience, was discouraged by what Theodore Roszak calls the myth of objective consciousness, which privileges external facts over the data of experience. And the final turn, from personal experience into the dimension of shared experience, or performance, violated a deeply inscribed cultural puritanism, which associates performance and ritual with superstition, subjection to authority, flakiness, and mere entertainment—a mind-set that is especially pronounced among scientists and in academic circles.

These observations helped me understand why the conservationists of my parents' and grandparents' generations had underestimated the value of restoration, and why the environmentalists of my own generation had ignored and resisted it. Restoration raises many questions. Some of these, like those that led Keith Wendt and me to the notion of restoration ecology, were merely technical or ecological questions about the process of restoration and the ecology of the ecosystems being restored. But others were more fundamental. What, for example, does the metaphor of restoration—or "standing up again"—mean when we apply it to a dynamic, living system such as an ecological community or ecosystem? If such a system is a moving target, with a complex history and an unpredictable future, what does it mean to restore it? How should we choose the historic ecosystem or landscape we want to use as a model, and how can we describe or define it so that we will know whether we have succeeded in our attempt to reproduce it? Even assuming that we can define an objective in some meaningful way, is restoration possible? Given the complexity of the work and the uncertainty of the results, wouldn't it be better simply to let a disturbed landscape alone, removing obvious sources of disruption and relying on natural processes to bring about recovery? What is the value of a restored landscape? And what sort of thing is it? Is it "nature," or merely a human artifact misrepresented as nature—at best a poor substitute and at worst a deception and a fake, as some have argued? What is the proper role of humans in the restoration—and by extension the management, and ultimately the ecology—of natural or historic landscapes? Is restoration the epitome of a responsible, nurturing relationship between ourselves and our fellow species and with the rest of nature generally? Or is it, as some have insisted, simply another arena for the exercise and aggrandizement of the human ego? What, more generally, is the proper relationship between ourselves and the rest of nature? If restoration, understood as compensation for "outside" influences on a landscape, is the indispensable paradigm for the conservation of historic ecosystems, what are we to make of the fact that it is difficult, uncertain and in some ways emotionally challenging work?

All these questions apply to all aspects of our relationship with nature, but many of them are easy to ignore in a landscape that is regarded as a "preserve" or found object. They are almost impossible to ignore in a restored landscape like that of the UW Arboretum. Thinking them over, I gradually realized that these questions were perhaps the most valuable thing about restoration, but that they were also the reason why several generations of environmentalists had either ignored or resisted it. Such questions point to our ignorance, which is troubling enough, but they also bring us face to face with our deepest uncertainties, and in doing so they challenge ideas about nature, about relationship, and about the nature of relationship that environmental thinkers have taken for granted since the time of Emerson and Thoreau.

In arguing for the value of restoration not only as an effective act—a way to recreate and maintain landscapes—but also as an expressive and symbolic act—a context for the creation of meaning—I want to be clear at the outset what I mean by restoration. Though restorationists have struggled in recent years to come up with a generally acceptable definition of this word, the difficulty here is not in defining "restoration," which is easy to do, but in describing what restorationists actually do and hope to accomplish, which is a more complicated matter.[4] Anyone who speaks English knows what the word "restore" means. It means to bring something back into existence or use, or to return it to some previous or "original" condition; "ecological restoration" simply means doing that to an ecological system, such as a prairie, for example, or a lake or a wetland.[5]

In the case of an ecosystem such as a prairie or a wetland, of course, this process has to be understood in a dynamic sense that is not captured by the word "restoration," which is derived from the Latin word for "to stand," a root it shares with words like "static" and "stationary." The restorationist's aim is usually not to arrest change or recreate a plant-by-plant replica of a historic landscape—what restorationists disparage as "snapshot" objectives or a "diorama"[6]—but rather to redirect it, getting

the system back on track, setting it in motion again, not only in an ecological, but ideally even in an evolutionary sense. The restored system
should not only look (more or less) like the "original" or model system,
it should *act* like it. It should undergo change and respond to disturbances in the same way. In the long run it should even support evolutionary processes, acting as a source of new species.[7]

Besides this, the process of restoration is itself dynamic, adding to the
dynamics of the historic ecosystem the new dynamics of its interaction
with the restorationist and the human society that he or she represents.
In order to emphasize this dynamic element and bring the rather abstract
dictionary definition a bit closer to the ground, I define restoration as
*everything we do to a landscape or an ecosystem in an ongoing attempt to com-
pensate for novel or "outside" influences on it in such a way that it can continue
to behave or can resume behaving* as if *these were not present.*

Several points are worth emphasizing here. To begin with, it should
be clear that I am defining restoration rather narrowly in certain respects.
I am especially concerned to distinguish restoration from land-
management practices that are merely restor*ative*. These include a wide
range of practices, referred to by terms such as "reclamation," "rehabilitation," "revegetation," and "recovery" (what practitioners sometimes
call "passive restoration"), or even more general terms such as "stewardship" or "management." Each of these protocols has a distinct value, and
what is distinctively valuable about restoration is that, while these other
protocols involve attempts to restore only selected features or qualities of
a system—productivity, for example, or diversity or beauty or even
health—restoration, understood as I am defining it here, is a deliberate
attempt to return *all* the features of the system to some historic condition, defined ecologically and with a studied disregard for human interests.

This is an important point. Restorationists often talk about the value
of their work as a way of beautifying a place, or creating habitat for rare
species, or improving water quality, or contributing in some other way
to what is often called "natural capital." Restoration projects usually do
provide these benefits, but that is not the defining characteristic of restoration. What is distinctive about restoration is the commitment it implies
to bringing the whole system back to a former condition whatever that
might happen to be—not just those features we find beautiful, interesting, or useful but also those that we consider uninteresting, useless, ugly,
repulsive, or even dangerous. This is what sets restoration apart from
other restorative forms of land management such as rehabilitation (the

restoration of function, or certain selected functions), or reclamation (rehabilitation, usually from a profoundly disturbed condition resulting from an activity such as mining or construction), or even healing (the restoration of health).

Restoration may overlap these other, related forms of land management, but it is not the same as any of them. The overlap with healing provides a good example. Usually, restoration entails an improvement in the health of an ecosystem (however that might be defined). But this is true only when the historic system that is being restored happens to have been healthier than the one that currently exists, which is usually but not always the case. In fact, far from healing, restoration may, in certain instances, involve injuring an ecosystem, or even killing it. This was actually the case in a recent project to restore part of a Nazi concentration camp to the condition it was in during the early 1940s.[8] This project involved taking out trees and plants that had invaded the area over the years in order to return a field of cinders to its former, ecologically sterile condition. This was obviously not healing. But it was restoration. Admittedly, this is a peculiar example, but it makes an important point. Restoration is not the same thing as making a landscape "better" or "improving" it.[9]

There are two reasons for defining restoration narrowly in this way, and for insisting on clear distinctions between the various forms of restorative land management. The first of these is ecological. Since, axiomatically, everything interacts with and influences everything else, preservation of an ecosystem is ultimately impossible. A landscape's condition and survival depend on our ability to identify and then compensate for novel or "outside" influences on it: they depend, in other words, on the way we define restoration. Define it loosely, in terms of health or integrity or selected functions, overlooking details such as "minor" species or inconspicuous processes, and those elements are liable to drop out as the landscape drifts in response to subtle and indirect influences from "outside."

The second reason for defining restoration narrowly has to do with its value and development as a context for creating meaning. Like other ways of interacting with the landscape, restoration is a form of technology, a way of creating a product. But it is also a game, a way of creating delight and meaning, and the kinds of delight and meaning a game creates depend on the rules of the game—that is, on how we define it. All the games we play with nature—reclamation, rehabilitation, healing, gardening, preservation—have their own value, both for the landscape and for the feelings and meanings they generate. But when we confuse the various games or blur the distinctions among them, we compromise their value as a context for generating feelings and negotiating meanings.

Traditional forms of gardening, for example, are valuable in part because they provide a context for a creative engagement with the landscape at the level of the ecological community. Ecological restoration, in contrast, is valuable as a special form of gardening that is—or at least aims to be—explicitly *noncreative* with respect to objectives, neither improving on nature nor improvising on it but attempting, blankly, to copy it. Most of the restorationists I know resist this characterization, insisting that restoration is creative work, and of course in many ways that is true. Yet in an important sense the aim of restoration *is* noncreative, and this commitment to noncreativity has its own value—one we often miss because we make a fetish of creativity. Once past that, the value of the deliberately *non*creative act as a stilling of the will, an expression of obedience and humility and the entrainment of consciousness to the gesture and movement of the other—an important element in religious practice—becomes clear. But this value is compromised or missed entirely so long as we insist only on the creative aspects of restoration and deny the commitment to noncreativity at its core.

It is important to note that both of these points are relevant anywhere, not just in places like North America or Australia, where the idea of restoration developed. Noting that restoration is to some extent a New-World idea, inspired by the idea of the pre-contact landscape as an unspoiled Eden, and the possibility of recovering or returning to it, some have argued that it is irrelevant in other parts of the world, which have longer histories or—more accurately—histories that are better documented and so harder to overlook. But restoration as I define it is not about a return to an Edenic "nature" outside history. It is about the re-creation and maintenance of *historic* landscapes defined in ecological terms, with or without reference to the ambiguous and in many ways problematic ideas of "nature" or "natural" or "native" ecosystems.

Others argue that restoration of historic, sometimes economically obsolete, landscapes is a luxury that many can't afford and insist that for this reason we should broaden the definition of "restoration" to include practices such as sustainable forestry or revegetation projects aimed at reducing soil erosion. Insisting on an "American" definition of restoration, they argue, is imperialistic.[10] But what I am talking about has nothing to do with either America or imperialism. Ideas have consequences and generate values that are independent of where they come from: to ignore this is not only condescending but entails a loss of meaning and value. If restoration is impossible or is a luxury that, say, Indonesian farmers can't afford, then the straightforward thing to do is admit that fact and face its ecological and political consequences, which include the inevitable degradation and loss of historic landscapes in Indonesia. This cannot be corrected by broadening or softening the definition of restoration, and I can see no reason for using the word "restoration" to describe a rehabilitation or reclamation or revegetation project unless it is to sell the project or make people feel good about it. That is just advertising talk that sacrifices meaning for feeling at the expense of the landscape. Of course euphemism and the weakening of language always come at a cost. In this case what is at stake is the future of the classic landscape.[11]

In any event, if restoration is a luxury in many parts of the developing world, it is a luxury in most parts of Iowa and Florida and California as well. Fortunately, as projects being carried out by people like Dan Janzen, who is spearheading restoration of thousands of acres of tropical forest in Costa Rica, and Narayan Desai, who is restoring forest shrines in India, clearly illustrate, there are reasons to believe that restoration can have a place in an economy dominated by subsistence farming.[12]

So far, my insistence on this point has done little more than gain me a reputation among my colleagues as a kind of word-Nazi. But if my definition of restoration is narrow in one sense, it is broad in another, since it applies not only to the intensive, from-the-ground-up projects that have traditionally served as models of restoration, but to any form of management involving an attempt to keep an ecosystem on a historic trajectory in the face of "outside" or novel influences, however subtle or indirect.

Restoration projects vary enormously in both scale and intensity. In some cases, restorationists practice what amounts to horticulture, manipulating the ecosystem or landscape virtually on a plant-by-plant basis. When working on a larger scale, they often practice a kind of ecological jujitsu, using an element such as fire, or introducing a predator to achieve a large effect with a minimum of effort. Practitioners usually use the terms "management" or "stewardship" when talking about projects of this kind, reserving "restoration" for smaller-scale, more labor-intensive projects. But the distinction is an arbitrary one, and it is also misleading, since it suggests a qualitative difference between an ecosystem that has to be restored and one that merely has to be managed. This allows everyone involved to ignore the hard questions about ends and means that a hard-edged term like "restoration" raises, and also to overlook the troubling, permanent dependence of ecosystems on deliberate human effort that the act of restoration implies. For all these reasons, if a project fits the definition of "restoration" I outlined above, it is best to call it a restoration project, whatever its intensity and whatever the scale on which it is carried out. Obviously you can use the word "restoration" any way you want to. But if you care about the survival of classic ecosystems, which will ultimately depend on the practice of restoration as I have defined it, you had better hold on to *some* word that means just that and nothing else.

In any event, I am not being a fundamentalist here. My point is not that there is or ought to be some rigid, classic, or essentialist definition of the term "restoration," but rather that acts and ideas have consequences, and that the acts and ideas distinctive of "restoration," as I define it, are important.

Perhaps the best way to handle a practical, working description of restoration is the way lawyers define a point in law, by pointing to precedents—in this case, projects that practitioners generally regard as exemplary. Asked about this, many restorationists who are familiar with work in the United States and Canada would think immediately of the tallgrass prairies of the Midwest, where some of the earliest restoration projects were carried out, and where the best projects are still widely regarded as models representing restoration in its purest and most ambitious form.[13] Highly regarded examples from this area with which I happen to be familiar include Greene Prairie at the University of Wisconsin-Madison Arboretum, and Ray Schulenberg's prairie at the Morton Arboretum in Lisle, Illinois. Prairie remnants being "rescued" and restored by Chicago restorationist Bob Betz in old cemeteries and along railroad rights of way are also excellent precedents, because they make the point that there should be something—an altered or degraded system—there to restore. (When there isn't, the terms "creation" or "re-creation" may be more appropriate.)

By itself, restoration is not a satisfactory conservation strategy or paradigm for our relationship with the rest of nature. In recent years, as restoration has gained visibility as a conservation strategy, there has been a tendency to hold it up as *the* model or protocol for conservation generally. This is a mistake, not least because it involves stretching the idea of restoration to the point of sacrificing some of its distinctive meanings. Restoration is not *the* model for conservation. It is, however, the best paradigm for the conservation of historic or classic landscapes, and the best way we have of coming to terms with the conservative aspect of our relationship with nature—our best tribute to the landscape we did not make but have simply inherited. This makes it an important game. But it is certainly not one that we will want to play everywhere. Other games, other rituals, other sacraments of relationship emerge from our engagement with nature in its other aspects—as a resource, for example, or as a partner in creation.

CHAPTER 2

The Challenge of Reinhabitation

In the century that environmentalism has existed as a recognizable social movement, it has put forward a succession of ideas about our relationship with the rest of nature. All have value. But none offers any real hope that in the foreseeable future—say, a hundred or two hundred years from now—anything much will be left of the natural landscape outside a few scattered preserves, or that our relationship with those bits that remain will be anything like the rich, deeply engaged, often troubled relationship that has always existed between our species and the rest of nature.

These ideas fall into three broad categories. The first, historically speaking, was the idea that our relationship with the natural landscape is, or ought to be, essentially *colonial*. Nature in this view is primarily a resource, and the value of a particular landscape depends first and foremost on its value as a source of goods and services. This was the philosophy, or at least the philosophical emphasis, of the conservation movements of the first half of the twentieth century, and it was the basis for conservation programs that managed natural ecosystems such as forests, grasslands, and lakes more or less as farms for the production of goods such as food, fuel, timber, clean water, fish, and game. The great value of this form of environmentalism was that it took the natural landscape seriously rather than taking it for granted. It fostered an ethic of stewardship over land, and it provided the basis for a robust economic—and so genuinely *ecological*—relationship with it, including actual work in the woods and fields. Its great drawback, so far as the natural landscape was concerned, was that, seeing nature in utilitarian terms, as a source of goods and services for human benefit, the conservationist typically had little interest in conserving other species or natural ecosystems for their own sake. Thus, under conservation management a landscape might remain healthy and productive even as a handful of agricultural crops growing in fields interspersed with habitat for a few favored species of fish and game replaced its original population of plants and animals.

The second idea about our relationship with the natural landscape that has played an important role in the environmental thinking of the past century is in many respects the polar opposite of the first and developed in part in reaction against it. This is the idea that the natural landscape is best regarded as a *sacred place,* ascribing to the plants and animals that inhabit it a value in and of themselves that transcends economic or other purely human interests. The great prophet of this idea was nineteenth-century naturalist John Muir, who broke with the Calvinist religion of his Scottish ancestors to discover God in nature and proclaim wilderness areas God's most perfect cathedrals and sanctuaries.

This view was a prominent feature of the environmentalism that took shape in the 1960s and 1970s and, together with conservationism, remains an important factor in environmental thinking today. It is important because it brings to environmentalism a clearly articulated sense of the value of other species that had not been a feature of conservationism. Its great drawback has been that, by idealizing the pristine, untouched landscape as nature at its most natural, it confines humans to the role of visitors—at best admirers and at worst consumers and vandals—in the natural landscape, fostering a dispiriting sense that humans don't belong on the earth at all, and that the planet would be better off without us. In keeping with this view, it advocates a limited repertory of ways to engage nature, principally through scientific research and low-impact (yet ultimately consumptive) activities like hiking and birding, which provide the basis for only a limited constituency for conservation. And by fostering doubt about the ability, or even the right, of humans to manage nature, it discourages the processes of identifying and actively compensating for "outside" influences on historic landscapes. This is no mere academic issue. Preservation alone, in most instances, is not an adequate prescription for the conservation of ecosystems. In many cases it can lead to their outright destruction, as our experience on the prairies and in the ponderosa pine forests of the Southwest has shown.

Both ideas about our relationship with the natural landscape are now widely recognized as inadequate. They lie at opposite ends of a spectrum of responses to the nature-culture question—one end granting humans preeminent status, the other denying them any special value in the polity of nature. Neither, most now agree, offers the basis for a satisfactory relationship between humans and the natural landscape. Far more promising is a third idea, which falls somewhere between these other two and combines elements of both. This is the idea that the relationship between humans and the rest of nature is best defined in terms of membership in a *community*.

The idea that all species properly make up a community, and that human beings have a moral obligation to expand their idea of community to include other species and, ultimately, even inanimate objects and natural processes, was first clearly articulated during the 1930s and 1940s by pioneer conservationist Aldo Leopold. Trained as a forester, Leopold graduated from Yale in 1909 and spent the early years of his career with the Forest Service, directing the management of forests, wolves, and game populations with the confidence and enthusiasm characteristic of conservationists of the time. His gradual transition to a more nature-centered philosophy, which became decisive during the years immediately following 1933, when he accepted a position as professor of game management at the University of Wisconsin, has become one of the defining legends of environmentalism. Picking up on the idea, then current in ecology, that ecological systems are tightly integrated systems in which all the parts play important roles and no single part is of paramount importance, Leopold developed a philosophy that accorded moral value not only to other species, but also to inanimate features of the landscape such as mountains and rivers, to natural processes such as the cycling of water and nutrients through ecosystems and, on a longer time scale, to the formation of new species through natural selection. Eventually this culminated in his "land ethic," a formulation of responsibility to the environment grounded in an appeal to four values: the integrity and stability of the land community, its beauty, and—centrally—community, and the land conceived as a community of organisms.[1]

Leopold's thinking was unusual in its breadth and balance and remains valuable today in part because he avoided the extremes of utilitarian conservationism and hands-off preservationism. Rejecting simplistic systems of value at either end of the spectrum of environmental thinking, he wrote on a wide range of issues, from agriculture and game management to wilderness preservation, outdoor recreation, and the esthetic value of natural landscapes, dealing with them in ways that balanced ecological and economic considerations against higher values such as beauty and community. His writings are marked by a sense of moderation and an undogmatic respect for diverse cultural traditions combined with a passionate commitment to the well-being of the land community.

No doubt partly for this reason, Leopold's message, though regarded by some as radical in its insistence on moral consideration for other species, has proved both durable and widely appealing. His later essays, collected under the title *A Sand County Almanac,* in which he sets forth the principles underlying his land ethic, are now canonic in environmental circles and are required reading in ecology and environmental philosophy courses throughout the world. In recent decades, the ideas he developed there have played a foundational role in the development of environmental thinking. Today they inform the broad mainstream of environmentalism and provide the philosophical basis for policies and programs in schools, environmental organizations, and agencies, not only in the United States, but in other parts of the world as well.

This, clearly, is a major achievement. To have provided both basis and inspiration for so much thought and action, and to have done so without recourse to the extremes of preservationism or human-centered utilitarianism, is a contribution of great importance. Some regard it as the single most important contribution to the environmental thinking of the twentieth century. Yet few would argue that it has been enough, or that the philosophy developed by Leopold and his followers has proved equal to the task of ensuring the conservation of natural areas or of achieving Leopold's ideal of human membership in the larger community of plants and animals. Today, half a century after Leopold's death, and a generation after his book became a popular classic, the great interconnected problems of conserving the natural environment and achieving a healthy relationship with it are, if anything, more urgent than ever. We have achieved some successes, of course, in the preservation of natural areas and in protecting them from influences such as chemical pollution. Yet in most areas the destruction and deterioration of classic landscapes continues, even in areas where entire ecosystems are approaching the vanishing point. Equally important—and ultimately inseparable from this problem—prospects for a healthy, gracious relationship between ourselves and other species remain dim. And the constituency for conservation, though platitudinously broad, is notoriously thin and politically inadequate to the task at hand.[2]

The question is, why? Part of the answer to this question obviously lies outside environmentalism, in economic circumstances such as capitalism and the development of advanced technologies and industrial means of production; in political institutions such as the nation-state; in cultural traditions represented by certain religions or worldviews or philosophical systems; or simply in the human ego and the propensity of our species for greed, violence, and indifference to the well-being of others. But part, I have come to believe, lies within environmentalism itself, and in the ways our various environmentalisms have dealt with these circumstances and the challenges and—we might suppose—the opportunities they offer.

I have already mentioned a few basic limitations of the first two of the three environmental paradigms discussed above—the ideas of the natural landscape as a colony, and as sacred space. Few now regard either idea by itself as a satisfactory basis for a healthy relationship between our own species and the rest of nature. But what about the third—Aldo Leopold's idea of the land as a community to which we properly belong?

In my view, this is a far more powerful metaphor. It provides, as the others do not, for a relationship between ourselves and the landscape that is both engaged and participatory and at the same time respectful of nature for its own sake, and not merely as a resource. It is also immensely appealing, drawing as it does on an experience that has always provided much of the meaning and richness of human life. Yet my reflections on restoration, and on the relationship with nature the restorationist enacts, have led me to believe that there is a limitation here—not in Leopold's idea of the land as a community to which we belong, but rather in the idea of community itself, what it is and how it is achieved, that Leopold and environmentalists generally have taken for granted.

Leopold's achievement was to take the idea of community that ecologists had borrowed from the cultural commons seriously enough to insist that it had ethical as well as purely ecological implications. In doing so, he linked the old idea of moral value with the idea of a transhuman community suggested by the newly emerging science of ecology, establishing the basis for a moral and ethical relationship between humans and other species. This was an important achievement. What Leopold's interpreters have generally overlooked, however, is that everything—the entire import and value of the land ethic—depends on our conception of the ideas that make up its value base: the ecological values of stability and integrity, certainly, but also the transcendent values of beauty and community.

Concentrating for the moment on the last of these, we need to consider exactly what community is. What distinguishes it from other forms of association? How do we achieve it, and at what cost? How does what we know about community among members of our own species relate to the task of expanding community to include other species? And what might the idea of extending community in this way mean for a society that has, by all accounts, been in full flight from both the experience and the institutions of community for at least two hundred years, a society in which the practice of community, at least in its tougher, more demanding forms, has been decisively marginalized, flourishing only on the fringes of society, among the poor, for example, or in organizations such as gangs?

Given the key role the metaphor of community has played in the environmental thinking of the past half-century, it is remarkable how little critical attention has been given to these questions. While environmental philosophers have devoted considerable attention to criticizing and revising the two ecological values on which Leopold based his land ethic—the stability and integrity of the ecosystem—they have paid far less attention to the other two—the transcendent values of beauty and community. Yet as soon as we begin to consider this matter we realize that words like "community" and "beauty" are very old words that have been virtually drained of meaning, or at any rate have had their meanings radically revised in modern contexts, and that are used today largely for their powerful positive connotations, rather as words like "home" and "freedom" are used in advertising, as "positives" that are used to convey a feeling rather than an idea or an experience, and that can be taken to mean almost anything. Thus community for Leopold was a loving association of members. It was also egalitarian, humans being cast in the role of "plain members" of the larger biotic community. It was nonhierarchical and also broadly inclusive, since the land ethic called for creation of what would amount to a universal community. This idea of community is obviously an appealing one, and some version of it has been implicit in virtually all the environmental thinking of the past half century, from the most radical versions of deep ecology and ecofeminism to the blandest environmentalism of the agencies. Its great value has been that it has provided a way of thinking about "nature" and the natural landscape that includes humans and insists on a principle of respect and responsibility that reaches beyond our own species. Yet it has at least two obvious limitations. The first of these is that, seeing community in entirely positive terms, this idea offers no way of identifying, much less dealing with, the difficult or troubling elements that presumably limit the formation of actual communities.

The second, closely related, problem is that this entirely positive conception of community has little basis in actual experience. Psychology, for example, together with the vast record of art, history, and religious experience, all make it clear that community, however valuable and important it may be, is among the most problematic of experiences. And even a brief look at the literature of sociology shows that the idea of community as a congenial form of association, relatively free of the problems of hierarchy and inequality, has not withstood studies of actual human communities. Summing up what he calls the "community studies tradition" of the past eighty years, sociologist Steven Brint writes that these studies have produced few useful generalizations about community but "have gained dramatic power from their tendency to undermine the romantic image of warm and mutually supportive community relations." He elaborates:

An often repeated message of the community studies literature is that communities are not very community-like. They are as rife with interest, power, and division as any market, corporation, or city government. And people in even the most enclavelike communities do not necessarily associate with one another more than they do with people outside the community.

Early on, community studies researchers discovered the inequitable effects of social stratification . . . and emphasized the structure of privilege as the hidden truth underlying nominally cohesive communities. Subsequently, the comforting image of community-centered governance was replaced by discovery of a self-interested and self-reproducing power structure ruling from behind the scenes.[3]

Some will object that Brint's comments are irrelevant because the communities that sociologists study are embedded in modern, technologically advanced societies in which the institutions of community have been compromised or degraded. But we find exactly the same thing in anthropological studies of premodern and traditional societies. In a recent overview of research on hierarchy in simple, "egalitarian" societies, anthropologist James Flanagan writes that "the blanket characterization of a wide variety of non-Western societies as 'egalitarian' has come under increasing scrutiny in the recent anthropological literature. Not only has such a characterization appeared inadequate to deal with the changing circumstances and newly emergent social order in these societies, but it has also been seen to ignore the historical tensions within these societies and the interpersonal power struggles that form a part of daily existence." Flanagan argues that the idea of egalitarianism as a natural condition, a default position or starting point for the development of human societies, was an invention of Enlightenment thinkers, who secularized and literalized the medieval idea of human equality before God and made it a political ideal that became the basis for relatively egalitarian societies such as those of the modern democracies. Valuable as this "naturalizing" of a theological idea has been, Flanagan notes that for roughly a century it caused anthropologists to ignore egalitarianism and to concentrate their attention on "social inequality . . . as a product of sociocultural mechanisms" and so "a fit topic of sociocultural research."[4] Rather than regarding egalitarian behavior as natural and "given," Flanagan writes that many anthropologists now see it as a product of culture—actually an *achievement* of hierarchical societies—that entails considerable emotional and cultural cost, and that results not in uniformly egalitarian societies, but rather in conditions of *relative* equality within certain components of a society.

The point is that, while egalitarianism certainly exists as a principle of social relations, it is not in any useful sense "natural." In fact, it goes against "nature" in representing a "conquest" of nature of sorts, so that when egalitarian elements are found in a society, the question to ask is not how they were *preserved,* but how they were *achieved,* and how and at what cost they are maintained. In an account of the social life of the !Kung San of southern Africa, for example, anthropologist Richard Lee notes that egalitarian habits and institutions characteristic of this and many other foraging societies "are not achieved effortlessly, but rather require a continuing struggle with one's own selfish, arrogant and antisocial impulses," supported—we might even say compelled—by the customs and rituals of the society.[5]

Rituals themselves, then, though often understood as a sign of concord and harmony, are perhaps more accurately understood as the means by which a society manages discordant and divisive elements, both within the individual and among individuals, in order to achieve a measure of harmony, experienced as a value such as community. Indeed, one way to get an idea of what community means in a practical, operational sense is to ask how, in traditional community-based societies, a person becomes a member of the community or, alternatively—and in line with Leopold's idea of a community of human and nonhuman subjects—how a community extends the rights, prerogatives, and obligations of membership to new members. Doing this, however, and considering specifically traditional and premodern societies of the kind often proposed as models of both community and a harmonious relationship with the landscape, we find an array of institutions, rituals and, in many cases, arduous disciplines, not always entirely voluntary, that commonly involve dietary and other disciplines, enclosure or some other form of separation from the community, dramatized differentiation of gender, reprogramming of personal values and attachments, and, especially for boys, ordeals, ritual humiliation, and mutilation of the body.[6]

Equally revealing, and even more directly relevant to the idea of extending community beyond our own species are practices that pertain to a society's relations with other species. These naturally entail a principle of respect, caring, and attribution of personhood. But they also quite commonly include practices such as ritual sacrifice that incorporate and dramatize the violence that ultimately defines the relationship between predator and prey.

Practices such as these are a scandal to the liberal imagination that has played so large a role in the development of environmental thinking.[7] These practices vary widely from culture to culture, as ritual scholar Ronald Grimes points out. Nevertheless, their recurrence as common elements in a wide range of cultures does tell us something about what community means for societies that take community seriously. It suggests, first of all, that there is little warrant in traditional societies for the idea that community is either inclusive or easily achieved. A community, it would seem, involves a measure of exclusiveness that defines it and gives it much of its meaning. There are psychological, social, and biological barriers around a community, and crossing them is neither easy nor "natural," but is difficult and involves hard emotional work. People do not, for the most part, carry out this work on their own, but in the context of cultural institutions, which provide the tools, techniques, and, to some extent, even the incentive people need to confront the difficulties involved and deal with them in a productive way.[8] Community may be a great, even an irreducible value, but like other values and virtues— beauty, say, or charity or chastity—it is not the solution of a problem but is rather the problem itself: of *course* community is a good thing; the problem is how is it achieved and maintained? This is why it is of so little value to survey religious and cultural traditions in an abstract or philosophical spirit for evidence that community is valued. Of course it is valued, since in the abstract it represents the concord that is arguably the aim of all religion, perhaps all human aspiration. What is of interest here is neither the abstract principle nor the universally shared goal or vision of community, but the particular means that particular cultures have devised for realizing it—the protocols and practices of the culture and its art and religion, including the mythologies and theologies and the often demanding elements of religious practice. It is only our denial of the difficulties involved in the creation of community, supported by the marginalization of community in our own lives, that has allowed us to speak glibly about the extension of community in the absence of means for dealing with these difficulties.

Philosopher A. L. Herman has criticized Leopold's conception of community on the grounds that it rests ultimately on an appeal to altruism. This may seem a forgivable weakness, especially since it is one that Leopold shares, in Herman's critique, with such moral luminaries as Gandhi, Martin Luther King, and the Buddha. Yet clearly there is something missing from Leopold's land ethic. In setting out its value base, he drew from nature but did so selectively, overlooking negative elements. Just as he defined the ecological values of "stability" and "integrity" by reference to idealized wilderness, he also defined the human values of beauty and community in terms of a similarly selective reading of human nature. While acknowledging the elements of fear, pride, envy, shame, and selfishness mixed with altruism, courage, humility, and other more positive aspects of human nature, he did not provide ways of dealing with them, implying that they are somehow incidental, and that eliminating or somehow outgrowing them is the key to a healthy relationship with nature. The result is a sentimental, moralizing philosophy that insists, on both ecological and Darwinian grounds, on the naturalness of humans, and that celebrates the relational self—the self experienced as essentially constituted by and inseparable from a network of relationships with other selves—but that neglects or downplays the radical difficulty of achieving such a sense of self, and also downplays the role of culture and cultural institutions in carrying out this work.

Our own experience, to say nothing of psychology, anthropology, sociology and the record of political life and religious experience, all make it clear that there is a profound dissonance, a radical conflict of interest, between the demands of a community and the desires and interests of the individuals who make it up. Unless we are prepared to argue that this somehow distinguishes our own species from the rest of nature, we must assume that this, too, is natural and expresses at the human level of awareness a negative or destructive principle that is at the heart of creation itself. Nature may be beautiful. It may even include an element of altruism. But it is also terrible and shameful, and it is only by confronting and coming to terms with this—with what mythologist Joseph Campbell called, in an arresting phrase, "the monstrosity of the just-so"[9]—that we achieve the deepest kinds of relationship with it.

This, however, is exactly what our various environmentalisms have consistently failed to do. All of them insist on a heightened sense of respect for other species. All call for restraint and humility in our relations with them. Yet none has provided adequate means of confronting and coming to terms with the negative, troubling aspects of relationship that this entails, not because humans are in any sense unnatural or outside nature, but because limit and tension are inherent in nature itself. Most prescribe changes, often radical changes, in values and in ways of thinking and living. Yet none has dealt effectively with the anguish involved in bringing about a change in values—in suffering what Emily Dickinson called, using the image of a physical wound, an "internal difference / Where the meanings are."[10] Judged in comparison with any serious religion or important art, or even a sport or game considered in its more serious aspects, environmentalism has offered a story that is thin and sentimental and that fails to deal with our profoundest doubts about the world and our place in it.

An example is the failure of our environmental thinkers to provide ways of coming to terms with the experience of consumption. Consumption is a form of violence that involves a radical violation of the "other," who is consumed. It is also, however, a paradigm of creation, an immediate encounter with the fact that all creation is destruction, and that all animal life proceeds out of death and depends on it. There are good reasons for supposing that this is a source of profound anxiety for anyone who is genuinely in touch with these facts of life. In traditional or premodern cultures, however, the act of killing is commonly an occasion for rituals through which participants confront the monstrous aspects of their relationship with the other and, in doing so, achieve the deepest kind of relationship or communion with it. Indeed, what would *community* amount to if it did not take this aspect of a relationship into account—if it did not provide a way of inhabiting the emotionally challenging middle ground between self and other in which the other becomes sacred *because* we kill it? Yet our environmental thinkers have consistently failed to do this. Instead, they have urged an ethic of minimal consumption, of taking only what one "needs," of "living lightly on the land." But these ethical formulations, valid in their own way, are not enough. There are more fundamental issues here, concerns that lie behind and beneath ethics. And since, at the deepest level, we all know this, the admonition to take only what we "need" is, in the absence of ways of dealing with these aspects of experience, ultimately nothing less than a counsel of despair.

Environmentalism has also failed to provide means of dealing productively with the negative and troubling aspects of change. Environ-

mentalists celebrate changes of a certain kind—in the progress of the seasons, in the weather, in a landscape, or in the cycle of life, but only when they perceive them as "natural" and cyclic or reversible. What we might call radical change—change that is irreversible and decisive—is another matter. Environmentalists often insist that our primary responsibility is never to foreclose possibilities, to keep all our options open. But nature doesn't work that way. It constantly takes one path to the exclusion of others—in the generation of species, for example. And a decision that doesn't limit options is not really a decision at all—that is, etymologically, a cutting off. We might even say it isn't action at all. It is a mere hedging of bets and contributes nothing to evolution. This is not to suggest that decisions that may have important consequences should be taken lightly. The point is that it is in making such radical decisions that we participate most fully in the monstrous and beautiful process of creation itself, and the inevitable foreclosing of possibilities it entails. This is naturally troubling and shameful. Yet it is a principle of creation and, properly handled, it too can be the source of beauty, community, and meaning.

Our own history bears out our species's increasingly self-conscious contributions to the violent process of creation. Perhaps the prime examples are the domestication of animals and the invention of agriculture. These are a profound imposition on nature and our fellow species, which decisively deepens the shame of our relationship with those species on which we depend for food, and there is good reason to believe that this is a source of profound existential anxiety for those who carry it out in a sensitive, reflexive way. Yet traditional agricultural societies have found ways of dealing with this that are a source of great beauty, deep meaning, and, arguably, profounder communion with the rest of nature. An example is ritual sacrifice, the deliberate killing of the innocent victim, which is a common feature of traditional agricultural societies but seems exotic from a modern perspective. Some scholars have interpreted sacrifice as an extension of rituals of the hunt, and therefore ancient or "primitive" in origin. Historian of religion Jonathan Z. Smith, however, has argued that this is not the case, that sacrifice did not develop as an extension of hunting rituals but was an invention of agriculturists as what he calls a meditation on domestication—a way of dealing with the cold-blooded, premeditated murder of the domestic animal, and what I would call the intensification of shame this entails.[11]

This, then, provides a key to a relationship with nature that is not backward looking, reactionary or nostalgic because it is a way of dealing in a psychologically and spiritually productive way with the scandal of

creation and our collusion in it. The key lies not in any particular way of life, but in the means culture provides for dealing with *changes* in the technical and economic basis of life and the intensification of shame or the new kinds of shame these entail.

This idea is important for us because it provides a way out of the primitivism and creationism, the habit of seeking the ideal in the origin or the "original," that have characterized much of the environmental thinking of the past half-century. To be effective, an environmentalism must confront the scandal of creation—including the killing and the inventions and innovations by which we ourselves participate in and contribute to creation—and must provide ways of dealing with it in a productive way. Yet this is precisely what environmentalism has consistently failed to do.

Here we come to the root of all so-called environmental problems, and also to the reason for the inability of environmentalism to deal with them effectively. This reason, we can now see, lies not in greed or alienation or technology or institutions or prejudice or the invention of artificial categories of thought, all of which have always been part of human experience. It lies rather in a structural flaw in the very foundations of environmental thought—in an idea of nature that has dominated environmental thinking for a century and a half. This is the idea, traceable to the biblical account of creation, in which shame, trouble, and badness are introduced into the creation peculiarly late and as a result of a human failing, the idea that nature itself is innocent and therefore morally discontinuous from human beings, whose lapse introduced shame, trouble, and evil into creation.

Beginning with Ralph Waldo Emerson, environmental thinkers have consistently rejected the old idea of Original Sin (or, more often, have taken its rejection for granted) but have retained the peculiar biblical idea, figured in the Garden, of a creation prior to trouble and shame, and this has made it impossible for them to account for or to come to terms with the human experience of alienation. Insisting, as good evolutionists, that creation is ongoing, they have overlooked the message of mythology, which characteristically represents creation and origin, not necessarily as evil, but always as troubled, destructive, and shameful.

Nature, the myths explain, is radically at odds with itself in the very act of creation. Whether this creative first act is figured as the slaying of a cosmic dragon or, more abstractly, in the collapse of infinite possibility into limited actuality figured in the Big Bang (itself a figure of creative cosmic destruction) or even the wildest and most thoughtless and destructive of human innovations, creation is trouble. Or, as in the old joke about the

turtles—if the world rests on a cosmic turtle, what does the turtle stand on? Well, it's turtles all the way down—creation is trouble all the way down. But environmentalism, like classical liberalism generally, has never been able to accommodate this idea, and the result is a kind of creationism, a denial of evolution in its monstrous and radical destructiveness.

It is, I argue, this inability to confront productively, not the basic facts of creation but rather the human response to those facts, that has limited the success of environmentalism. A philosophy or religion that ignores the destruction and shame inherent in creation and urges "minimal impact" without providing means for dealing in a psychologically and spiritually productive way with the impacts that we *do* make simply won't work. It won't work because it denies or downplays those troubling aspects of experience that provide opportunities for communion with a creation that is monstrous and shameful (and, as we shall see, *therefore* beautiful). And it won't work because it places human beings in a psychologically and spiritually incoherent situation that no one can tolerate for long, and to which no healthy-minded person can afford to make an ultimate commitment. This, I will argue, is why the constituency for environmentalism, though broad, has remained inadequate to the task of bringing about real social change. Lacking a robust, reflexive awareness of shame, a way of confronting it somewhere near the center of the economic interests that define our relationship with the landscape, and of dealing with it creatively, environmental thinkers have typically sought communion in exactly the wrong places—in parables and models of harmony rather than in those troubling aspects of life and relationships in which the shame and tensions inherent in them are revealed and made accessible.

The marks of this aspect of modernism are clearly evident in the idealization of the classic landscape, and in the paradigms of relationship that environmental thinkers have put forward over the past century, each of which fails in its own way to come to terms with the most problematic aspects of our relationship with the rest of nature. We are, we say, natural insofar as we live in harmony with the rest of nature, but inexplicably "outside" nature when we don't, forgetting both the radical contradiction inherent in creation itself and the tensions, both objective and subjective, that exist between us and the rest of nature, which are in fact the most natural thing about us.

Unable to deal in a coherent way with the ambivalence of creation, we have naturally also been unable to deal productively with the experiences of killing and consumption, which are our most intimate encounter with creation. Conservationism, for example, treats the problem of consumption matter-of-factly. Killing to eat is okay, the conservationist says, because it is "necessary" or "natural," disregarding the fact that that is precisely what makes it an *existential* crisis.

The situation becomes more interesting when we turn to the other two major environmental paradigms, since, far more than conservationism, they evoke higher values—the idea of nature as sacred, and Leopold's idea of the land as a community. The record of religious experience makes it clear that both of these values have at least two aspects. The experience of the sacred can be a more or less spontaneous apprehension of the unity underlying the manifest diversity of creation; or it can be the outcome of acts such as killing that outwardly appear to violate that unity. There are, to put it another way, two kinds of sacredness—one that we discover, and one that we actively create. Both are important, but it is the second of these that is most complete in the sense that it includes, and is the result of our most intense *ecological* engagement with the world. Yet since the time of Emerson, Thoreau, and Muir, environmental thinkers have emphasized the first to the virtual exclusion of the second.

The same may be said of the idea of community that is implicit in Leopold's writing, and that environmental thinkers have generally taken for granted. Community for Leopold is a "positive," and he has little to say about the more troubling, psychologically challenging aspects of life in an actual community. His idea of community reflects the romantic conception of *Gemeinschaft* developed in the 1880s by sociologist Ferdinand Tönnies—community as the warm, intimate, trusting association of the band, tribe, or village, as opposed to the more abstract and alienated structures of *Gesellschaft,* or society. Thus Leopold writes that conservation, conceived in a spirit of community, is "a state of harmony between men and land."[12] While community necessarily entails hierarchy and inequality, including the radical hegemony of predator over prey, Leopold downplays this, developing an egalitarian idea of community. A human, he insists, is simply "a plain member and citizen" of the land community—a formulation that simply papers over the difference, whatever it may be, that is the whole reason for the conversation. In a crucial passage in "The Land Ethic," headed "The Community Concept," Leopold mentions one problematic aspect of relationship—competition—but only fleetingly. The rest of the passage is devoted to a cataloging of human uses of natural landscapes cast as a form of conquest or exploitation. The fact that all life depends absolutely on "conquests" of this kind slips into the background. It is not that Leopold, hunter, forester, and manager of game and of land, was ignorant of the more troubling aspects of even the most benign of human relations with the land. It is simply that, seeing them as facts of life, he treats them matter-of-factly and has nothing to say about the shame that arises from any killing, as from any encounter with death, dependence or necessity. What Leopold implies here is a distinction between "use" (which is "necessary," and therefore legitimate) and "exploitation" (which is "unnecessary," and therefore egregious). This distinction is a commonplace in environmental thinking even today, despite the fact that, as A. L. Herman has pointed out, the distinction is a meaningless one, since "most use is already a form of exploitation, the taking advantage of another for one's own purposes and ends."[13]

Similarly, while community entails exclusion as much as inclusion, Leopold implies that community can include—and indeed ought to include—everything, and that extending to everything the moral status of membership in a community is the key to solving environmental problems. He betrays little awareness of the sense of the radical other, the chaos and ontological inferiority that lie beyond the psychological membrane surrounding a traditional community and give the community much of its meaning and importance. Crossing this membrane is a difficult, emotionally demanding process, as the initiation practices in traditional societies make clear. Yet Leopold takes membership in community for granted as something that may be achieved simply by declaration or good intentions. What is called for, he writes, is "an internal change in our intellectual emphasis, loyalties, affections, and convictions." But he seems unaware that such a change—essentially a transformation at the deepest levels of the self—might itself constitute an existential crisis that is beyond the reach of ordinary experience. "Perhaps," he writes, "such a shift of values can be achieved by reappraising things unnatural, tame, and confined in terms of things natural, wild, and free,"[14] a suggestion that, reduced to its essentials, amounts to saying that we would have different values if we had different values. Ultimately, of course, Leopold's answer to the question of how one enters community lies not in any particular statement but in the body of his work and the experience it recounts. The key, this work implies, is learning to live closer to the land.[15] Surely this is a first step toward community. Yet just as surely it is not enough, as the initiation practices of premodern societies—or for that matter, of gangs or military organizations or fraternal societies, or any group that takes community seriously—make abundantly clear.[16]

Indeed, if we are going to take the metaphor of community seriously as a basis for our relationship with other species and with the landscape generally, the place to begin is with the human community, since that is the community we know most immediately and experience most deeply, the one in which we are best able to develop an idea of what "community" might mean, and what sorts of tensions and psychological challenges it might entail. Yet, despite a tradition of communal *agricultural* pastoral from Brook Farm and the Shaker and Amish and Mennonite sects in the nineteenth century down to the bioregionalism and back-to-the-earth movements of our own time, our favored strategy for communion with wild—or "original"—nature has been a movement, not through the human community, but around and away from it, evading the emotional, not to mention economic, demands that other humans make on us. Our canonic environmental literature, from Henry David Thoreau and John Muir on, depicts withdrawal from the human community as the essential first step toward entry into the biotic community. This is true even when the facts of the experience itself are otherwise—as Thoreau, for example, downplays his visits home in *Walden,* or as other people are eerily absent from Leopold's account, in *A Sand County Almanac,* of what was, in fact, a series of family outings on his rural property. Neither Thoreau nor Leopold was attempting to mislead. But both were working within a rhetorical tradition that made it difficult to account for social experience or to place the human community in the natural landscape. Here Herman Melville, in his great pastoral *Moby Dick,* offers an alternative in a fable of the exploration of nature and the wild in which the protagonist is not alone but is a member of a ship's crew working—not playing or visiting—in what was essentially a factory, dealing with the vagaries and ambiguities of life in an actual community.

If environmentalism is to succeed at its central task of providing the basis for a healthy relationship between ourselves and the rest of nature, it must, as Melville's Ishmael does, confront the difficult, emotionally challenging aspects of such relationships. Yet, with a few scattered and partial exceptions, our environmental thinkers have had little to say about this. Leopold is by no means a peculiarity here. The weak, elastic, essentially sentimental idea of community he takes for granted is entirely consistent with what sociologist David McCloskey calls the three modern myths of community—that community is harmonious, homogeneous (made up of individuals who are all essentially alike, with common interests), and solidary (based on a common value system).[17] This "mythology" is characteristic of environmental thinking, a reflection of the idea that relationships are "naturally" and fundamentally free of genuinely challenging elements. The problem with this is that it makes the experience of alienation from nature, or a fundamental anxiety about any aspect of our relationship with it, into an intellectual and spiritual error or mistake—anthrocentrism or nature/culture dualism, perhaps—rather than a vital aspect of our experience of the drama of creation.

In fact, these myths conceal their own nature/culture dualism, since they rest on the idea that what we might call relational anxiety is a peculiarly human experience, isolating us from the rest of nature. It is this fundamental dualism, hidden beneath the conventional insistence on the unity of creation, that accounts for the nostalgic, backward-looking character of environmentalism, its tendency to locate the good in the past, in "nature," or in traditional or archaic societies, and to disqualify human invention and innovation, with all their costs, from natural creation. It also accounts for the tendency to sentimentalize creation, prettifying what premodern societies commonly figured as the primordial murder of a cosmic beast as a blossoming out, or trivializing the terrible majesty of the Big Bang by softening it into a mere "flaring forth."[18] And it accounts for the hatred of history and the mistrust of civilization that emerge in writings across the environmental spectrum—perhaps most vividly in philosopher/zoologist Paul Shepard's prescriptions for a return to various aspects of Paleolithic ways of life.

There are exceptions. Thoreau, for example, does confront the problem of killing in his writing and at times comes close to providing a robust means of dealing with it, as I will show later, in chapter 6. In our own time the writings of both Loren Eiseley and Annie Dillard reflect a vivid awareness of the monstrous in nature. Though both witness rather than engage with it, both at least confront it courageously.[19] Shepard and poet Gary Snyder take up the troubling aspects of our relationship with other species, particularly as experienced in the acts of killing and eating, and prescribe ritual and art as a means for dealing with it. But their treatment is consistently primitivist: they idealize the "old way" of confronting the horror of creation in classic acts such as killing for food but fail to come to terms with the horror of ongoing creation evident in novelties such as agriculture or science or the rise of industrialism, the modern nation-state, modern medicine, or the computer. This is also true of the practice of neopagans like the Wiccan Starhawk. Though historian Catherine Albanese suggests that Starhawk's practice "negotiates the divide between real and ideal with grace," it is still by and large backward looking.[20]

Nowhere, so far as I am aware—either in mainstream environmentalism or in its inflections in deep ecology, ecofeminism, environmental justice, or neopaganism—has anyone clearly articulated or fully realized the "strong" idea of creation and change or of relationship and community that I am dealing with here. The idea that there is an essential link between an ultimate value such as community and negative feelings such as fear, horror, or shame is foreign to environmentalism, as it is to modern thinking generally. It is this failure to confront the trouble and shame of creation that has limited what environmentalism has been able to accomplish. It is why, for more than a century, environmentalism has shifted uneasily, unproductively, and often even destructively between the poles of an alienated preservationism and a resource-oriented conservationism, and has proved incapable of inhabiting the middle ground where community is achieved as selves confront each other, first to acknowledge and then somehow to transcend the irreconcilable differences between them. This, I believe, explains why environmentalists have argued for community but have made so little progress in the task of strengthening the human community, much less expanding it to include other species.

In this book I explore a conception of relationship that provides an alternative to this generally accepted and clearly inadequate paradigm, but it is one that I am sure many readers will find troubling and even offensive. This is the emotionally demanding conception of relationship that I have taken, for the most part, from the work of literary critic Frederick Turner, which is based in part on the work of his parents, anthropologists Victor and Edith Turner—the idea that there is an essential, unbreakable link between the experience of transcendent values such as beauty, meaning, and community and the experience of shame that arises from our awareness of the world and the sense of limitation and difference this awareness entails. Shame here, it is important to emphasize, is distinct from guilt. It is not the response of the conscience to what we *do,* but of our consciousness of what we *are:* "I am ashamed," Sartre writes, "of what I am."[21]

Shame, in this sense—what I call existential shame—may arise from wrongdoing, but it is not associated only with moral failure. It is rather a sense of existential unworthiness, the painful emotion a person naturally feels on encountering *any* kind of shortcoming or limitation, beginning with the infant's discovery that he or she is not omnipotent but is instead one of many others and dependent on those others for every kind

of pleasure and satisfaction, and even for life itself. This shame is inseparable from any experience of relationship for the simple reason that any
relationship forces on us an awareness of difference, and therefore of limitation. It is a worse feeling than guilt, because guilt is the emotional register of a debt that might be repaid, or at least a failing for which we are
responsible and of which we are therefore "in charge." Shame, on the
other hand, is the emotional register of our natural, radical, existential dependency and a debt for which we are not responsible and which we cannot repay.[22] Repayment is not an option, and neither are an increase in
competence or wealth, or an improvement in health, or the reflection
that, death and suffering, though inevitable, may be deferred to an in-
definite future. As William James notes,

Our troubles lie indeed too deep for *that* cure. The fact that we *can* die, that we
can be ill at all is what perplexes us; the fact that we now for a moment live and
are well is irrelevant to that perplexity. We need a life not correlated with death,
a health not liable to illness, a kind of good that will not perish, a good in fact that
flies beyond the Goods of nature.[23]

As heirs to a modern, liberal culture that typically represses shame, we
like to think that shame is unnecessary, simply an emotional tool that culture uses to manipulate individuals. In fact, critic James Hans argues,
whatever use a particular culture may make of it, the experience of shame
is a universal part of human experience, and what is distinctive about the
West is not its use of shame to control behavior, but its habit of denying
shame and rejecting or downplaying the performative technologies
needed to deal with it productively.[24] Hans locates the origin of this habit
of thought in the thinking of Plato and Socrates, with their explicit attack
on both shame and the myths and rituals that had been invented to confront and deal with it productively. Indeed, it is the traditional, myth-
making cultures that environmentalists often point to as models for a
healthy culture that are typically most deeply in touch with their shame,
and provide the richest means of articulating it as the pathway to value.
Consider, for example, the eloquent litany of existential shame recited by
Old Torlino, a Navajo priest, as he begins a recital of the story of creation:

I am ashamed before the earth;
I am ashamed before the heavens;
I am ashamed before the dawn;
I am ashamed before the evening twilight;
I am ashamed before the blue sky;

I am ashamed before the sun;
I am ashamed before that standing within me which speaks with me.
Some of these things are always looking at me.
I am never out of sight.
Therefore I must tell the truth.[25]

The experience of existential shame is not peculiar or unusual but is universal, an inescapable (though deniable) aspect of human experience, not because we have done wrong, but because our limits are a scandal to our ego, and because, as Sartre argues, "shame . . . is shame of *self*; it is the recognition of the fact that I *am* indeed that object which the Other is looking at and judging," and then asks, "What sort of relations can I enter into with this being which I am and which shame reveals to me?"[26] Shame, in other words, is inseparable from the performative interaction that is the basis for the relationship between the self and the other. Summarizing this insight, philosopher Cheryl Foster notes that shame is the mechanism by which we come to see that part of ourselves that can only be revealed through noticing another looking at us. In other words, the look of the other causes a feeling of shame because we see in that look how we appear as objects in the world—not free, choosing, transcendent subjects, but objects in the consciousness of others.[27]

The ultimate example of this is our own death, the moment when we cease to be subjects and become objects. But occasions for this experience of existential shame are literally everywhere in a differentiated, impermanent, limited—and therefore shameful—creation, and we deal with this shame for the most part by denying or repressing it. This is a psychological skill that is necessary for sanity but that can stand in the way of communion with a creation that is defined by limit. It is important, then, to seek out carefully selected occasions for confronting shame and dealing with it productively, and this is the function of religion and the arts. Indeed, Turner has argued that, properly managed through the spiritual and psychological technologies of ritual and the arts, the experience of shame turns out to be the indispensable pathway to the experience of beauty, which for Turner is the comprehensive "value of values."

From this perspective, the experience of all the higher values—the pang of beauty, the hope that arises from the apprehension of meaning, the deep sense of connectedness and completion that we achieve in community—are the neurological rewards evolution has provided for the hard work of dealing with shame. What Turner has in mind is not the simple beauty of a sunset or a tree full of flowers, but the tougher beauty that humans achieve through rituals such as the bullfight or the Mass, or in tragic drama, and that, Turner argues, lies at the heart of all experiences of beauty and of the transcendent values generally, which he regards as inflections, or facets of the experience of beauty.

One of the best places to find warrant for this idea is in mythology, of course, but also in those close relatives of myth—fairy tales and children's literature. Adults are generally adept at repressing existential shame. But children confront it constantly as they explore the world and find themselves incompetent and inadequate in practically every way, and the experience of shame in the face of difference, inequality, and incompetence is a common theme of children's literature from classic fairy tales to Harry Potter.

Consider, for example, the episode in E. B. White's *Charlotte's Web* in which the pig, Wilbur, as he comes to know his spider friend, Charlotte, and to admire her weaving ability, decides that he, too, will create a web, tries bravely, and winds up throwing himself absurdly and ignominiously off the dungheap in his pen with a bit of string tied to his tail. "You needn't feel too badly," Charlotte later tells him. "Not many creatures can spin webs. Even men aren't as good at it as spiders." Wilbur consoles himself by exulting in his own excellent sense of smell, only to be mocked by a lamb for being "the smelliest creature in the place"—a double encounter with shame, both in the awareness of his body as an object and in the experience of being so regarded by others. Finally, troubled by the prospect of his own death, he is comforted by Charlotte, who says she has a plan to save Wilbur. That plan turns out to be the message she writes in her web—a performance in which she magically transcends her own spider nature to achieve a momentary stay against confusion.

Like any good art, good children's literature deals with the shame of difference and incompetence honestly, revealing it as a condition of life but one that, properly handled, with pluck and grace and imagination, leads to higher values, such as Wilbur's deepening friendship with Charlotte.[28] This, as Bruno Bettelheim has pointed out, is why stories such as the one about "the little engine that could" are so unsatisfactory: they suggest that it is possible to avoid shame through competence, and in so doing sidestep the essential problem of dealing with the incompetence and inadequacies that actually define our lives and our relationships with others.[29]

Everything is defined by difference—that is, by shortcoming. Fred Turner sees this universal shortcoming and the shame that arises from it as a principle of nature, and entropy, the ineluctable running down of the universe, as a physical manifestation or correlate of shame. He speaks of the heat still radiating from the Big Bang as "the hot blush of universal shame"—the blush, of course, is a trope for beauty. And in his poem "Prima Vera," Rainer Maria Rilke makes the link explicit, writing "and the beauty is shame."

What all this suggests is that an environmental or social philosophy that lacks a reflexive sense of shame is very much like a physical science that lacks a conception of entropy. This is the context in which I explore the practice of ecological restoration—not only as an environmental technology, but as an encounter with the shame of creation, and so as a performing art and a context for the creation of the higher values. Since community is arguably the key value on which Leopold's land ethic is based, and since I have found it easier to think about than beauty, I concentrate on it. I argue that restoration is important for a number of reasons. It is important because it is a way of returning classic ecosystems to the landscape, allowing us to go on the offensive in the struggle to ensure their long-term survival. It is important because it provides a unique context for a positive, active relationship with the classic landscape. It is important because it offers a way of rebuilding the ecological capital of soil, air, water, biological diversity, and productivity that is the basis for all human economies. But it is also important for exactly the reasons that four generations of environmentalists have been skeptical about it: because it is at every point an encounter with shame. Restoration is shameful because it involves killing and a measure of hegemony over the land; because the restoration effort is never fully successful and never complete; because it dramatizes not only our troubling dependence on the natural landscape, but—equally troubling—its dependence on us; and because it dramatizes the restorationist's complicity, not only in the destructive acts he attempts to reverse, but, more fundamentally, in the shameful process of creation itself, in which he presumes to participate. Attempting to rescue the landscape from history, the restorationist moves inevitably toward the discovery that there is no escape from history, just as there is no escape from ecology. Beginning as an attempt to reverse or obliterate time, restoration concludes by accommodating it. Sometimes criticized as an exercise in nostalgia, it is, at its best and most deliberate, quite the opposite of that—not a daydream of the past, but a troubling encounter with time and change. It shows that the classic ecosystem can survive and flourish, as we had hoped it might, but only on radically new terms.

◆   ◆   ◆

Gradually, as these ideas took shape, I put together an idea of the process of community building, or entry into community. This eventually included four steps or stages, each of which involves a challenge to the self and the experience of shame. The great value of ecological restoration, I now believe, is that it provides an ideal, even unique context for negotiating these stages in the development of a relationship between ourselves and the classic landscape. These steps are:

First, achieving awareness of the other. A human infant regards itself as omnipotent or co-terminus with the world, making no distinction between what it desires and what the world has to offer. The breakdown of this illusion of an all-inclusive self, as the other appears on the horizon of awareness and the demands of the ego are thwarted or denied, is a psychological trauma from which, anthropologist Ernest Becker suggests, few ever fully recover.

According to psychologist Jean Piaget, and very significantly for us, the infant's radical incompetence actually fosters the illusion of the omnipotent (and so shameless) self because it sabotages purposeful effort— it is emerging *competence* that leads inevitably to frustration, the encounter with limit and the experience of shame. In the same way, restoration deepens our awareness of the landscape and the intractable other that sometimes responds to, sometimes resists our efforts.

Second, getting a job and learning the language. This is the ecological or economic stage of relationship, the purposeful exchange of goods and services with the other, and also the classic, biblical trope for the fall into the experience of shame. This is not a problem in a working agricultural, urban, or pastoral economy, all of which provide contexts for engaging nature economically through productive work. But the classic landscape poses a dilemma here, since traditional forms of manipulation aimed at production, beautification, or control of processes for human purposes all compromise the value of such a landscape as the embodiment of nature-as-given. Restoration solves this problem by providing ways of working in the landscape that are defined, insofar as possible, by reference to the condition and needs of the landscape itself, and with a studied disregard for human interests. At the same time, since, like any action, restoration has expressive as well as effective value, the restorationist enters into a dialogue with nonhuman nature in its own language—the language of action and performance that precedes human speech.

Third, the exchange of gifts. The exchange of goods and services carried out in the course of work provides the economic basis that necessarily underlies any truly ecological relationship. But the relationship defined in this way is limited to a reciprocal relationship that yields only ecological values. To step beyond this, we replace the quid pro quo of the economic transaction with the offering of a gift. In contrast with the merely ecological transaction, the value of the gift is not openly calculated, and the gift itself is offered with the pretense that nothing is expected in return. The result is an open-ended exchange that, at least in principle—and in contrast with a merely ecological or "commercial" exchange—transcends the purely economic and is likely to deepen and intensify as each party involved increases the value of his gift in an attempt to ensure that he is "keeping up his end." Restoration provides a context for this development because the restorationist does offer nature a gift in nature's own kind, both in the restored ecosystem and in the greater understanding and increased self-awareness that the act of restoration, properly conducted, contributes to the landscape and that constitutes its distinctively human element.

Fourth, resolving ambiguity. Since the value of gifts is never accounted for, none of the parties involved can ever be sure that the value of the gift he offers is commensurate in value with the gift he receives in return. As a result, the cycle of gift exchange generates a deepening sense of ambiguity and uncertainty about the equity of the relationship. Since this ambiguity cannot be resolved in literal terms, it is necessary to step outside the literal and into the figurative dimension to deal with it. This is the prime function of ritual and those other technologies of the imagination, the arts and religious practices, which provide the means for Turner's productive passage through shame to beauty.

If this seems exotic, excessively demanding, and unappealingly negative, that is because community in its tougher, classic sense has become for the most part obsolete, as Fred Turner argues that beauty has been obsolete in the West for at least two hundred years. We are living, by this argument, in a postvalue society, much as philosopher Alasdair MacIntyre has argued that we are living in a postvirtue society. It may be that the higher values of beauty, community, meaning, and the sacred are no longer available to us. It may even be that this is inevitable—a natural outcome of evolution. But if that is true, if the old experiences of community and beauty, bought at the price of the knowledge of shame, really are obsolete, then it is our job to invent satisfactory substitutes for them, and it is a dangerous mistake to go on using the old words, as we now do, sentimentally. Purified of their shame and drained of their tougher meaning, they serve only to reassure, distracting us from the task of inventing something entirely new.

Quite possibly, given the constitutive limitations of classical liberalism in this respect, this may have to come from outside the liberal tradition. Perhaps the flourishing of evangelical religion, with its linking of community feeling and personal obligation, represents a step in that direction. At all events, if the question is how a culture generates the truly new, it makes sense to begin, as the restorationist does, with a look backward because, after all, we have been through this before.

The process of value creation has ancient roots in the rituals that people living in premodern societies use to deal with the existential dilemmas posed by facts of life such as predation, reproduction, coming of age, and death. The hunter, for example, encounters "nature" most deeply in the act of killing, and a healthy hunting culture provides means of dealing with the misgivings this arouses through rituals of atonement, of giving back, and of retrieving the spirit of the slain animal. Farming — the first industrial revolution — raises the ante, replacing the hot-blooded killing of the hunt with the even more troubling cold-blooded killing of the barnyard and the systematic mass-murder of cultivation and harvest. But, as I noted, agricultural societies have invented ways of dealing with this through institutions such as ritual sacrifice.

Our even more technically advanced industrial and postindustrial societies have raised the ante yet again, extending the creative killing beyond the levels of the individual and the population to the level of entire ecosystems. Restoration enters here as the key to resolving the uncertainty attending this even-greater taking from nature, countering the destruction of whole ecosystems with the offering back of whole ecosystems in a cycle that corresponds to the classic cycles of ritualized taking and giving back developed by hunting and agricultural societies.

In an early essay, theologian Teilhard de Chardin called for "a Mass on the world" in which we not only acknowledge but actively participate in the killing and destruction that are part of the creative process, but do so in the context of a redemptive cycle of taking and — even if inadequately — giving back.[30] If the Mass in its traditional form is rooted in the act of sacrifice as a way of dealing with the horror of creative death, figured in the killing of a single creature, or even of God, then a Mass on the world would provide a way of dealing, in symbolic terms, with both the killing and the resurrection of entire ecosystems. Restoration clearly provides a context for such an encounter with the rest of nature — and an occasion for what Emerson called its terrible and beautiful condensation.

CHAPTER 3

Paradigms of Community

In his 1970 book *The Invisible Pyramid,* naturalist Loren Eiseley wrote an eloquent plea for reentry into the "first world" of nature, figured as a thicket of sunflowers that grew along a creek near his boyhood home in Nebraska.

[Man] must make, by way of the cultural world, an actual conscious reentry into the sunflower forest he had thought merely to exploit or abandon. He must do this in order to survive. If he succeeds he will, perhaps, have created a third world which combines elements of the original two and which should bring closer the responsibilities and nobleness of character envisioned by the axial thinkers who may be acclaimed as the creators, if not of man, then of his soul.[1]

Eiseley's is not the first such statement. Artists, priests, and shamans have been concerned since ancient times with the problem of achieving a more intimate and more satisfactory relationship between our own species and the rest of nature. But Eiseley's statement of the challenge is especially useful. For one thing, he carefully avoids a naive and sentimental primitivism, a prescription merely to abandon civilization, throw down our tools, and reenter the forest. An evolutionist, Eiseley knows that history, like evolution, is irreversible. Though reentry is essential, he recognizes that we will have to achieve it not in spite of, but actually *by way of* the achievements of civilization—which he refers to as "the knowledge gained on the pathway to the moon." For another, his way of putting the challenge, using a vivid yet somewhat fanciful metaphor to make a specific demand on us and our society, prompts an obvious question: what, in practical terms, would it actually mean to reenter the sunflower forest? What would it mean for a truck driver, say, or a dentist or a school-teacher actually to reinhabit a wetland, an oak forest, or a tallgrass prairie—not merely to know it and admire it and care about it but actually to form a working, ecological relationship with it? And beyond that, what might it mean to become part of the forest in a deeper psychological and spiritual sense, becoming what Aldo Leopold called a member of the land community?

In his 1980 book *The Rights of Nature,* environmental historian Roderick Nash traces what he sees as the expansion of community through the progressive enfranchisement and extension of rights and citizenship to an expanding circle of subjects, which might eventually include other species and even nonliving elements of the world.[2] Like Eiseley's formulation, Nash's scheme raises basic questions about the nature of community and the process by which it is achieved. Nash finds a basis for these developments in classical liberalism, and he sees movements such as the environmental, women's, and civil rights movements as progress toward realization of an expanded conception of community and as a form of moral progress. Historically, however, liberalism, like modernism generally, has tended to define social values individualistically, in terms of the rights of individuals, and to be unfriendly to community. And while liberal thinkers may talk about the value of community and, as Nash points out, liberalism has led to the extension of certain rights to a widening circle of people, it has done so by and large at the *expense* of community, trading the organic and spiritual bonds of communal relationship for legally defined rights and the more abstract linkages of citizenship and political enfranchisement. Furthermore, the concept of rights goes only so far in defining relationships and fails completely when it encounters the more problematic aspects of relationship, such as that between people and the plants and animals they kill in order to stay alive. This being the case, it would seem that liberalism is ill-equipped to deal with the problematic aspects of relationship and community that I mentioned in the previous chapter: the crisis of individual identity inherent in any relationship; the inequity inherent in the exchange of goods and services that is the economic—or ecological—basis of community; and the fact that a community is defined as much by what it excludes as by what it includes.[3]

It is one thing to describe a community at the ecological level as an exchange of goods and services. It is quite another to come to grips with the implications of that exchange for those involved in it. Consider, for example, the network of relationships that ecologists blandly describe as a food chain or food web. This involves, quite simply, eating—or being eaten by—other members of the community. Such a relationship is obviously deeply problematic. It becomes even more so to the extent that one attempts to enfranchise other creatures, grant them rights, and regard them as brothers and sisters. Yet it is precisely the act of killing to sustain one's own life that provides the paradigm of relationship we see being explored in classic expressions of relationship and community: rituals of the hunt, food shamanism involving the spiritual preparation of food to remove dangerous elements from it, and the sacrificial rituals of many premodern people—the Eucharist in Christian tradition, the Sun Dance of the Plains Indians, or the world-renewal rites of the Australian Aborigines—that reenact in a ritual manner the violence inherent in relationship and, for that matter, in creation itself.

These are the answers of particular cultures to questions that cannot be answered by ecology, which offers only an analysis and interpretation of the hardware, or objective aspects of relationships. Nor can they be answered by liberalism or, for that matter, by any political system or philosophy. In fact, this central task of environmentalism—the creation of relationships and the building and extension of community—is ultimately a religious task in the fundamental sense that religion is the art and discipline of dealing with the problems of relationship at the psychological and spiritual levels.[4] It is in religious tradition that we find the most profound experience and the most deeply felt and deeply considered ideas regarding the fundamental issues of relationship: how have humans come to be—or feel—separate, or even alienated from the rest of nature? What stands in the way of communion, which we may define as the deepest level of experience of the other, the real, or the sacred? Beyond that, what actually *is* the sacred or the really real that we apprehend in moments of communion? Where does the sacred come from? Is it discovered, inherent in creation, or is it a quality that in some sense we create? And what is the source of the moral and spiritual energy—or grace—needed to achieve it? Religious traditions and debates have much to teach us about these matters. Whether we are aware of it or not, they condition the ideas about relationship that we have inherited and generally take for granted. This being the case, exploring the roots of these ideas in religious tradition may well lead us to insights into our own ideas about nature and community and the limitations of those ideas.

Curiously, one of the most helpful guides I have found to thinking about this is a small book by literary scholar R. W. B. Lewis titled *The American Adam: Innocence, Tragedy, and Tradition in the Nineteenth Cen-*

tury (1955).[5] This book is not explicitly about the environment but offers a valuable perspective on figures—notably Emerson and Thoreau—who have played key roles in the development of American environmental thought. Lewis discusses this development in terms of the idea of origi-nal sin and the Fall in the Garden of Eden—a central metaphor for nineteenth-century Americans. If we are inclined to adopt a condescend-ing attitude toward this way of posing the problem of the relationship be-tween humans and the rest of nature, this, as we shall see, is in large part because we are the heirs of one of the schools of thought that emerged from this discussion.

In his account of the birth of American literature, Lewis writes that two basic questions facing writers early in the century were, who exactly was the American who would be the protagonist in the American story? And what would the story be about? Writers of fiction, along with philosophers and social critics like Emerson and Thoreau, Oliver Wendell Holmes and Henry James Sr. (the father of Henry James the novelist and William James the psychologist), historians like Francis Parkman and William Prescott, and religious leaders like theologian Horace Bushnell were united in the idea that the American protagonist was the new man represented by the biblical Adam, and that the American story would be the story of his encounter with the New World, figured as Eden.

The question, then, was how to tell the story—how, in particular, to deal with the story of sin and the fall from grace that is at the heart of the story of the biblical Adam and Eve? Closely related to this question were the issues of shame and innocence, time and the past, memory and tra-dition, hope and redemption, all of which are "religious" matters which, broadly understood, are directly related to the question of our relation-ship with nature. Central to all of them is the question of redemption. How, having fallen from grace, is one redeemed back into unity with the world represented by the garden?

Lewis writes that thinkers of the time were divided into three schools of thought on this question, which he designates the party of Memory, the party of Hope, and the party of Irony. The first of these, the party of Memory, represented what remained of puritanism, the form of Calvin-ism that had been the dominant religious influence in New England dur-ing the colonial period.

To the question of redemption the Calvinist's answer was bleak: the burden of the past is both immense and unavoidable. As a result of the sin in the Garden, not only humankind, but all of nature is fallen. So far as humans are concerned, in the end some will be saved and others will be damned, in accordance with an inscrutable divine will, but this has nothing to do with human merit or virtue. For the Calvinist, the individual is both spiritually unworthy and powerless to effect his own salvation.

While puritanism had to a considerable extent lost its hold on the American imagination by the beginning of the nineteenth century, elements of the Calvinist worldview survived and have influenced American views of the world and American institutions and social movements, including environmentalism. This is clearly evident, for example, in the work of canonic environmental writers such as Emerson, Thoreau, and Muir, all of whom consciously reacted against the Calvinist sensibility. We can see it, for example, in Muir's emphasis on the corruption of human nature in contrast to a nature that he regards as a repository of purity and innocence. While the Puritans had seen all nature as fallen before God, Muir saw humans as fallen before nature, which he came to see as divine. We can also see the mark of Calvinism in the tendency of a long line of environmental thinkers beginning with Emerson and Thoreau to reject human institutions, bypassing them in order to seek salvation through the unmediated personal experience of nature.[6]

Even more important for environmentalism, however, was what Lewis (somewhat misleadingly, it turns out) designates the party of Hope, in which the leading figures included both Emerson and Thoreau and poet Walt Whitman. Reacting against the stark doctrine of their cultural forbears, the party of Hope—which for convenience I will call the Emersonians—rejected the idea of the Fall and of inherited—or original—sin. For them humans may be fallen—in fact, they saw civilization itself as the outcome and expression of a fall from grace. But nature remained morally pristine, a repository of innocence. Thus redemption was possible and could be achieved by withdrawing from civilization, divesting oneself of the accouterments and distractions of civilized life and immersing oneself in nature. We see this idea in Emerson's determined rejection of the past with its burden of shame and guilt—in his "lop off all superfluities and tradition, and fall back on the nature of things," for example, or "Here's for the plain old Adam, the simple, genuine self against the whole world" (6). We see it in Thoreau's ritualistic retreat to Walden Pond, and in Whitman's lusty celebration of himself, unclothed, anticipating redeeming contact with nature as with a lover: "I will go to the bank by the wood and become undisguised and naked, / I am mad for it to be in contact with me."[7]

All these are expressions of the conviction that redemption is achieved, not through history and social institutions, but by *renouncing* history and society in favor of nature, an act that is redemptive precisely because nature, though it is flawed, is nevertheless innocent—and therefore morally discontinuous from human nature. If humans are living in chains, imprisoned in the strictures of history, Thoreau "prescribes the following cure: the total renunciation of the traditional, the conventional, the socially acceptable, the well-worn paths of conduct, and the total immersion in nature" (21). If we experience alienation or perceive a problem in our relationship with others or with the rest of nature, Thoreau implies, the problem lies in a propensity for alienation or waywardness that is peculiarly human. Thus the key to communion is to set aside this human sense of difference and become attentive to the ultimate oneness or unity of things. "The only sin is limitation," Emerson wrote in "Circles," succinctly expressing the confusion between shame and guilt characteristic of modernism. And while he is clear that this "sin" is inherent in nature, he suggests that it is rather easy to escape its consequences, writing in "Compensation,"

The radical tragedy of nature seems to be the distinction of More and Less. How can Less not feel the pain; how not feel indignation or malevolence toward More? . . . It seems a great injustice. But see the facts nearly and these mountainous inequalities vanish. Love reduces them as the sun melts the iceberg in the sea. The heart and souls of all men being one, this bitterness of His and Mine ceases. His is mine. I am my brother and my brother is me.[8]

The formula here is simple and, apparently, psychologically undemanding. The difference is not "real." It lies merely in the eye of the beholder and can be resolved by waving toward it words like "love" or "humility" or "compassion" or "respect," forgetting that compassion means suffering and that love itself, we have reason to suspect, is a crucifixion. Actually, Emerson frequently dealt with the experiences of pain, loss, and shortcoming. Yet, while some have argued that he achieved a view that comprehended both the tragedy and the comedy of creation to achieve "an ultimate serenity, a sheer gratitude for being," critic Irving Howe suggests that what Emerson managed to achieve was only "in one charmed glide, an *effect* like unity" (emphasis added), an effect he achieved in large part by rejecting the contingencies and vicissitudes of physical circumstance. He aimed for unity, Howe, argues, yet acknowledged that he "beheld two" in the waste and drag of daily life, noting characteristically, "Alas . . . infinite compunctions embitter in mature

life the remembrance of budding joy . . . all is sour if seen as experience."
Inevitably, the sense of unity Emerson achieved was fragile.[9]

There is warrant for the Emersonian reading of the world as ideally
free of shame in the biblical creation story, which at least by some readings not only recounts a creation that is "out of nothing" and therefore
eerily innocent of destruction but also posits, in the Garden, a place outside trouble, prior to shame, that has provided the West with a basis for
utopian and primitivist fantasies for nearly two thousand years. By making humans responsible for all the trouble in the world, this story casts
them as morally discontinuous from nature. And in attributing the Fall
to sin (rather than to mere being or existence), it conflates shame and
guilt, providing no basis for making the morally and psychologically crucial distinction between the bad feelings I have because of the limited and
dependent thing I am and the bad feelings I have because of the evil I
have done. Thus when a liberal thinker like Emerson rejected the idea of
original sin, as he was bound to do, he could not account for the shameful aspects of life. These, however, are peculiarities of a particular reading of the biblical creation story, in contrast to the creation stories of
many premodern cultures, in which there is no Eden, no time prior to
shame, since the creation itself, figured in the murder of a god, the slaying of a primal beast, the blundering efforts of an inept maker, or the
pranks and misdemeanors of a trickster, is understood to be an existential scandal, both sublimely destructive and shamefully ridiculous.

Our own idea of evolution by genetic mutations—of which only a tiny
fraction survive the trial of selection to become part of the creation—reflects the ambivalent consequences of natural violence and destruction.
Awareness of these is at the core of mythology, which Joseph Campbell
describes as "a verification and validation of the well-known—as monstrous."[10] It is precisely this deep sense of a continuity of universal shame
that is missing from our environmental thinking. Thus, ecotheologian
Thomas Berry characterizes human violence as a "new violence," different
in kind from natural violence, which, he implies, is unambiguously creative: "if in prior ages the violence of the natural world was essentially creative in the larger arc of its unfolding, the violence associated with human
presence on the planet remains ambivalent in its ultimate consequences."[11]

What we have forgotten, if not the primal murder itself, are its continuity with human action and its implications for communion. Thus
Berry sees "the communion of each reality of the universe with every
other reality in the universe" as a principle of creation, but he has little to
say about how to realize this communion in the face of his first principle,

which is differentiation—difference. Science, he writes, has produced a vast body of information and insight that is consistent with an ancient intuition of unity in the world.[12] This may be both suggestive and inspiring. But it begs the question. The problem for humans has never been the ultimate oneness of things but the manifest and troubling differences— Emerson's "mountainous inequalities"—among them. Difference, we say, is good—but only so long as it really makes no difference.

Similarly, the theologian Rosemary Reuther writes, "An ecological spirituality needs to be built on three premises: the transience of selves, the living interdependency of all things, and the value of personal communication." She acknowledges that the letting go of the ego these premises imply is important, yet she is critical of spiritual traditions that have "emphasized the need to 'let go of the ego,' but in ways that diminished the value of the person." What she offers in their place is essentially what Berry offers: a meditation on the material continuity of the universe in the context of pleasant experiences of birds and plants in a garden.[13] Through such reflections, she suggests, we achieve compassion. But it is a compassion without passion—without suffering or participation in a nature that is at odds with itself in the very act of creation.

Here again, simply to declare our radical naturalness is not to solve the problems of difference and of relationship. "The separateness of the parts," Robert Frost once suggested, "is as important as the connection of the parts."[14] And Spanish poet Antonio Machado writes,

The other does not exist: this is rational faith, the incurable belief of human reason. Identity = reality, as if, in the end, everything must necessarily and absolutely be one and the same. But the other refuses to disappear; it subsists, it persists; it is the hard bone on which reason breaks its teeth. Abel Martín [Machado's fictional alter ego], with a poetic faith as human as rational faith, believed in the other, in "the essential Heterogeneity of being," in what might be called the incurable otherness from which oneness must always suffer.[15]

In the same vein, though in more concrete terms, pointing out the role ritual plays in the "transduction of information between unlike systems," anthropologist Roy Rappaport writes,

Despite the fact that they share components, local ecological systems and regional political systems are "unlike," and the same may be said of individual psychophysical systems on the one hand and social systems on the other. Local ecological systems are "about" trophic exchanges, energy flows, soil depletion and replenishment. Regional political systems are "about" war, women, land and the exchange of goods.[16]

Difference, in other words, is real. And the psychological tensions associated with difference are not the result of a peculiarly Western—or modern—nature/culture dualism. Whatever categories a culture uses to make sense of the world, it encounters difference and finds it troubling. The presence of others, all perfectly natural yet unlike ourselves, is a fundamental problem, not only for the philosopher trying to make sense of the puzzle of the one and the many, but for the self confronting a world full of intractable "others." And it is not a problem we can solve simply by declaring or insisting on our identity with the world or our membership in a universal community of subjects.

The idea that this problem can be solved in this way is characteristic of what literary scholar Harold Bloom calls "the American religion." In a recent book by that name, Bloom argues that there is a distinctively American religious sensibility, quite unlike that of the "old" European religions. Emerson, Bloom suggests, is its chief "theologian," but it is shared in some measure by all Americans, whatever their formal religious affiliation.[17] This sensibility is essentially subjective and personal. It places great emphasis on the experience of personal rebirth or regeneration and, in its explicitly Christian versions, on a personal relationship with Jesus as the basis for redemption. In interpreting the biblical narrative of redemption, it characteristically emphasizes the resurrection and downplays both the crucifixion (the American religionist's Christ, Bloom writes, "is a Jesus who barely was crucified") and the role of Christ as redeemer, making him less a savior than a "resurrected friend, walking and talking, one-on-one, with the repentant sinner." Bloom argues that this sensibility affected American versions of Christianity and of Eastern, Native American, and other non-Western religious traditions as well. If this is true it should not be surprising that environmentalism reflects this sensibility, especially since environmentalists have often been skeptical about traditional religions and unself-conscious about the explicitly religious aspects of their own thinking and might therefore be expected to have adopted a prevailing religious sensibility uncritically.

In any event, it is worth taking note of Bloom's reading of American religious culture, if only to remind ourselves that there are other kinds of religious sensibility, ones that stress the objective and communal; that emphasize performance—expressive action—rather than unmediated personal experience; that place more emphasis on the problematic and tragic aspects of life; and that for this reason may be better prepared to deal with the trouble—and tragedy—that is inseparable from it.[18]

From a social, literary, and religious point of view, there are both strengths and weaknesses in the Emersonian view of nature and redemption. Its great strength is that it brings ultimate value—the sacred or divine—down to earth, locating it in nature, and so providing a basis for a loving, communal relationship with the natural world. Its weakness is that by idealizing innocence, driving shame out of nature and celebrating the individual ego, it precludes communion with a creation that is defined by its shameful limitations.

Summing up the social and psychological implications of what he calls the "religion of the self," Bloom writes, "What the American self has found, since about 1800, is its own freedom—from the world, from time, from other selves." But this freedom comes at a high price "because of what it is obliged to leave out: society, temporality, the other. What remains, for it, is solitude and the abyss."[19]

In Lewis's reading too, the Emersonian formula for redemption proved in the end to be not a formula for communion at all but rather a prescription for loneliness and alienation. Speaking of Whitman, whom he sees as carrying the Emersonians' idea of the American Adam farthest of all, Lewis writes, "Whitman's dominant emotion, when it was not unmodified joy, was simple, elemental loneliness . . . of course he was lonely, incomparably lonely; no anchorite was ever so lonely, since no anchorite was ever so alone." He adds that "Whitman's image of the evergreen 'solitary in a wide, flat space . . . without a friend a lover near,' introduced what more and more appears to be the central theme of American literature, in so far as a unique theme may be claimed for it: the theme of loneliness" (48, 49).[20]

The crucial point here is the relationship between loneliness and innocence. Innocence is, in the end, a prescription for loneliness. It precludes community and communion because, knowing no harm, it cannot relate to a nature that is full of harms, and also because its egotism isolates it, as we can see clearly in the self-absorption characteristic of a child. Community depends on the knowledge of harm and also on the setting aside of the ego—actually, on what philosopher Octavio Paz calls contamination of the self—an experience that, religious tradition suggests, is both difficult and painful. Hope too depends on transcending the ego, since for the individual self there is no possible end but the oblivion of death. Thus, in idealizing innocence and celebrating the ego, the Emersonians precluded community and, for all their praise of the world and of nature, Lewis sees in their work the foundations, not of an artistic tradition of redemption and communion but of the modern literature of alienation (9).[21]

In other words, by replacing the old virtue of hope with "the human quality of hopefulness" (175), Lewis points out, what the party of Hope offers is not hope at all, but at best a fragile optimism. Hope, after all, is not a good feeling based on confidence that things will turn out well. It is, rather, a virtue rooted in the discovery that, despite the worst that can happen to *me,* in some transcendent sense "all manner of thing shall be well."[22] This, however, depends on the setting aside of the self in identification with something larger—family, friends, ecosystem, or god—that flourishes and grows despite—indeed, because of—the suffering and mortality of the self. Thus, by idealizing innocence and celebrating the self as spiritually "original" and self-sufficient, the party of Hope actually cut itself off from hope, as well as from community and from access to other transcendent values.

Far more promising as a basis for community and hope is the third major response to the problem of the past and original sin that Lewis identifies in nineteenth-century America as the party of Irony. The Ironists, Lewis writes, were represented by a group of thinkers, notably the elder Henry James and writers Herman Melville and Nathaniel Hawthorne, who found the speculations of the Emersonians unsatisfying and proposed a radical alternative. This idea, first developed in a philosophical way by James, was that the world itself contained a negative, monstrous principle, and that redemption—or the full experience of community—actually depended on the experience of this monstrousness. Thus for James, "in order to enter the ranks of manhood, the individual (however fair) had to *fall,* had to pass beyond childhood in an encounter with 'Evil,' had to mature by virtue of the destruction of his own egoism" (55).

Here was an interpretation of the Fall completely different from that of either the Emersonians, who sought to identify with the prelapsarian Adam, or of their intellectual descendants today, who reject the story of the Fall as a tragic, even morbid misconstrual of reality. In response to Emerson's toast to "the plain old Adam," James argued that "nothing could be more remote . . . from distinctively *human* attributes . . . than this sleek and comely Adamic condition" (6). He disparaged Adam as "a dull, somnolent, unconscious clod . . . an imbecile, prosaic, unadventurous" (58). While the Calvinists saw the Fall as a moral catastrophe that could not be reversed by human effort, and the Emersonians dismissed it or regarded it as a peculiarly human problem that could be solved by human effort, James celebrated the Fall, which he saw not as a calamity at all, but rather as the necessary first step toward the knowledge of badness that is prerequisite to adulthood and so to redemption and community. And where a modern-day ecofeminist like Carolyn Merchant is critical of the biblical story because it depicts a fall or "declension" and because it ascribes primary responsibility for the Fall to a woman,[23] James saw the prelapsarian Adam as representing the moral infancy of the human race and argued that "the first and highest service which Eve renders Adam is to throw him out of Paradise" (58). In this way the Ironists exculpate both Adam and Eve for the Fall, not by denying the Fall in a search for innocence but by identifying it as a story of the coming of age of the human race—the loss of innocence that is prerequisite to communion with nature and the other.

Though the party of Irony remained a tiny minority among American thinkers, James was not alone with what Lewis calls his "big idea." In very different ways, writers like Hawthorne and Melville worked their way toward the same idea. In *The Scarlet Letter,* for example, Hawthorne explores the idea that redemption from pain could be achieved by flight into the forest but concludes by suggesting that it is only through a return to the scaffold of shame that a measure of transcendence is achieved. Later, in *The Marble Faun,* he explored the theme of redemption through knowledge of the past and acceptance of its burden of both shame and guilt. Lewis finds a similar development in Melville's work. The great white whale of *Moby Dick* represents the monstrous element inherent in nature; and the madness of Ahab, the Quaker sea captain, is the madness of the innocent Adam who has encountered the monstrousness of the world, but whose culture provides no way of dealing with it.[24] Only later, in *Billy Budd,* written some forty years after *Moby Dick,* does Melville fully explore the resolution of this experience through the sacrifice of the innocent victim, the novel's protagonist Billy Budd, in the context of images evoking the sacrifice of the Mass (146).

This view of the world may strike many as excessively negative, even morbid. A number of colleagues with whom I have discussed it say that it simply represents an unhealthy state of mind. Yet Lewis's interpretation of these various literary experiments suggests that the reverse is true and raises serious doubts about any environmentalism built on foundations laid by the party of Hope. In his concluding chapter Lewis probes the limits of that party's "simplified and sunny theology" by contrasting the ideas of two Unitarian theologians, Theodore Parker and Orestes Brownson, and their implications for community. Parker made the rejection of history the central tenet of his minimalist theology, insisting on a theology based entirely on personal inspiration and independent of history and tradition. Brownson, in contrast, stressed community rather than personal inspiration and insisted on the importance of history in achieving it (188). At a time when "hopefulness and nostalgia had conspired to cut the American spirit off from those crucial resources, with pathetic and potentially tragic consequences," Lewis writes, Brownson and the party of Irony offered a vision of communion and community that embraced history as a form of intimacy with "the common experience and common reality of the human race" (192).[25]

While Brownson's idea of community as a value that is achieved only through culture and history (and the loss of innocence) ran counter to the current of thought that would eventually most influence environmentalism, it is far from idiosyncratic. In fact, this tougher idea of community is so much a part of the actual experience of community that it is inscribed in the word "community" itself. I had supposed that this word was derived from the Latin words *cum* (with) and *unus* (one), so that at root it meant something like "at one with." This, however, is not the case. The *cum* is there, of course. But the other root is not *unus* but *munus* (this accounts for the second *m*), which has an interesting cluster of meanings denoting first, a *duty* or *service* such as soldiers or citizens owe their country; second, a *gift,* reflecting the essential role of the gift in establishing solidarity; and finally a *sacrifice,* with its implication both of giving something up (ego, for example, in the process of initiation) and of giving something back by destroying it (as in sacrificial ritual).[26] More deeply, *munus* is derived from the Indo-European root *mei,* which denotes "exchange" and, even more generally, "change."

Thus the word "community" actually implies or carries with it the whole range of acts leading up to—or into—community, from the simple exchange of goods and services, through the exchange of gifts, to the sacrificial act by which the individual comes to terms with aspects of relationship that are both troubling and—at least in literal terms—irresolvable. "Containing" the root idea of "change," it also reminds us of the dynamic process by which a community evolves out of experience and the vagaries of ongoing interaction with others.

The formidable barriers that surround and define a community are dramatized by the rites many communities impose as a condition of membership. But they are dramatized even more clearly by the institution of gift exchange, which is embedded in the word "community" and, unlike initiation, is a universal institution, found in all human societies. In his classic essay *The Gift: The Form and Reason for Exchange in Archaic Societies,* French sociologist Marcel Mauss outlines a theory of the creation of relationships through the exchange of gifts.[27] Examining the institution of gift exchange in ancient Roman, Hindu, Chinese, Celtic, and Germanic societies, and also in a number of traditional societies of the Pacific islands and the Pacific Northwest, Mauss views the exchange of gifts—carried out on the principle that "I give in order that you may give back"—as distinct both from charity and from straightforward commercial transactions such as barter. He sees it as a step beyond the detached relationship implicit in these forms of exchange toward a deeper and less abstract relationship, which he called solidarity. In these societies, a relationship begins with the offering of a gift—an act that, precisely because of the obligations it entails, is itself a sensitive matter, calling for a gift in return, the "clinching gift" that confirms the relationship. Once the return is made, Mauss writes, a relationship exists and must be maintained indefinitely by a constant, more or less compulsory exchange of gifts on appropriate occasions.

Several features of this idea of solidarity are of special interest to us here. For one thing, it is not a transaction between individuals but among "collectivities," legal entities such as villages or units of a tribe or other social group. Second, it occurs in public in a ceremonial context, not, as are many commercial transactions, as a private matter between two individuals. Third, unlike commercial transactions it does not end with a settling of accounts but sets in motion a succession of exchanges that do not merely represent but in a sense constitute the relationship between the parties involved. Fourth, it is not without self-interest (Mary Douglas notes in her foreword to *The Gift*, "If we persist in thinking that gifts ought to be free and pure, we will always fail to recognize our own grand cycles of exchanges, which categories get to be included and which get to be excluded from our hospitality").[28] Fifth, the gift is not negotiated. Instead the giver must *guess* what the recipient will regard as appropriate. (This is a step toward the internalization of the relationship and also accounts for the practice of wrapping presents and offering them as a surprise, dramatizing their unnegotiated character.) Sixth, the gift must "move"—that is, it must always be passed on, and in this sense given up or foregone by the recipient. Sixth, the exchange is not voluntary—except for the more or less hypothetical initial gift, both the giving and the accepting of gifts are obligatory (this is why, as Mauss points out, citing an old Scandinavian proverb, the miser always fears the gift). And finally, though it is not voluntary, the act of exchange must *seem* voluntary—a pure expression on the part of the giver of bounty, generosity, and high regard for the recipient.

This last point is crucial. It means that the exchange of gifts, which Mauss sees as the basis for social solidarity in the societies he is dealing with, necessarily entails a measure of *dissembling*—is, in fact, an act or performance, not only in the sense that it is carried out in a ceremonial or ritual context, but also in the sense that it entails a measure of pretense. Roy Rappaport reinforces this point, writing, "While it is perhaps obvious it is worth reiterating that insincerity and the possibility of deceit are intrinsic to the very acts that make social life possible for organisms that relate to each other in accordance with voluntarily accepted convention rather than in ways more narrowly defined by their genotypes."[29]

In this ritual "insincerity" we encounter the radical ambiguity that lies at the heart of relationship, the dilemma of self and other that is a fundamental concern of psychology. Even at the level Mauss describes as solidarity, relationships are in a fundamental sense problematic, involving tensions and ambiguities that cannot be resolved in purely rational or even literal terms but must be dealt with by recourse to make-believe or playacting in a subtle, highly reflexive form of deception. In other words, relationships depend on the exchange of gifts, but in the act of exchanging gifts we inevitably encounter the tensions, uncertainty, and ambiguity inherent in any relationship that moves beyond the level of a purely economic—or ecological—transaction.[30]

And if this is evident in the dissembling of the gift exchange, it is evident in other aspects of gift exchange as well. Consider, for example, the claims on the recipient implicit in the acceptance of a gift. In the societies Mauss describes, this entails a permanent obligation to participate in what may, depending on the coefficient of exchange characteristic of the culture, escalate in a relentless price-inflation to the climax of destructive giving exemplified by the potlatch of some of the pre-Columbian peoples of the Pacific Northwest. This may be an extreme example but, as is often the case, the extreme tells us something about the norm. Gift exchanges always involve obligations and so are in a way always an imposition on the recipient. Besides this, offering someone a gift is necessarily an emotional risk because it dramatizes the donor's willingness to give away something the receiver wants—and presumably lacks—compounding the affront of economic advantage with an implication of moral superiority.

Seeing these problems as a universal feature of human relationships, Mauss specifically rejects the notion of a society of any kind based on a natural, unself-conscious—or innocent—exchange of goods and services: "Apparently there has never existed, either in an era fairly close to our own, or in societies that we lump together somewhat awkwardly as primitive or inferior, anything that might resemble what is called a 'natural economy' in the sense of an economy based on a system of simple exchange among individuals."[31]

Ultimately, the exchange of gifts brings us face to face with issues of identity and worthiness we cannot resolve. In his book *The Culture of Hope,* Turner argues that every exchange of gifts is fraught with uncertainty, which he expresses in terms of the shame or sense of unworthiness that is inseparable from an exchange of gifts.

We are never quite sure whether we have given the right gift, or given a gift when we should not have, or not given a gift when we should; and we are shamefully anxious about whether we have been given the right gift. We are ashamed of what we have made, whether because of uncertainty about its worthiness or because of the obligation we incurred to those parts of the world we destroyed to make our new contribution to it.[32]

Though Turner's reading may seem extreme, it is not mere poetic hyperbole or scholarly overinterpretation. We can all recall occasions when a well-intentioned exchange of gifts failed for some reason, resulting in feelings of intense shame.

These observations raise serious questions, not about the desirability of community, but about its practical value as a model for relationships in a society so out of touch with what is arguably the basic psychology of community, and so dedicated to replacing the troubling bonds of obligation, solidarity, and communal association with the more abstract linkages defined by political, legal, and economic transactions. Community in the strong, classic sense, is hard work and, given a choice, most choose emotional convenience over the demands of community and the other transcendent values.

This idea is radically at odds with what most of us take for granted. Leopold defined his land ethic in terms of four values — stability, integrity, beauty, and community — and our culture encourages us to suppose that beauty and community are closely associated with, and even dependent on, a more or less comfortable way of life — including ecological values such as stability and sustainability. But Turner suggests that exactly the opposite is true. In the last analysis, he argues, we have to choose *between* stability and higher values such as beauty. This assertion may seem exotic, and even perverse. Yet it coincides precisely with the core insight in Aldous Huxley's classic dystopian novel, *Brave New World,* expressed by the World Controller, who explains to the Savage why beauty no longer exists in a world in which the motto of the World State is Community, Identity, Stability, and in which a central social dogma is that "every one belongs to everyone else."

"We haven't any use for old things here," the World Controller says. "Even when they're beautiful?" the Savage asks. "Particularly when they're beautiful," the World Controller replies, later adding, "That's the price we have to pay for stability. You've got to choose between happiness and what people used to call high art. We've sacrificed the high art."[33]

Huxley's idea that there is a necessary trade-off between beauty and "happiness" (or what I would call emotional convenience) seems strange, even perverse to us because arguably we are living in a version of Huxley's brave new world and take for granted a deeply sentimental idea of value. We think of Saint Francis preaching to the birds, our relationship with a favorite pet, or the boy in the Disney film learning to talk with dolphins; or we talk about a person walking in the woods "communing" with nature, or of a person like Thoreau who has, through patience and attention, gained a measure of rapport with animals so that they will come at his call, perch on his shoulder, and so on.[34] Such experiences are important, and they can be beautiful and rewarding. But they are only the first and, for a shame-denying culture, perhaps the easiest step into relationship. They fall short of communion because, like our attenuated rituals of initiation (getting a driver's license, graduating from high school), they fail to come to grips with the more problematic aspects of relationship.

If these considerations lend support to the Ironists' view of the dynamics of redemption—the "plot" or drama by which redemption of the individual into community is achieved—so do several relevant lines of religious thought expressed both in myth and, more abstractly, in theology. Lewis notes that Henry James's interpretation of the story of Adam and Eve in the garden coincides exactly with a much earlier interpretation of the same story. "For," Lewis writes,

what James had hit on by the sheer force of his speculation was a variation on a very ancient theme: the theme of the "fortunate fall." In the history of Christian theology, the theme can be traced back almost to the fourth century A.D., and its most enduring formulation came in the medieval hymn which is sung during the Holy Saturday Mass. The hymn is exultant; it is known, indeed, as the "Exultet"; it is the most poetic and transcendently hopeful answer that Christianity ever contrived to the old puzzle about the experience of evil in a world created by a benevolent God: "O felix culpa!" the hymn exclaims; "quae talem et tantem meruit habere redemptorem" (O happy sin! to deserve so great a redeemer). (61)

The idea, Lewis comments, is that happiness (we may say redemption or communion) *depends* on the sin of Adam and Eve because it depends on the experience of badness followed by the discovery of hope—not in the expectation of good fortune, but rather in the midst of the most profound trouble and existential crisis, represented in the Christian tradition by the crucifixion.

Ultimately, what Lewis's account of these literary experiments suggests is the inadequacy of any environmental philosophy based on the premises of nature's innocence or the moral discontinuity of humans from the rest of nature. This is especially true with regard to the "natural" or classic landscape that is our special concern here. Seeing such a landscape as the embodiment of nature's unspoiled innocence, proponents of this philosophy will seek above all to preserve that innocence. They will not set up the exchange of goods and services that constitutes the basis of a truly ecological relationship with a landscape but will dismiss it as exploitation and the corruption of innocence. They will resist active management, including restoration, and, if it is carried out, will downplay or deplore it. Unable to provide a context for the reflexive experience of shame or means for coping creatively with the shame of consumption (ecological engagement) or the dependence of a natural landscape on management by humans, they can urge only that we use nature parsimoniously, taking only what we "need," leaving open the ultimate question: need for what? to survive? to live in a house? to drive a car? to wear shoes? to send flowers to a friend? "O! Reason not the need," Lear cries, having discovered in his extremity the desperate futility of such counsel.

> our basest beggars
> Are in the poorest things superfluous:
> Allow not nature more than nature needs,
> Man's life is cheap as beast's.
> *King Lear,* 2.4.264–67

As for the gift and the step into a solidarity with nature, the idea of nature's innocence precludes them too, since anything we offer nature violates its purity. In this view we can take from nature but can never give back. We accept its gifts of food, materials, place, and beauty but never offer back the clinching gift that would establish a basis for solidarity. And finally, because we never risk the offering of a gift, we have no need for sacrifice, the ritual in which we confront and pass through the ambivalence, fear, and shame of the gift exchange to communion.

In fact, while enjoining us to live lightly on the land, our various en-

vironmentalisms have had little success in providing ways of living deeply
with the classic landscape because at every point living deeply involves a
violation of what we have taken to be the purity and innocence of that
landscape.[35] For the same reason it generally fails to come to grips with
other troubling aspects of life in the world, including difference, inequity,
inequality, change, hegemony, and hierarchy—all of which we encounter
in particularly high relief in acts such as predation and the use of natural
resources generally. Seeking a place outside shame, environmental
thinkers have consistently looked in the wrong places—not at the occasions where shame is most intense, but rather in places where it is least
conspicuous and most easily overlooked. In these cases, shame has either
been repressed, or means of dealing with it have been more or less rou-
tinized so that it is easy to overlook. (This is what Thoreau has in mind,
for example, when he comments on fishing, "I did not perceive that my
feelings were much affected. I did not pity the fishes nor the worms. This
was habit.")[36] Thus environmentalism has tended to romanticize traditional and premodern cultures, and to overlook or misconstrue the hard
cultural work they carry out in order to come to terms with the emotionally troubling aspects of relationship. It offers instead an ideal of harmony and community and does not take into account the fact that, as
Rappaport has pointed out, harmony itself is the result, not of relaxation,
but of tension and careful tuning. Withholding the gift, environmentalism has, as restorationist Dave Simpson says, taught us to withhold part
of our souls.

Restoration, precisely because it entails the loss of innocence, provides
a context for all four phases of the move into community with the classic
landscape. To begin with, it forces us to become aware of ourselves as
ecologically effective inhabitants of a world populated by others—the infant awakening that is the first step into relationship and the knowledge
of shame. Beyond this, it allows—and in fact requires—humans to interact with these others, by actively participating in the ecology of the natural landscape. Furthermore, by providing a way to compensate for our
influence on the natural landscape, it in a sense "redeems" acts of consumption and use, allowing them to become the first phase in the cycle
of giving and taking back that is the ecological foundation for any relationship. As for the gift, the basis for solidarity with nature, the restored
ecosystem is perhaps as close as we can come to paying nature back in
kind for what we have taken from it. The fact that this gift is still inadequate and in certain respects unworthy, we now see as a characteristic of
all gifts and an integral part of the structure of any relationship. Finally,

the act of restoration, precisely *because* it is inadequate and *because* it implicates the restorationist in the universal scandal of creation, provides a context for achieving communion with creation. Indeed, as we will see in chapter 7, the work of restoration resonates powerfully with classic rituals of initiation, communion, and world renewal, providing a new context for accomplishing the ritual work of community making and world building. In all these ways it provides a context in which to confront and perhaps resolve the predicament, carried over into our own time, of Emerson, of Whitman, and of Ahab.

CHAPTER 4

Awareness

Restoration as a Way of Seeing, and as Work and Play

After a day of tree-planting, I feel physically exhausted but
spiritually invigorated.

Seth Zuckerman, "Pitfalls on the Way to Lasting Restoration"

We talk easily of community but, Piaget tells us, are born alone, naked,
and lost in a vast, overweening, and complacent individualism. In his 1973
book *The Denial of Death,* Ernest Becker argues that an infant comes into
the world in a condition of radical narcissism, a "magician," who takes for
granted not only the immediate satisfaction of every wish, but also his or
her "cosmic specialness" as "*the* one in creation." For such a creature,
Becker argues, awareness of the other, its prerogatives, the demands it
makes on the self, and the challenge it poses to one's presumed omnipo-
tence is psychologically intolerable. From the moment awareness is
achieved, he suggests, the self is primarily concerned with the construction
of a "character," the essential purpose of which is to protect the self from
what he calls "the reality of his world as miracle and as terror . . . the real
overwhelmingness, the stark majesty of the objects in the child's world."[1]

Here culture functions to supply the conceptual software, in the form
of myth, symbol, ritual, and story needed for the construction of this
"vital lie." When, however, this task is not carried out successfully, the result is the "all or nothing" mentality of the person who cannot "partial-
ize the world" in this way.[2] This takes the form either of megalomania or
of what Becker calls "wormhood," a debilitating feeling of unworthiness
and shame. Applied to the formation of relationships with other species,

we might suppose that the first of these two responses might take the form of an overweening disregard for the other, while the second might be expressed as a rigid preservationism based on a sense that the best we can do for the other is to leave it strictly alone. Restoration is important here because, by demanding both that we manipulate the other and that we maintain total respect for it, it draws us into the middle ground that lies between these two alienated alternatives. It is precisely because it places us in the field of tension between these two extremes that it is so valuable as a context for the invention of the rituals and stories needed to move toward the formation of a mature relationship.

Once the self has taken on the difficult task of inventing a way of accommodating the other, the next step in the building of a relationship is the work of perceiving—of listening, watching, feeling, smelling, and touching to discover exactly who the other is. This is the phase in the development of our relationship with the natural landscape that our environmental thinkers have dealt with most effectively, producing, in the work of writers and thinkers like Thoreau and Muir, John Burroughs, Sigurd Olson, Loren Eiseley, Barry Lopez, Annie Dillard, E. O. Wilson, and Gary Snyder, a large body of literature exploring and celebrating nature from an observer's point of view. From this perspective, restoration looks less like a way of appreciating nature than a way of manipulating it. The restorationist does manipulate the natural landscape and may even be said to intrude on it. Yet it is important to keep in mind that restoration properly begins where preservation begins, with an awareness of the others in nature, and with a profound respect for the classic landscape and a desire to ensure its survival, insofar as possible on its own terms. But to do this we have to know the landscape. We have to see it clearly and sympathetically. And one way to see a thing clearly, as anyone who has ever tried to make a drawing of something knows, is to try to copy it or make a representation of it. The reason this is so valuable an exercise in the formation of a relationship is that it involves a measure of self-abnegation, an emptying out or setting aside of the ego in the act of pure attentiveness to the other. This, of course, is an essential step in any religious practice, comparable to the self-naughting of Christian practice, or the Zen disciple's setting aside of self to let the world—the other—work through him. "In Zen," Becker writes,

it is the primal powers that . . . are supposed to take over, to act through the person as he opens himself up to them; he becomes their tool and their vehicle. In Zen archery, for example, the archer no longer himself shoots the arrow at the target, but "It" shoots; the interior of nature erupts into the world through the disciple's perfect selflessness.[3]

This is exactly the aim of the restorationist—to let nature work through him on its own terms, speaking, we may say, in its own language.

As restorationists undertake the task of reproducing the natural landscape or ecosystem, observing it and formulating ideas about it, they test their ideas as artists or inventors or scientists do, by reducing them to practice in the form of reproduction, working model, experiment, or representation. In this way, the work of restoration can become a way of *intensifying* awareness, appreciation, and understanding and may even be said to provide a means for the intellectual, emotional, spiritual and esthetic discovery of the landscape being restored.

That this is true is evident from the accounts that the more articulate restorationists give of their work. I recall, for example, a characteristic outburst by Bob Betz, one of the grand old men of the restoration movement in the Chicago area. We were standing in a parking lot at the Morton Arboretum late on a winter afternoon, and someone happened to mention monarch butterflies. Immediately, Betz took hold of the conversation, recalling how as a boy he had watched the monarchs in the fields near his home each autumn, how their numbers have diminished over the years, and how he learned to rely on monarchs in his search for rare milkweeds in the hay meadows of Kansas and Nebraska.

"Some of those milkweeds are hard to find out there," he said. "So I started watching the monarchs. When a female came along, I'd follow her with binoculars, and I found that when she got near a milkweed, her flight would get erratic. Then, she would disappear into the grass, and I'd go over and find her laying her eggs on a milkweed."

In general, the task of faithfully following the model, trying to get the restored ecosystem just "right," requires an attention to detail that leads not only to insight but to a beautiful intimacy. On a recent visit to areas in the northwestern part of Michigan where forests are being clearcut to create habitat for Kirtland's warbler, I learned of attempts to imitate the effects of the fires that ordinarily create the clearings these warblers require for nesting and foraging. One attempt mimics what foresters call roll-vortex strips: stands of trees left when the convection currents set up by a fire create a horizontal tornado, causing the fire to leap over sections of the forest, leaving—as if providentially—peninsulas of mature trees in stands that run like hedgerows through burned-over areas and serve as sources of seed for their regeneration. Working to reproduce this effect, restorationists achieve intimacy not only with a small bird, but also with an elemental force of nature.

The enchantment in such stories is in part the enchantment of partnership—real collusion with other species—participation in natural processes, and the awareness and understanding that go with it. And such stories are far from unusual. I recall similar stories from Steve Packard about the work that led to his new idea of the oak savannas; from Ron Panzer, holding an audience spellbound with accounts of his work with prairie insects; from Freeman House discussing restoration of salmon habitat in California; or from Ed Collins, discussing the history and ecology he encounters in the process of breaking up drain fields on farmland in northern Illinois in order to restore it to wetland.

What these accounts reflect is awareness and observation heightened by purposeful engagement, and by the fact that success in restoration depends mainly on the "work" done by the ecosystem being restored. As restorationists often point out, in most cases the system, not the restorationist, does most of the work, and in all cases it does the essential work of reproduction, growth, nutrient uptake, recycling, and other life processes that lead to its recovery. As a result restoration, like any craft, is not in the last analysis a matter of simply letting be, but rather the more difficult matter of knowing exactly how and when to let it be—a kind of wisdom that the restorationist learns through practice and through close attention to the system itself.

The key to this wisdom—and to good restoration—is the same as in any relationship: a beautiful combination of manipulation and attentiveness, of action and responsiveness. Restoration can be hard work. But in the end it is *mostly* stepping back, letting be, listening, waiting for the system to respond and go about its business. At its best, restoration can become an intimate dialogue with an ecosystem, in the course of which the restorationist can learn from it as from a close friend. It is in this stepping back and waiting for the other's reply that Noelle Oxenhandler, in a beautiful essay on waiting, finds a source of grace: "some of my most pleasurable moments have come when I allowed myself to sink into the feeling that something was taking place without—or in the aftermath of—my conscious intervention. . . . The precious 'while' that follows when you have done your part, and surrendered the work of your hands to powers as great as sun, air, time."[4]

This is the grace of the first step into communion. It begins in pure attentiveness, in attentiveness to the other without purpose that Simone

Weil saw as the essence of prayer. But it matures and ripens toward communion through purposeful engagement. Oxenhandler's "precious 'while' " comes only after you have done your part—mailed the letter, planted the seed—and *then* stepped back, waiting for the response.

And engagement leads us to the experiences of work and play. In a recent essay, historian Richard White argues that modern environmentalism has failed to provide means of connecting with nature through work and suggests that the result is an attenuated relationship, not grounded in an ecological transaction.[5] Properly undertaken, restoration solves this problem. It is work and it can also be play, a way of communicating with other species and with the landscape, a mode of discovery and a means of self-transformation—a way of both discovering the natural landscape and discovering ourselves in that landscape. Any work, any kind of play, any experience naturally changes the participant, and what I want to consider here is how the experience of restoration might be expected to transform the restorationist.[6] This might be called the alchemical aspect of restoration, since in one interpretation the purpose of alchemy was not really to convert base material into gold, an emblem of the golden age before or outside history, but rather to serve as a ritual through which the alchemist could achieve his own personal transformation and redemption from history through heightened awareness of the other.[7] In the same way, and quite apart from the fact that under favorable conditions the restorationist, unlike the alchemist, may actually succeed in an objective, literal sense, we may see the restorationist, like the alchemist, as engaging in a self-transforming attempt to return a piece of land to some earlier condition, not outside history but independent of the restorationist, and therefore outside his ego.

> It is believed that by the judicious use of fire or other biotic
> controls, fairly complete associations of each of the formations
> can be established and maintained within the 1,400-acre limits
> of the Arboretum: it is hoped that much information of value
> concerning the dynamics of formation boundaries can be
> obtained in the course of such establishment.
>
> John T. Curtis and Max L. Partch, "Effect of Fire on
> the Competition between Blue Grass and Certain
> Prairie Species"

What kind of work is ecological restoration? And how might it affect the restorationist and her relationship with the ecosystem being restored, with the landscape and with nature generally? One way to answer these questions is to consider what kinds of work restoration is related to or borrows from. Of these, perhaps the most obvious is agriculture. But restoration is also related in significant ways to other kinds of work, including the aboriginal work of gathering and hunting, the mimetic or representational arts, and of course the science of ecology. Let's take these up one at a time, beginning, if only because I did, with ecology.

When I began thinking about restoration in 1977, one of the first things that occurred to me was that it is a way of learning about the ecosystems being restored. This was a direct result of my consideration of the Arboretum's restored ecological communities and their value for research. Originally, the Arboretum planners had intended to create these communities in order to have them available for research. But the project hadn't worked out that way. No one really knew, in 1934, how to restore a prairie, a maple forest, or a freshwater marsh, and, not surprisingly, the results were uneven. All the Arboretum's restored communities were defective in some way. Even the most successfully restored communities, such as the prairies, not only had defects that were well documented, such as missing species and infestations of troublesome exotic species but presumably had other, less conspicuous defects that had not been recognized, all of which limited their value for research.

These defects in turn limited the value of the Arboretum itself, since its primary purpose was to serve as an outdoor laboratory and classroom. Mulling this over out on Curtis Prairie one day during my first summer at the Arboretum, however, it occurred to me that while the various defects in the Arboretum's restored communities might be a disadvantage in one way, in another they might actually be an advantage.

What I had in mind was this. As long as you looked at a restored community such as the prairie as just a prairie—a given—and attempted simply to describe or analyze it, its value as a subject for research was limited. You could study it, but there would always be a question about the relevance of your results to an understanding of a natural prairie. If, on the other hand, you stopped pretending that the restored prairie was just a "given" and regarded it as an ongoing experiment in community reassembly or ecosystem reconstruction, then the very defects that limited its value for descriptive research became the most valuable, most interesting, most *revealing* things about it.

Look at it this way. Over the years, a succession of restorationists had worked on the prairie, trying to put it back together using the best available descriptions of the prairie as a guide. What worked—that glorious swath in the middle of Greene Prairie, for example—testified to what they got right or at least came close enough to getting right that the plants and insects and bacteria could take over and make it right. But there were glitches—the big patch of sweet clover that had taken over several acres on the north side of Curtis Prairie, for example; or the aspens that were taking over in other areas, pushing out other prairie species; or the ubiquitous bluegrass, the exotic lawn grass that persisted in many parts of the prairies; or the honeysuckle and buckthorn that had invaded many of the woodland areas, crowding out understory species. Each of these was an emblem of failure. Yet for this very reason, each could be seen as a kind of probe or marker, pointing to some looseness in structure of the community, some niche space unfilled, something the restorationists had failed to account for in putting it together.

Looking at the Arboretum's collection of restored and partly restored ecological communities from this perspective, I realized that while the value of a restored ecosystem as an *object* of research might be limited, the *process* of restoring it might be one of the most effective ways of raising questions and testing ideas about it. In fact, once this occurred to me I realized that the research that had been carried out at the Arboretum during the previous forty-odd years clearly illustrated the value of working with these imperfect, partly restored ecological systems. The classic example was what we sometimes referred to as the "discovery" of fire. When the restoration of Curtis Prairie began in the mid-1930s, the Arboretum planners were aware that fire had been a common event on the prairies in pre-contact times, but, despite a good deal of speculation, no one really understood the importance or the exact role of fire in prairie ecology. It was not until Ted Sperry, the young ecologist hired to supervise restoration of the prairie, had completed several acres of prairie plantings, only to discover that they were being overwhelmed by weedy, mostly exotic species, that he and John Curtis began a series of experimental burns in the prairie plantings.[8] The results, published in 1948, clearly demonstrated the value of fire as a tool for prairie restoration. Equally important, they also demonstrated the crucial role fire plays in the ecology of prairies, shaping the community by favoring some species while discriminating against or excluding others.

But this was not the only lesson that had come out of the Arboretum's restoration efforts. As I became familiar with research that had been carried out at the Arboretum over the years, I realized that many of the most significant projects had been carried out, not in spite of the various defects and deficiencies in the restored communities, but because of them. In fact, many of these projects could not have been carried out at all in a pristine, natural ecosystem. In addition to the work with fire, for example, the restoration of Curtis and Greene Prairies had set the stage for a long-term study of the dynamics of prairie vegetation—the way various species of plants interact and move around on a prairie over the years—that would have been difficult, if not impossible to carry out on a natural prairie.[9]

Similarly, the failure of attempts to recreate pine forest at the Arboretum, a hundred miles or so south of the natural range of pine forests in Wisconsin, had led to insights into the subtle climatic factors that influence the development of the ground-layer vegetation in these forests. It turned out that the critical factor was precipitation—not the *amount* of precipitation, but the quantities in which it was delivered. In areas where rain comes mostly in small showers, less water reaches the forest floor under pines than in areas where it comes in heavier downpours because the needle clusters of pines act as small paintbrushes, picking up the first few millimeters of a shower, reducing the amount of water that reaches the forest floor and affecting which species can grow there. It would have been difficult to discover this in a natural forest. It was the attempt to create a pine forest on an ecologically *inappropriate* site that had created the opportunity to achieve this insight.[10] Other studies, occasioned at least in part by defects showing up in the Arboretum's growing collection of communities under restoration, led to insights into the role of ants in the dispersal of woodland wildflowers, the ways different forest types handle and recycle nitrogen, and the physiology and ecology of many of the weedy exotic species that inevitably turn up in restored communities and that are often the restorationist's most serious and most challenging problem.[11]

In some cases descriptive studies alone might have led to these insights. But observation rarely reveals the exact role of elements or processes, which cause which, or which are of primary and which of only secondary or incidental importance in the ecology of the system. To determine such matters, it is necessary to do complementary experiments—taking an element away, then putting it back in—as Sperry and Curtis had done, though at first unintentionally, in their work with fire on the Arboretum's prairies.

As a technique for basic research, then, restoration not only takes from ecology, it has much to contribute to it as well and therefore has important implications for the practice of ecology. For one thing, it represents a way of bringing ecology back to its roots as a healing art. In his book *Nature's Economy,* environmental historian Donald Worster discusses how early ecologists thought of their discipline as a healing art, rooted in natural history and a tradition of reverence for nature represented by writers like Wordsworth and Thoreau.[12] After World War II, however, this conception of ecology was eclipsed by a more mechanistic attempt to describe the behavior of natural landscapes in mathematical terms. Worster sees this as a betrayal of the promise of ecology to be the discipline that would depart from the paradigms of reductionist science to provide an intellectual basis for true community, including some form of communion between humans and the rest of nature. From this perspective, restoration ecology, the restoration and creation of ecosystems for explicitly heuristic purposes, represents a return to this earlier, more organic conception of ecology and its healing mission.

This return has profound implications for the science of ecology, and therefore for one of our most important ways of knowing and relating to the world. While a mechanistic ecology denies any commitment to values, restoration ecology represents a technique for basic research that explicitly links ecology to values such as beauty, community, and the well-being of the ecosystem. And while mechanistic ecology, taking its lead from classical physics, adopts the modern notion of the scientist as a detached observer, the restoration ecologist not only acknowledges but actively promotes, takes advantage of, and even celebrates the scientist's active role in the complex phenomena under investigation. In this sense restoration ecology is to mechanistic ecology roughly what quantum mechanics is to classical physics. Similarly, while mechanistic science has been criticized as being excessively "masculine" in its approach to nature, relying as it does primarily on observation and analysis, operations which enact a voyeuristic, manipulative or exploitative relationship with nature, restoration ecology is explicitly synthetic and even nurturing in its approach to discovery.[13]

This does not mean compromising the intellectual objective of ecology—the understanding of ecological systems. Indeed, British ecologist Anthony Bradshaw has suggested that restoration represents the "acid test" of ecology.[14] Clearly, we need to take this metaphor with a grain of salt since ecological systems, being alive, participate in their own restoration in ways that the restorationist may not even be aware of. Yet to the extent that it is valid the intellectual and ethical objectives of ecology overlap: what ecologists *want* to know in order to understand the system is the same thing they *need* to know in order to manage or restore it. So it is a mistake to think of restoration as merely "applied" ecology, an intellectual spin-off of more "basic" research. It makes more sense to think of it as the organizing principle for ecology, a basis for the planning, evaluation and criticism of ecological research. The move beyond the mere description of ecosystems into the diagnosis and treatment of ecological disorders is no intellectual compromise, since these processes actually provide more stringent tests of ideas than does purely descriptive work.[15]

I eventually realized that the heuristic value of restoration extends far beyond even the ample boundaries of ecology. If restoration provides a powerful way to explore the ecology of an ecosystem, it also provides a powerful way to explore its history, since any attempt to restore or recreate a thing entails an attempt to reenact or reverse its history. In this way, it draws the historian out of the library and into the field, and it draws ecologists and horticulturists into fields such as history, geography, and anthropology.

Again, the "discovery" of fire on the prairies serves as an example. It not only revealed something of overriding importance about the ecology of the prairies, it revealed the role that pre-Columbian peoples played in the ecology and development of the American prairies. Thus it represented an important, if still underappreciated, contribution to research in geography, anthropology, and environmental history.[16]

Thus, though it has not been systematically exploited in this way, restoration provides a basis not only for synthetic ecology, but also for a kind of synthetic, or reconstructive history and anthropology as well. And as an attempt to reverse history or turn back or reset the ecological clock, restoration can be a source of wisdom about time and change. Many people, I have found, are uncomfortable with the idea of restoration because they see it as a sentimental attempt to recover the past.[17] They miss the point: in *attempting* to return to the past—in playing the *game* of reversing time—a restorationist explores the very nature of time and change and winds up achieving a certain wisdom about it. The impulse to return to the past may be defensible on ecological or cultural grounds, or it may be quixotic, sentimental, and nostalgic. But by actually doing the work, confronting hard, present-day realities, the restorationist escapes sentimentality and nostalgia, and learns to discriminate between changes that are reversible and changes that are not. He also learns something about the costs of change, and the investment in effort, skill, time, and materials required to reverse or compensate for it. One result is a refining of ideas about the ecosystem involved and its replaceability. Environmentalists have tended to think of classic ecosystems as irreplaceable. But as we will see in the next chapter, while some kinds of ecological change *are* irreversible, others are fairly easy to reverse. The point is that it is through the attempt to reverse change that the restorationist learns to discriminate between these various kinds and degrees of change.

Besides this, in attempting the paradoxical trick of reversing and re-living history in order to escape it, the restorationist creates a context in which to explore, experience, and perhaps even reconcile cyclic and pro-gressive time. In fact, this double experience of time is implicit in the word "restore" itself. The "re-" suggests the cyclic and dynamic, while the "-store" indicates the stable, the stationary, and the unchanging. Com-bining the two—the circle for return and regeneration, and the line for progress and change—generates the figure of the rising spiral or helix of evolution, each turn of which marks a return to the old and "original," but at a higher level of self-awareness.

Properly conceived, restoration takes the evolutionary helix into ac-count and dramatizes it. Philosophers and scientists since Heraclitus have insisted that the world is intrinsically dynamic, an insight that "new ecol-ogists" like Daniel Botkin and Steward Pickett are now bringing back into the foreground of ecological thinking. A few critics have objected to restoration on the grounds that it is characteristically defined by statically conceived objectives—the "snapshot in time" that restorationists in fact disparage. Of course it is true that restoration, like any historical inquiry, can be undertaken in a merely antiquarian spirit. But to assume this is the essence of restoration is to overlook several of the most important things about it. For one thing it is to overlook the dynamic terms in which prac-ticing restorationists actually define goals for their projects. It is also to overlook the dynamic element that is involved in attempting to guide an ecological system back to a historic condition and sustain it there, against the pressure of "outside" influences. It is to overlook what we can learn from this effort, and the insight that it generates. And it is to overlook the value of restoration as a kind of game in which, in a spirit of play and humor and inquiry and irony, we attempt to reverse what we know can't be reversed, to revisit a time we know is forever past. There is value in this—ecological value, as I have said, but also a higher value. The restora-tionist is in this sense like a child building a dam in a gutter, playing with the running down of time itself, figured in what Robert Frost called "the stream of everything that runs away."[18] Or like the narrator of Frost's "Brook in the City" who, reflecting on time and the change figured in urban development, recalls how he once "dipped a finger length" into a brook, "And made it leap my knuckle," a gesture of symbolic interrup-tion and reversal that expresses his fretful reflection on the ineluctability and irreversibility of change. This is why the idea that the goal of restoration is a "self-sustaining" ecosystem is so misguided—not only because the idea is ecologically untenable, but also because it is precisely the effort of sustaining the ecosystem against the pressure of novel influences that accounts for much of the value of restoration as a way of defining and making us aware of our relationship with it.

This may be put another way. Since the changes a restorationist tries to reverse have usually been brought about by human beings, restoration is a powerful way to explore our own influence on the landscape, and in this way to gain a clearer idea of who, in ecological terms, we are. To see this, recall the definition of restoration I offered in chapter 1: the attempt to compensate for novel influences on an ecosystem in such a way that it can continue to behave or can resume behaving as if they were not present. To do this it is necessary to understand exactly how these novel forces have influenced the system, and then to figure out how to compensate for these influences in an ecologically effective way. Since these forces are usually of human origin, doing this commonly entails an increase in our awareness and understanding of human influences on the system. Furthermore, because the cycle of influence and compensation is intellectually asymmetrical—we can influence an ecosystem without understanding (or even being aware of) the nature of our influence, but we can't compensate for this influence or change the system *back* without understanding that influence in ecological terms—restoration forces us to become aware of aspects of our relationship with an ecosystem that we might otherwise have overlooked. In this way restoration amounts to the discovery and dramatization of the precise nature of our relationship with the ecosystems we attempt to restore, each act of compensation representing—in negative, as it were—some element of that relationship. Properly and reflexively carried out, it generates nothing less than an ecological definition of who we are—that is, a definition of our species, or of a particular human community, expressed in terms of how it has influenced and interacted with other organisms and with whole ecological systems over a particular period of time.

Once again, the restorative act of burning the prairies serves as an example. In carrying out this beautiful and evocative work, restorationists define themselves as

> members of the species that burned the prairies for thousands of years, playing a role in their creation,
>
> members of the civilization that stopped the fires, very nearly putting an end to the prairies, and

members of a community that returned fire to a particular prairie, bringing about its restoration.

One by one, other restorative acts both acknowledge and dramatize the elements and aspects of our influence on the landscape, whether deliberate or not. Thus,

> the attempt to remove exotic species such as bluegrass or sweet clover from a prairie, iceplant from a California coastal community, or carp from a lake in Ohio dramatizes the fact that Europeans introduced these species to these areas in the first place, and at the same time forces us to acknowledge the ecological consequences of our role as habitual transporters of species, inveterate openers of the ecological Pandora's box;
>
> the breaking up of drain tiles in an old field to reestablish historic drainage patterns draws our attention to the heroic, and in some ways tragic, history of the tiling and ditching done by the early settlers in many areas;
>
> the attempt to reduce the input of pollutants or nutrients to a lake or stream dramatizes the story of their introduction, and the resulting changes in the watershed; and
>
> attempts to reintroduce an extirpated species evoke the story of how it came to be extirpated, drawing attention to its ecological importance and the implications of its extirpation in a constructive rather than a critical or despairing way.

In this way, restoring a landscape is like grinding a corrective lens: it corrects for a deviation by complementing it in a precise way. In the process of creating (or, more precisely, becoming) such a "lens" for a landscape, the restorationist is forced to refine her ideas about how that landscape has changed, and about her species's role in causing those changes.

Restoration also has value as a means of discovering the beauty of a historic landscape, or of ecosystems or processes that had been considered ugly or repellant. Again, the prairies provide an excellent example, since prairies had little place in the American landscape esthetic until restorationists began working with them. But the same thing is true of other landscapes as well—wetlands, for example, or the coastal dune and scrub ecosystems of southern California. The desert ecosystems of the Soutwest are another example. Though Americans have always admired the austere beauty of these landscapes, their value as elements in formal landscapes has been largely the discovery of landscapers and restorationists.

Significantly, the pioneers in the exploration of this esthetic frontier were landscape designers like Jens Jensen, Wilhelm Miller, Elsa Rehmann, and Ossian Cole Simmons, who began creating landscapes modeled on prairies and other natural landscapes during the early decades of the twentieth century. These designers were also among the pioneers of restoration, and it is important to keep in mind that restoration was an artistic enterprise well before it became a scientific one.[19]

> But another element of the vision compelled us to want to see what we had so often read of, something that no longer existed anywhere—the rich grassland running up to, and under, and through the oaks. A prairie with trees.
>
> Steven Packard, "Just a Few Oddball Species"

If restoration is a way of doing research and of learning about an eco-system or landscape, it is, even more obviously, a form of agriculture.[20] The restorationist propagates plants. She practices cultivation and other means of preparing soil for planting and controlling weeds. She supplies fertilizer, applies mulch, and may use irrigation as a way of getting a plant community started under unfavorable conditions. In some cases she may even practice a kind of animal husbandry, rearing birds, insects, or other animals for reintroduction into a community.

Many restorationists resist the characterization of their work as a form of agriculture. "I am not a gardener," Chicago restorationist Bob Betz will thunder, standing in the prairie he has planted and weeded for fifteen years. "Oh, I'd never do that," another will say. "That's just gardening."

Restorationists have good reason for distinguishing their work from that of gardeners and those practicing other, more traditional forms of agriculture. Restoration simply doesn't look or *feel* like gardening because its aims are different. While agriculture ordinarily involves bringing nature under control to a certain extent, simplifying an ecosystem in order to ex-ploit it more effectively for some human end, restoration does just the op-posite, recomplicating the system in order to set it free, to turn it back into or over to itself, with a studied indifference to human interests. Yet resto-ration *is* a form of agriculture, even if it is agriculture in reverse, so to speak, and there are good reasons for insisting on this as well. One of these is that doing so is a way of pointing out the positive, nurturing element in agriculture, the beautiful intimacy a good farmer or gardener achieves with the land and with plants and animals. Another is the value of agriculture as a paradigm of the relationship between our own species and the rest of nature. So long as humans lived by hunting and gathering, they were merely participants in the scandal of creation, which they confronted in acts such as killing to sustain life. With the invention of agriculture, however, humans ceased to be mere participants and became active agents or engineers of the ongoing creation. This was a crisis in our relationship with the rest of nature, but it was a "natural" crisis—the distinctively human expression of the creative energy of nature generally. And culture after culture has dealt with this successfully, making agriculture the basis not only for an ecologically satisfactory relationship with nature but, arguably, a deeper, more troubled, but also more beautiful relationship with it.

The key, of course, is ritual—both the ritualized giving back of first fruits, which recalls the gift a hunter makes to the slain prey, and also the institution of ritual sacrifice, which, as I noted earlier, may be understood as a creative response to the shame of domestication and agriculture, both of which exemplify our complicity in the shame of creation. Thus Joseph Campbell has suggested that sacrifices are best understood not as a giving back to nature so much as a "fresh enactment, here and now, of the god's own sacrifice in the beginning, through which he, she or it became incarnate in the world process." Both readings of sacrifice point to a single element of experience—the shame, anxiety, and ambivalence associated with killing—what Campbell calls "the qualm before the deed of life"[21]—intensified by the act of domestication.

Either way, the restorationist is in an extremely interesting position. Because restoration is a form of agriculture, the practitioner is implicated in the natural crime of agriculture, with its assumption of hegemony over other creatures.[22] Yet because it is reconstructive agriculture, it offers a new way to seek the redemption of agriculture, not by offering back the first fruits of the harvest but by offering back whole ecosystems to replace those that have been destroyed by traditional forms of agriculture. Traditional agriculturists dealt with the anxiety of domestication mainly at the level of the population or the individual organism, leaving their influence on the landscape, which was often profound, unredeemed. Restoration provides a way of redeeming agriculture (and so ourselves), first, because it makes the destruction of the ecosystem explicit, being, as it were, a meditation on the exploitation (if not exactly the domestication) of whole ecosystems, but also because it offers back to nature a gift, worthy or not, in return for the gifts we receive from it, and because it is a

gesture of respect and deference toward nature, as restorationist Cindy
Goulder notes in her poem "Volunteer Revegetation Saturday."

> After all the stabbing at
> slick clay soil in the rain,
> and all the hands, backs,
> eyes, knees, working the plants in
> in the mud,
> and after passing pots, picks,
> spades, cups, bagels, chuckles, shovels,
> and so many how-to's and
> how-come's and
> all too simple explanations,
>
> the last thing we did was
> back out,
> driving live stakes into the
> ground as we went,
> erasing our own
> route in.
>
> If it is the path
> that makes the garden,
> and the garden that
> civilizes the wild,
> we are disengardening now,
> turning on our past
> and our pioneering ways
> to make amends for the
> scythe that went too far,
> to say a thank you
> audaciously
> for the future.[23]

For a period in the mid-1980s I devoted quite a bit of thought to the idea
of restoration as a form of agriculture before it occurred to me that I was
overlooking something. Then one fall afternoon as I watched a group of
volunteers gathering seed out on Curtis Prairie, it occurred to me that,
besides being a kind of agriculture and a way of doing ecological research,
restoration includes the experience of gathering and, to some extent, even
hunting as well.

The restorationist gathers seed in order to propagate plants for new
projects. In this way he or she acquires the intimate knowledge of plants
that comes from purposely searching them out, handling them, and tak-

ing from them. At times he also hunts—to control populations of species such as rabbits or deer in the absence of their natural predators or, less bloodily, to acquire animals for reintroduction to new projects. In this way he shares the experience of the hunter, Ortega y Gasset's "alert man," whose searching out, killing, sharing, and eating of game provides a classic paradigm for the experience of communion with nature.[24]

Restoration includes these experiences, but as in the case of ecology and agriculture, it also transforms them from an activity that is essentially consumptive—a taking from nature—to one that is essentially constructive—a giving back. This change in sign is crucial at a personal level because it allows the restorationist to shift for a moment from the feeling of satisfaction (and shame) at consuming a part of nature to the pleasure and joy (and also shame) of giving something back to it. It is also important at the social level because by changing the sign of the relationship between nature and culture from negative to positive it opens the way to participation by large numbers of people.

The realization that the restorationist is at times a gatherer and at times a hunter adds another element to our consideration of the value of restoration as an experience. It completes an evolutionary catalog of human experience, recapitulating the principal modes of our relationship with nature, from the primal experience of the gatherer and the hunter, through the attempts of the gardener and the farmer to reshape nature, to the scientist's attempt to understand it in a more abstract way.

In a single season, or even a single afternoon, the restorationist can explore all these experiences and can try out all these relationships in the most effective way possible—by reenacting them. The experience goes beyond the reenactment of history I discussed earlier to a reenactment of the deeper history of cultural evolution—an exploration not of the history of a particular people in a particular landscape, but of our species and its relationship with the rest of nature. It is perhaps here that we can see most clearly the extent to which restoration provides opportunities to engage nature fully and in a psychologically comprehensive and satisfying way, using all our abilities, including those acquired, in Loren Eiseley's words, on the pathway to the moon.

> To enter the river and attempt to bring this strong creature out of its own medium alive and uninjured is an opportunity to experience a momentary parity between human and salmon, mediated by slippery rock and swift current.
>
> Freeman House, "To Learn the Things We Need to Know"

But if restoration provides work in the classic landscape, it also provides that other prerequisite for an economic and sociable relationship with the community of nature—a language in which to communicate with the rest of nature and, at the deepest level, with ourselves.[25] This point is well illustrated by Thoreau's accounts of his own efforts to achieve redemption through communion with nature, and by the limitations of his approach—limitations of which he himself was very much aware.

Thoreau celebrated the fishermen who came to Walden Pond—"wild men," who knew how to find bait for fishing in winter, who got their living by barking trees, and whose lives "pass deeper in nature than the studies of the naturalist penetrate."[26] He undertook the famous experiment in agriculture reported in the chapter "The Beanfield" in *Walden* in part because, as he wrote, he was "determined to know beans." Yet the conclusions Thoreau drew from this experiment were generally downbeat.[27] Planting and hoeing his beans, he experienced agriculture as an intrusion into nature, and while he mentions the "intimate and curious acquaintance" with beans (and also with various weeds) he achieved in his beanfield, the comment is tinged with irony. Certainly, he never took this idea of agriculture as a way of gaining intimacy with nature seriously enough to apply it to his attempts to achieve an intimate relationship with the natural landscape. There, skeptical of agriculture, Thoreau confined himself to the role of observer. As Donald Worster remarks, Thoreau's accomplishments as an observer were prodigious. As he immersed himself in nature, in some cases entering the habitat of other species and acting out their role in it, he became, Worster notes, "like the muskrat, a limpid eyeball peering out of the sedges of a flooded meadow."[28] Yet Thoreau himself sensed the limits of this approach and toward the end of his life sometimes expressed regret that he seemed to have lost some of his former ability to achieve closeness to nature through sheer contact with it and immersion in it. He attributed this to his own increasingly scientific approach to nature. But perhaps Thoreau's real problem was not that he became too "scientific" in his approach to nature, but that he didn't push his idea of himself as a muskrat or a fox far enough. If he had, he might have tried his skill at cultivating the marsh, because that is what muskrats *do*. A muskrat is not merely a "limpid eyeball" peering at the marsh, but a busy participant in its *creation*.

The restorationist is Thoreau's muskrat, liberated from the role of a mere observer of the marsh to become an active participant in its ecology. Thoreau seems to have toyed with the idea of getting involved in this way, and on occasion he undertook small restorative acts of his own. In

1859, for example, he planted white pines on the site of his former bean-field, establishing a grove of trees that flourished there until it was destroyed by a hurricane in 1938.[29] But such acts remained marginal to his thinking about nature and his place in it.

Though understandable, Thoreau's skepticism about agriculture is unfortunate because, as we have seen, it is precisely through action, including the acts of the farmer, that nature communicates with itself and that we communicate with nature at the deepest and most elemental level. It is action, the language of nature, that enables a practitioner such as a farmer, a hunter, a scientist—or a restorationist, whose work incorporates the experience of all three—to come closer to nature than a person can ever come through pure observation, or through words alone. Thoreau was aware of this. He celebrated not only his own immersion in nature as a perceptive, intensely aware observer, but also the experience of others, like the fishermen and ice cutters on the pond, whose direct, economic engagement in natural processes he somewhat envied. At the same time he spent his entire life exploring the value of language as a means of communion with the world, and he was keenly and deeply aware of its limitations. The problem, he saw, is that language is too abstract, too metaphorical, too far from concrete reality. And so he sought "the language which all things and events speak without metaphor," words "so fresh and true and natural that they would appear to expand like the buds at the approach of spring."[30]

That language is the language of action, of mimesis, of participation and identification through sympathetic and imitative action, and the restorationist is learning to speak it. He is Thoreau's muskrat, inhabiting the marsh more fully than the mere observer. He is also the wolf, carrying out the wolf's job of killing deer, learning to see deer from a wolf's point of view. He is a pollinator and disperser of seed, filling in for various birds and insects in their role of creating and maintaining an ecological community. He is a crane, teaching young cranes to fly by clumsy example, or dancing with them to promote mating.[31] And, firing the prairies and woodlands, he takes on the role of Aboriginal people, and of the elemental force of lightning itself.

I, Lightning

Bending to this act I think I see
A flash of lightning striking that old tree
Off there on the horizon, then
A crash of thunder, then

A distant crackle and clatter of flame moving
In brush and grass, adding a thread of smoke to the dull sky;

Or a party of Sauk or Winnebago
Talking, perhaps arguing. Then one stoops
To touch fire to grass;
The men watching as the flame rises,
Spreads black in a widening circle, rushes downwind,
The men calling to one another in a foreign tongue.

I lightning, I one of a party of Sauk or Winnebago,
I, too, stoop to dry grass,
Bringing fire: the scratch and spurt of match
The eager orange plasma spreading,
The widening black patch—
This our High Mass.[32]

It is precisely through this sympathetic imitation of nature (including copying, which we might regard as zero-order imitation) in the attempt to recreate the natural or historic landscape that the restorationist comes not only to know it better but also to care more deeply about it. In his discussion of eighteenth-century Italian philosopher Giambattista Vico, political philosopher Isaiah Berlin explores Vico's idea that we can know, in the deepest and surest sense of attaining to truth, only those things that we make. This, Berlin notes, was not an original idea in Vico's time. But earlier thinkers who employed this idea had applied it only to entities such as mathematical propositions, which the mathematician understands in the same way that God understands the world, because he creates it. Vico extended this idea into the realms of history and language, disclosing to philosophy a new way of knowing based on imagination and participation. This is a knowledge that adds to the knowledge of the observer who merely describes phenomena, what Berlin describes as "the knowledge of the actors, as against that of the audience, of the 'inside' story as opposed to that obtained from some 'outside' vantage point."[33]

Scientists do this, Vico realized, when they carry out experiments, which may be seen as performances—attempts to understand the world we are given (and therefore do not make and do not understand) by recreating it in carefully calculated ways. Experiments, in other words, are acts of mimesis, ways of coming to understand nature by imitating it. In undertaking the imitation and even the copying of the natural, or "given" landscape, the restorationist extends this deeper "maker's knowledge" outward from the realms of mathematics, history, and politics into the realm of nature-as-given in the form of the natural landscape.

This perspective is important here for several reasons. For one thing, the "maker's knowledge" Vico described leads past the more abstract ways of knowing by description and analysis toward the experiences of "empathetic insight, intuitive sympathy, historical *Einfühlung* (empathy), and the like." For another, it led Vico to an idea of knowledge and of culture that falls between a strict relativism that denies our ability to know the other at all and an absolutism based on a conception of unchanging truth. This is the idea that we make our own knowledge, but that we do so not arbitrarily, but through performative interaction with other subjects. And this provides a way of resolving the debate now under way in environmental circles over whether nature is "real" or is "merely" a construct of the mind. Behind these opposed entities it shows us reality as a construct—not a purely mental construct like mathematics, but rather one that emerges from performative interactions, an idea that I explore further in the next three chapters.

There remains, of course, the question of presumptuousness. While I regard restoration as an act of humility before nature, there may be a measure of arrogance in the restorationist's willingness to join the gods of the landscape in their work of creation. Yet if we want to conserve natural landscapes, we have no choice. What are we to make of this? Only, I would say, that the ambiguity we face here is the ambiguity inherent in creation itself, which is inseparable from our role as self-conscious partners in creation.

Here we may learn something from mythology. Defying the gods and presuming on their prerogatives is a common theme of mythology. Indeed, according to Herbert Howe, the University of Wisconsin classics professor who made the translations for Barry Powell's *Classic Myth,* in Greek and Roman mythology, it is the predominant theme of all the Olympian myths—the myths, that is, that deal with the relationship between humans and the gods. This, after all, is the human dilemma, and it is one the restorationist faces in an especially dramatic way. Making a prairie or a wetland—playing god, some have called it—what presumption! What arrogance! What wicked conceit! Yes—and how inevitable. How dangerous. How shameful and—in the end—how beautiful.

One after another the Greek myths reaffirm the repayment of presumption with pain and also with beauty. Consider the story of the titan Prometheus, for example. Prometheus is famous for stealing fire from the gods and bringing it to humans, placing in their hands the power of technology—of world making. For this Prometheus was punished by being chained to a rock. What we often forget is that the story offers a promise of redemption, as in the end Zeus, indebted to Prometheus for a favor, grudgingly allows him his freedom.

The gods, the story suggests, need us. And though in *their* pride and willfulness they punish us for our presumption, there is a higher law beyond even the gods that ensures that in the end we are rewarded and the world is made more beautiful as a result of our efforts.

Take another myth of pride and presumption that seems to speak directly to the restorationist in her work of world making—that of Arachne the weaver. Like Prometheus, Arachne presumed to defy a god, not only challenging Athena to a contest in weaving but unwittingly insulting her in the process. To make matters worse, Arachne does not lose. Her weaving is the match of Athena's, so that "not Pallas [Athena], not envy itself, could find a fault in the weaving."[34]

This, of course, is an affront far more serious than that of losing. Enraged, Athena strikes Arachne who, in fright, hangs herself, and then— bringing in the note of universal compassion—Athena takes pity on her, rescues her, and transforms her into a spider.

Messages for the restorationist abound in these stories. There is a risk in presuming to take on the work of the gods (we might substitute nature), but also an ultimate reward. Arrogance and insolence will be punished mercilessly—as will success. But pluck and skill will be strangely rewarded. We need not (as we cannot) give back all we owe, which is troubling. But in the end the debt is forgiven. The gods relent or at least, like Zeus, look the other way. Vengeance is mitigated. Prometheus is freed from the rock. And Arachne's fate, though frightening, is perhaps also the ideal of the restorationist—to become a member of the community of life, a humble skillful creature, weaving the world.

CHAPTER 5

The Exchange

*Restoration as Repayment, and the Gift
of Ecological Immortality*

Everything we have, we take from nature, sometimes by persuasion or collaboration, sometimes by outright theft. Either way, the debt we incur is, or at least ought to be, a constant concern. For many, restoration is an attractive idea because it offers a way of repaying this debt. But does restoration represent a fair or reasonable repayment of our debt to nature, or is it, as some have insisted, merely a hoax or a fraud, offering back to nature a shabby fake in exchange for the real thing?

Broadly speaking, this question breaks down into two questions: first, what is the value of the restored ecosystem (which in turn breaks down into the questions of its ecological quality on the one hand, and of its authenticity, inherent value or meaning on the other); and, second, what is the value of the act of restoration itself, considered as a way of giving back to nature something that is distinctively human?

Turning first to the issue of quality, we find that, as we might expect, the situation is complicated. To begin with, plenty of restoration projects have been carried out in a careless or ill-conceived manner and have produced ecosystems that are obviously ecologically inferior to—or at any rate different from—the "original" or model system. But it makes little sense to judge the craft by the results of such work. To gain a clearer sense of what restoration has to offer, and what the quality of the classic landscapes of the future will be, it is necessary to turn to the best examples, projects such as Greene Prairie at the UW Arboretum, or the most successful wetland projects in tidal marshes along the East and West Coasts and in freshwater wetlands inland. Doing so we find that there is no simple answer to the question of the ecological quality of restored ecosystems. Certainly the commonplace claim that restoration is impossible is discredited by the most successful projects. But so is any notion that restoration is an easy, or even reliable, process.

In fact, the success of restoration efforts varies widely, depending on the kind of ecosystem being restored, the nature and degree of the disturbance it has undergone, and the conditions under which the restoration effort has been carried out. While environmentalists once referred to all natural ecosystems as "irreplaceable," it is now clear that restoration of some ecosystems to a fairly high quality is possible under favorable conditions. And some ecosystems are easier to restore than others. Broadly speaking, the difficulty of restoration depends on the complexity and resilience of the community, the nature and severity of the disrupting or "outside" influence, and the difficulty of replacing elements (such as species or soil or nutrients) or reinstating processes that have been interrupted. Under favorable conditions, the vegetation of certain tidal marshes on the East Coast is relatively easy to recreate because it consists of just one species of plant—cordgrass—and because the ecology of such marshes is dominated by the tides, which in their Newtonian regularity resemble a violent, regularly applied mechanical operation such as mowing. How the tide affects the ecosystem depends almost entirely on the grade or slope of the shoreline. Get that right, and the wetland can be planted almost like a rice paddy, which in many ways it resembles. The animal component of such marshes, on the other hand, is more complex and may be difficult to restore or may recover slowly if at all once the plant component of the community is in place. Freshwater wetlands typically support a more complex assemblage of plant species than cordgrass marshes, generally have a more complex and variable hydrology, and are usually more difficult to restore.[1]

Other communities also vary widely in their restorability. Certain kinds of prairie lend themselves to restoration, at least in certain respects. Many prairie plants are relatively small, are easy to propagate and handle, and reach maturity fairly quickly. Prairies present, however, the challenge of bringing a large number of species together in the right combination and distribution and the problem of excluding—or finding ways to control—nonnative or particularly aggressive native species. Besides this, animals present special problems. In the past restorationists usually concentrated on the vegetation on the principle that once the vegetation was in place, the appropriate animals would show up on their own. It has turned out, however, that many species don't, and restorationists are now doing extensive work with mammals such as bison and prairie dogs and smaller animals such as insects, which actually make up the largest component of the biological diversity of many biotic communities.[2] In certain respects forests are more challenging than prairies, not only because trees generally take longer to reach maturity than prairie species, but because the more complex architecture of a forest complicates the task of community assembly. Should understory species go in before or after the dominant trees have reached maturity? And coral reefs are challenging to restorationists simply because, being underwater, they are difficult to work with. They are also immensely complicated systems that include enormous numbers of species, many of which, like some of the corals themselves, are not well understood and, like trees, are extremely slow-growing.

Work with such systems highlights the importance of time, a factor that is beyond the restorationist's control. Tropical forests pose formidable challenges, both because they are extremely complex and because they depend on a continuous, rapid cycling of key nutrients that, once interrupted, may prove difficult to reestablish. Deserts and other arid ecosystems are commonly difficult to work with because plant establishment is difficult and growth and other recovery processes generally occur slowly under dry conditions. Generally speaking, ecosystems such as prairies, savannas, or riparian (river-edge) forests that are subject to and dependent on frequent and severe disturbances such as periodic fire, flooding, or bulldozing by ice floes are easier to restore than systems that reflect lower levels of disruption. Aquatic ecosystems such as lakes and rivers, which have been subjects of classic work in restoration, pose special problems because of their size, complexity, and intimate relationship with their surroundings.[3]

Not surprisingly, the restorability of an ecosystem also depends on the nature and severity of the disturbance to which the system has been subjected. A prairie or forest that has merely suffered a few decades of protection from fire and still retains most of its species is easier to restore than one that has been more severely injured and has to be recreated from the ground—or even from bare rock—up. This is also true of wetlands. Several years ago, when I went looking for a project that would represent the best work of wetland restorationists, a colleague directed me to a tidal marsh on the estuary of the Salmon River along the Oregon coast. Here the only major disruption had been to drain the marsh seventeen years earlier to create pasture for cattle. Restoration, which entailed merely taking out the cattle and removing a dike to allow reflooding and the recovery of surviving native vegetation, has been spectacularly successful.[4]

Success also depends on the techniques employed and the conditions under which restoration is carried out. Prairie restorationists, for example, long ago discovered that it is easier to restore prairies on thin, droughty, or nutrient-poor soils than on heavier, more fertile soils because the heavier soils support a more luxuriant growth of weeds, which compete with the more abstemious and generally slower-growing prairie plants, making it difficult for them to reoccupy the site. Similarly, it is difficult—strictly speaking, it is impossible—to restore wetland on an upland site. Though this is often attempted as part of the process of compensating legally—or "mitigating"—for damage to a natural wetland, most restorationists regard this as an inappropriate and even unethical practice. It is not restoration at all in the true sense and generally results in the creation of an ecologically misplaced, and therefore short-lived, ecosystem. It is basically a form of environmental window-dressing, and an abuse of the craft of restoration.

Even when the match of system to conditions is perfect, other factors may complicate the restorationist's work or limit the quality of the resulting system. A good example is continuing input of pollutants or nutrients, which may be virtually impossible to stop or correct for and may preclude restoration of a historic system. This is frequently a problem in lakes, streams, and other aquatic or marine ecosystems, but it may be a problem for terrestrial systems as well. Some scientists now believe that increasing inputs of nitrogen resulting from atmospheric pollution are beginning to affect the normally nitrogen-lean ecology of the prairies of the Midwest, possibly making changes we cannot easily reverse in the prairie ecosystem and the plant community it supports.[5]

The variety and complexity of ecosystems is only one reason why restoration efforts are hard to assess. Another, more fundamental, reason is that the work often raises questions about the ecosystems being restored that ecologists are not prepared to answer. For example, a project may involve components of the system—an underground component like the peat in a wetland, for example—that ecologists do not understand very well. Or it may require an evaluation of information, a prioritization of the relative importance of facts and ideas, and an identification of causes and effects that they are not in a position to carry out. Most attempts to appraise the quality of restored ecosystems have concentrated on just one component of the system—the aboveground component of the vegetation. Little is known about the ability of mammals, birds, or other animals to reoccupy restored ecosystems. The high marks ecologists have given some restored tidal wetlands, for example, reflect their preoccupation with what is in this case an extremely simple plant community and their tendency to overlook the more complex community of insects, mollusks, crustaceans, and microorganisms that normally inhabit these wetlands. Relatively little is known about what goes on underground in most ecosystems. Similarly, though ecologists know a good deal about the dynamics of some ecological communities—how they change over time, either as a result of their own internal processes or in response to outside influences, and also about processes such as productivity or the handling of water and nutrients—these features are generally more difficult to characterize and track than features such as species composition, and they are often poorly accounted for in evaluations of restored ecosystems.

These are critical considerations because, like any living system, an ecosystem is not merely an assemblage of species and other elements, such as soil and water. It is characterized by networks of relationships among elements, by the way it functions, and by more or less distinctive patterns of change. Since all of these are crucial, defining characteristics of the system, the restorationist needs to take all of them into account when planning and carrying out a project, and also when evaluating its success. Restorationists are aware of this, and frequently warn against what they call "snapshot" goals for restoration projects—goals based on the condition of the model system at a particular moment or brief period in time. What they seek, ideally, is a motion-picture objective based on the way the system acts over a period of time. Most practitioners are very much attuned to this issue, and to the folly of defining project goals in static terms. Massachusetts restorationist Peter Dunwiddie draws out the cinema metaphor in an elegant and highly suggestive way, proposing that an even better model is live theater—perhaps even improvisational or experimental theater—in which the restorationist not only follows the script but helps write and rewrite it in response to unforeseen developments.[6]

This, however, is the ideal. In practice, objects are easier to keep track of than processes and events. As a result, goals for restoration projects are usually defined in terms of countable or measurable objects—numbers of species, for example, or the size and numbers of individuals—rather than functional or dynamic attributes.

Consider function, for example. Though generally easier to track than dynamic attributes, which may be revealed only over a period of decades or even centuries, an ecosystem's functional attributes can be difficult to track, and studies of the functioning of restored ecosystems are relatively rare. Some of the best examples are studies of restored wetlands, where the politics and economics of mitigation have provided both incentives and resources for such work. The ecologist Joy Zedler, for example, analyzed some of the functional attributes of several restored wetlands near San Diego, not only measuring indices of productivity and nutrient cycling but also assessing the suitability of the restored system as habitat for various invertebrates and for the light-footed clapper rail, an endangered bird. Her results reveal a mix of successes, partial successes, and downright failures. The restored wetlands scored lower than the reference systems with respect to some attributes, higher with respect to others. But of course both higher and lower scores represent a failure to reach restoration goals, and Zedler concludes that restoration was generally unsuccessful in these instances and is not an acceptable alternative to the protection of existing wetlands.[7]

While few restorationists would disagree with this in principle, not all accept Zedler's generally downbeat interpretation of her own results. For example, John Rieger, a restorationist who works for the California Department of Transportation, comments that the wetlands Zedler studied were immature systems, only a few years old, and should not be expected to resemble mature reference systems either in composition and structure or in functioning and overall performance.[8] Off the record, others question her choice of examples of the restorationist's craft. They suggest that the work on these projects was *horticulturally* naive, and that the resulting wetlands are hardly worthy of careful ecological evaluation.

In any event, Zedler's work is important because it represents an attempt to evaluate the quality of a restored ecosystem in a comprehensive and systematic way. Such efforts are rare. Until recently, only a handful of ecologists took restoration seriously enough to devote serious attention to it, so practitioners usually worked out their own indices of success. The few comprehensive studies of the quality of restored ecosystems that have been done have generally been carried out, as was Zedler's, to appraise the result of a legally mandated project, where there is both a clear motive and funding for follow-up studies of this kind. Unfortunately, few, if any, such projects are driven primarily by concern about the well-being of the ecosystem, the motive that might be expected to underlie the best work.

The point here is that there is no simple way to evaluate a restored— artificial—ecosystem because doing this raises fundamental questions about what the ecosystem *is*. These are not questions that can be answered simply by applying existing knowledge and theory to a particular situation. They are, rather, fundamental questions that challenge ecologists to move beyond the description and analysis of an ecosystem to identify the critical parameters that define it. What restoration demands is the ecological equivalent of the repertory of vital signs medical doctors use to evaluate human health. These indicators—pulse, blood pressure, body temperature, and so on—are easy to measure under almost any conditions and with a minimum of equipment. Yet their use reflects a deep understanding of the body and how it works. The development of such tests is not merely a clinical trick, or a form of "applied" physiology. It is the product of close collaboration between theory and practice and represents an important intellectual achievement. The attempt to assess the quality of ecosystems calls for similar insight on the part of the ecologist and, as we saw in the last chapter, provides excellent opportunities for finding answers to some of the basic questions of ecology. In other words, the ecologist's attempt to answer the restorationist's question about ecosystem quality tells us as much about ecology and its limitations and possibilities as it does about restoration and the artificial natural ecosystems that result from restoration efforts.

If the restorationist's success is limited by what he knows—or can know—about the ecosystem being restored, it is also limited by what he is able and willing to do—and ultimately by what a society is willing to pay—to restore and maintain a particular ecosystem or landscape. As in most endeavors, cost of one kind or another is an unavoidable consideration in restoration projects, which, without any exception that I am aware of, always compromises the objective of "pure" restoration for some "practical" reason.

Other limitations on restoration are not under the restorationist's control at all and may turn out to represent real upper limits on the practice of restoration. There are, for example, certain limits on what features of an ecological community are actually restorable. Many clearly are. Some may not be. Sometimes components have been lost, structures disrupted, processes interrupted, or conditions changed in ways that really are irreversible either practically or, in some cases, in principle.

Extinct species, for example, are for all practical purposes irreplaceable, and their absence may affect the ecology of a restored ecosystem profoundly. A good example is the chestnut forests that covered large areas in the Northeast until early in the twentieth century when a blight all but wiped out the American chestnut. Clearly, restoration of the chestnut forests is impossible, at least until a blight-resistant strain appears naturally, or until someone develops a resistant strain or finds a practical way to protect trees from the blight on an ecologically significant scale.[9]

Conversely, the introduction of exotic species can also be essentially irreversible. Some invasive exotics can be controlled reasonably well under some conditions, but others cannot. No one, for example, expects to see the elimination of exotic grasses from California, of loosestrife from wetlands in the eastern United States, of leafy spurge from rangelands farther west, or of carp, English sparrows, zebra mussels, exotic earthworms, or a host of other exotic species from North America, yet all these can profoundly affect the ecological communities in which they take up residence. The list of troublesome exotics seems—and probably is—endless. At the moment restorationists in my part of the country are deeply concerned about the expansion of populations of garlic mustard, a European adventive that is invading forest understories and that many believe may eliminate most species of understory herbs, including the spring wildflowers that are one of the most beloved features of our forests. The prospect of a monotonous layer of green rather than shaded acres of trillium, bloodroot, Dutchman's breeches, and wild geranium in all areas that are not constantly policed by restorationists is obviously a dismal one and at times challenges even my considerable faith in the promise of restoration.[10]

Elements of structure, too, can be all but irreplaceable. The wetland ecologist Cal DeWitt has shown that the movement of water in certain wetlands, obviously a crucial feature of their ecology, depends on the capillary structure of the underlying peat, which is probably impossible to reproduce.[11] Similarly, alterations in water tables or cycles of flooding may be essentially irreversible. When this is the case, restoration in the strictest sense is impossible, and the restorationist is forced to abandon or compromise the goal of restoration and to settle for a system that is adapted to existing conditions.

Another example of irreversible change arises from the fact that ecological communities are not merely assemblages of parts that we can take apart and put back together again at will, the way we might a shotgun or an automobile. They have histories, as human communities do, and are to a considerable extent an outcome and reflection of that history. Moreover, they are to some extent chaotic systems that generate unique, unrepeatable histories. Both facts have important implications for ecological restoration. For a long time ecologists thought of the development of ecological communities as an orderly process of "succession," with one assemblage of species preparing the way for and gradually being replaced by another in a more or less predictable manner. Such successional processes probably do account for some aspects of ecological change. But in recent years, as ecologists have become increasingly aware of the complexity of ecological systems and the chaotic aspects of their behavior, they have developed alternative ways of thinking about them. Some, for example, have interpreted the process of community development in terms of what they call assembly rules. The idea here is that a given ecosystem is actually the outcome of a sequence of developmental phases or events, each dependent on the presence of a particular combination of species and other factors, such as weather, moisture, and soil conditions. Creating an ecosystem, in this view, is not like mixing paint, in which pigments can be added in any order and only the amount of each color is important. Nor is it like the orderly, genetically programmed development of an organism. It is more like the history of a nation, a process in which sequences of events and networks of contingencies may be crucial. Seemingly minor influences or circumstances such as the presence or absence of a particular predator or pollinator early in the life of a system may have a disproportionate influence on its development, which may then proceed not toward a single, more or less predictable outcome as in the succession model, but toward any one of a number of alternate steady states.[12] While, for the same reason, most systems seem to be reachable by a variety of alternative pathways, as ecologist Stuart Pimm has pointed out, it is likely that some of the steps in the development of a community may depend quite strictly on a particular combination of factors. What this means is that if a necessary sequence is not known, or if the conditions for a particular step cannot be met, it may be impossible, not just in practical terms but in principle, to reassemble the community.[13]

Pimm calls these barriers to reassembly Humpty Dumpties, after the famous egg, and believes that Humpty Dumpties may underlie some of the difficulties restorationists have encountered in attempting to recreate specific systems. Humpty Dumpties may be of two kinds. There may be *community*—compositional or structural—Humpty Dumpties, such as missing, perhaps extinct species that may not actually be part of the model community but that played a key, or catalytic role in its development. Or there may be *ecosystem*—functional—Humpty Dumpties, combinations of environmental conditions that reflected historic climate or geological or hydrological circumstances that may not be understood or that could not be reproduced even if they were. For example, stands of reeds in certain northern lakes grow in water too deep to allow them to reproduce and may date back to a time when the climate was different and lake levels were lower.[14] Ecosystems or communities of this kind may be said to contain ecological ghosts, the deep imprint or "memory" of previous events, and attempts to restore them under present-day conditions may fail because these ghosts are now gone and cannot be summoned back or perhaps even identified. The lesson here is not that restoration of most ecosystems is impossible. It is that some kinds of change are reversible, while others are not. Since ecological systems clearly undergo both kinds of change, a fundamental task of ecology is to distinguish them and tease them apart.

Restoration offers an excellent way to do this. It is precisely by attempting to reverse ecological change that we are most likely to encounter the Humpty Dumpties that lurk in ecosystems, precluding their reproduction and teaching us something about their ecology. In any event it seems sensible to regard restoration not as a practice based on the simple-minded idea that any kind of change is reversible, but as a powerful way of exploring and characterizing the various kinds of change.

The results of this growing understanding will have profound implications for conservation policy, allowing us to prioritize protection efforts and allocate conservation resources more effectively. Ecosystems like the reed beds in a northern lake that prove to be irreproducible may deserve the highest priority. At the same time it is important to keep in mind that systems of this kind are in a sense sterile. Being both irreproducible and incapable of reproduction, they are no longer part of the ongoing process of creation and have in a sense dropped outside nature itself. This gives them a unique value in one sense, but it reduces their value in another, creating a dilemma with which environmentalists will have to struggle in the years ahead.

Beyond purely ecological factors, restorationists face a succession of other obstacles that limit the success of restoration projects and the quality of the resulting ecosystems. By definition, restoration depends on an understanding of the history of the system being restored, and of the historic system chosen as a model. Restorationists have drawn on a number of disciplines here, using sources ranging from climatology to the study of tree rings, deposits of pollen, and even animal droppings in their attempts to define and characterize the ecosystems that serve as models for their work.[15] Nevertheless historic information is often a limiting factor in restoration efforts.

This is especially so when the model ecosystem no longer exists or exists only in an altered or degraded condition. This is the situation restorationists faced twenty years ago, when they began attempts to recreate examples of oak savanna, an open, orchardlike community that, unlike the more or less treeless prairies, supports scattered groves of trees. Oak savanna once covered large areas in parts of the Midwest but is now virtually extinct there. Having only scattered and degraded remnants of savanna to serve as models, restorationists faced a challenge rather like that faced by those attempting to build replicas of historic objects such as Christopher Columbus's ships or Shakespeare's Globe theater, which no longer exist and about which we have only limited information. In such situations restoration is information-limited, and the restorationist's claims to accuracy must always be qualified accordingly, though the value of restoration as a way of refining our ideas about an ecosystem can apply even to ecosystems that no longer exist, as we shall see.

Next the restorationist encounters what we might call epistemological limits—limits not on what restorationists know about the system being restored but, more fundamentally, on what they *can* know about it. While the ecosystem itself does most of the work, restoration necessarily involves bringing the ecosystem through the epistemological bottleneck of human perception and understanding. We always see the world from a certain perspective, through the lenses provided by culture, temperament, and the paradigms we learned in school, and restorationists are no exception. The results of their work will always reflect their point of view, their idea of what was important about the ecosystem, what was worth measuring, going to get, or paying to have done. Restorationists' work makes them aware of the difficulty of interpreting the world, and they talk about it. Bill Brumbach once put it very neatly when, commenting on his work with woodland wildflowers at the Garden in the Woods in Framingham, Massachusetts, he told me, "I know the plants I wind up with are the ones that are adapted to *me*. And I also know that there's nothing I can do about that."

Restored ecosystems are, after all, partly artifacts. Like other artifacts, they have what art historians call time-style, unavoidably reflecting the restorationists' knowledge, ignorance, ideas, misconceptions, values, tastes, and assumptions. As a result they are likely to seem a bit quaint to later generations. At the UW Arboretum, current understanding of the importance of scale and the ways the various communities in a landscape interact makes the restored communities' small size and ecologically inappropriate juxtapositions look a bit old-fashioned.[16] Besides that, Baird Callicott notes, the early work at the Arboretum reflects a view of ecological communities as organisms with a high degree of integrity that eventually reach a relatively stable, or "climax," condition.[17] Now most ecologists see them as relatively loose assemblages of organisms that are highly dynamic at all stages of their development. Our understanding of such phenomena will always run up against an epistemological limit, and one of the benefits of the restorationist's attempts to get completely outside himself and be absolutely true to nature is that this puts him in a position to explore this limit, characterize it, and define its position more clearly.

The preceding discussion provides an idea of the extent to which restorationists are able to restore classic ecosystems on a modest scale, creating what might be called samples, or swatches, of natural landscapes such as Curtis Prairie or a patch of tidal wetland in Maryland. Overall, the idea that is emerging after a half a century or so of experience is that work at this level can be reasonably successful under favorable conditions. But what about the crucial question of scale? Granting for the moment the ability of restorationists to create or restore ecosystems on what we might call the horticultural scale of, say, an acre or two, or even the agronomic scale of a few hundred acres, what are the prospects for restoration on the scale that classic ecosystems actually exist—that is, on the scale of mountain ranges, or the watersheds of major rivers? To put this another way, can they restore ecosystems large enough to actually *work* more or less like their natural counterparts and so to achieve at least a degree of self-sufficiency?

This is a crucial question, in part because there is in ecology a fundamental, Pythagorean relationship between quality and quantity. An ecosystem comprises a network of events and interactions, each of which functions on a certain scale, in time as well as space.[18] An example is grazing. If a prairie, for example, is too small to sustain a viable population of bison, it will not be grazed by bison, and this will affect its ecology in various ways. The same is true of fire. If fire does not burn a tallgrass prairie every year or so, the chances are that oak forest will replace it within a few decades. Fortunately, it has proved possible to compensate artificially for the reduced frequency of natural fires simply by setting fires on a schedule calculated to imitate the pattern of burning that might have occurred on a large prairie in pre-contact times. It is much more difficult, however, to provide surrogate bison or antelope in an ecologically effective way on a small site, though research on this is being carried out by restorationists and managers working on larger sites farther west.[19]

In any event, the issue of scale, in time as well as space, is a crucial one.

Precious as they may be in certain respects—as local reservoirs of biodiversity, for example, or as miniature representations of historic landscapes—restored ecosystems such as Curtis Prairie, isolated in a landscape of cornfields and housing developments, are in no way ecologically or esthetically adequate substitutes for their natural counterparts.

So long as restoration efforts are limited to projects of just a few acres, their long-term environmental value is limited, and concern about this underlies environmentalists' skepticism regarding the value of restoration as a conservation strategy. I recall a conversation I had with Bob Jenkins, then a senior official with the Nature Conservancy, sometime in the mid-1980s. Jenkins was an early supporter of the idea of ecological restoration. He had been a leader in bringing restoration into conservancy thinking and had championed several milestone projects, including wetland restoration work on Chesapeake Bay and a major prairie restoration project at Fermi National Laboratory near Chicago. He was also, which was unusual for an environmentalist at the time, inclined to consider the question of the quality and authenticity of restored ecosystems in positive rather than negative terms—to see the glass as half full rather than half empty. Nevertheless, when I asked him about the role he saw for restoration in conservation, he shook his head. He simply could not imagine ecological restoration being carried out on a scale commensurate with the scale on which natural landscapes are being disrupted and destroyed.

Given the scale of most restoration projects that have been undertaken so far, and the expense of carrying them out, which can run into thousands of dollars per acre, there are good reasons for such skepticism. At the same time there is a certain danger in skepticism here, since it might lead to a dismissal of restoration, to a failure to develop restoration techniques and find ways of applying them, and a failure to come to grips with key issues such as quality or authenticity, or the ethical questions arising from the use of restoration to compensate for environmental damage. This is a form of complacency we simply cannot afford. Restoration is not merely one of several alternative strategies for conserving classic ecosystems. As *the* means by which preservation is actually achieved, it will determine both the existence and the quality or character of the classic landscapes of the future. The question is not whether restoration is perfect, or whether it can be carried out on a scale large enough to result in a more or less self-sustaining ecosystem. The question is how good a job can restorationists do, and on how large a scale. Will the best restored ecosystems always be small, like the Arboretum's prairies, and therefore dependent on relatively intensive restorative maintenance? Or might we expect restorationists to learn how to work successfully on a scale large enough to create more or less self-sustaining ecosystems?

Here again, the experience of prairie restorationists, though in some ways exceptional, is especially revealing, though for slightly paradoxical reasons. Precisely because prairies have never been afforded legal protection (as, for example, wetlands have in recent years), prairie restorationists have generally been motivated primarily by a desire simply to get the ecosystem back, and they have placed unusual emphasis on ecological quality and accuracy. At the same time, having few resources other than their own labor, prairie restorationists initially worked on a small scale. Back in the 1960s, for example, when horticulturist Ray Schulenberg started a prairie planting at the Morton Arboretum in suburban Chicago, he set out plants by hand, and weeded them on hands and knees for several years. The result was a prairie of spectacularly high quality. Adjacent areas that have been restored since, using less meticulous techniques, are still of somewhat inferior quality. The same thing has been true of larger projects, such as the 700-acre project at Fermilab, much of which has been planted by broadcasting seed onto tilled ground, using trucks equipped with salt spreaders. Though strikingly successful in certain respects, the Fermilab prairie still includes relatively few of the rarer, more conservative prairie species.[20]

This sort of experience, repeated in dozens of other projects around the Midwest over the years reinforced the idea—no doubt grounded in the experiences of both wildflower gardening and tillage-intensive, row-crop agriculture—that the restoration of prairies is basically a needlepoint operation, that success depends on intensive management, and that attempts to scale up necessarily entail either an increase in costs or a sacrifice in quality. And this naturally reinforced environmentalists' doubts about the value of restoration as a conservation strategy.

Fortunately, this is not the whole story. At least two considerations suggest that the quality-for-quantity trade-off is not fundamental, and that it might indeed be feasible to recreate classic ecosystems on an ecologically significant scale. One is the fundamental ecological relationship between quality and quantity I mentioned earlier—the fact that size is critical in ecology, and that the bigger an ecosystem is, the more complete it is ecologically, and the more likely it is to be more or less self-sustaining. Environmentalists have always drawn on this argument to support acquisition of land—and then more land—for conservation purposes. Large preserves, or preserves near large natural areas, or clusters of preserves linked by green corridors or by small, stepping-stone preserves, are generally more self-sufficient and easier to maintain than small ones, and the same principle applies in restoration. Though scaling up may lead to certain technical difficulties, if these difficulties can be overcome, the work is likely to become easier as elements are added, subsystems kick in, and the system begins to come to life, pulling itself along, taking over more and more of the work, and to some extent directing its own development. This suggests that as projects increase in size, restorationists might anticipate a certain economy of scale, which will take the form both of reductions in subsidies to the system and of higher-quality results. This effect is already evident in some projects on the Great Plains, where the larger scale of prairie-restoration projects has made it possible to include bison on some sites, the result being a more complete, and more self-sufficient, ecosystem.

The second consideration involves the development of new techniques that provide a way around the quality-for-quantity trade-off. These typically involve finding ways to replace agricultural effort with ecological processes—the trick of knowing how to let nature do most of the work, which is the essence of any craft.

An excellent example is the work of a Montpelier, Ohio, river manager named George Palmiter whom I met in 1983. A railroad switchman who spent his spare time canoeing and hunting ducks on the slow-flowing rivers of northwestern Ohio, Palmiter got involved in river and stream management during the 1960s when the elms around Montpelier started dying from Dutch elm disease and falling into the rivers, spoiling them for canoeists. Palmiter organized a canoe club to remove the dead trees. Supervising this work over the years, he gradually developed a system that virtually eliminates the bulldozers, gabions, revetments, riprap, and other hardware of conventional river-management methods. With gentle intelligence Palmiter manages waterways, not by pushing them around but almost by suggestion and innuendo, tweaking them, and, as he says, letting the river do the work.

The result is a kind of magic, like that worked by the keystone of an arch or an airfoil, or by vitamins or vaccines—all technologies in which an understanding of the system enables the practitioner to work with the system as a colleague, achieving the synergy that emerges from genuine collaboration, creating something out of nothing—or, in Palmiter's case, out of sunlight. A former heavy-equipment operator, Palmiter now uses sunlight to move sediment, using the canopy of trees over the river like an awning. To create a bar, he cuts down a tree, opening up a hole at a strategic point. Sunlight falls on the bank; vegetation appears and begins to trap silt, building a bar or extending a bank. To get rid of a bar, he plants a willow, which in a few years casts the bar into shade, weakening the vegetation and letting the river carry the silt away. Basically, Palmiter is minimizing the use of heavy machinery by using solar energy in three forms: in the river current, which is Palmiter's substitute for a dragline; in the sunlight itself, which he uses to control the vegetation that ultimately shapes the channel; and in the trees, which are the tools he uses to manage the sunlight. Overall, the result is an approach to the management—or restoration—of waterways that respects the system and, by replacing heavy equipment and gasoline with muscle power, sunshine, and an intimate understanding of the system, makes the whole process less costly, more democratic, more elegant—and feasible on a larger scale.[21]

Another example of this sort of elegance and the economies it entails has recently emerged from work on the tallgrass prairies that, some restorationists now believe, has profound implications for the future of these ecosystems. From the very beginning prairie restorationists have tinkered with a variety of methods. One of these, tried by several of the restorationists who worked on the Arboretum's prairies during its early years, seems almost laughably simple. Working on tracts of overgrown pasture and abandoned plowlands occupied by a dense growth of weeds, on several occasions Henry Greene tried to establish prairie vegetation without plowing. He simply threw seed of prairie plants into the turf, raked it in, then waited to see what would happen. What happened was surprising, though it seems no one paid much attention at the time. Prairie species introduced in this way actually established well, gradually elbowing out the existing vegetation and coming to dominate the site.[22] Others tried more or less the same thing over the years with similar results, but the method, so different in "feel" from conventional plow-and-cultivate agriculture, did not catch on. Apparently, no one fully realized its significance and, even at the Arboretum where Greene had done his experiments, restorationists continued to rely on the more intensive, tillage-based approach to their prairie projects.

Recently, however, a few restorationists have experimented with the seed-into-sod method more seriously, and have begun to appreciate its implications for prairie restoration. One of these is Steven Packard, who does restoration work in the Chicago area. Packard began experimenting with what he calls successional restoration in the late 1970s, mainly because, like George Palmiter, he had limited resources and was looking for an effective, low-tech way to reestablish and upgrade prairies. What he found was not only that, given time, prairie species introduced by sowing seed into existing sod can make their way against existing vegetation, gradually replacing it, but that those conditions actually favor many of the fussier, rarer, or more "conservative" prairie species such as purple prairie clover, lead plant, prairie dropseed, and the yuccalike rattlesnake master, which are slow-growing and tend to be relatively rare in natural prairies. These species are often absent from prairies restored by traditional till-and-sow methods. Packard and his colleagues now find them in abundance on sites where successional restoration began on old fields five, ten, and fifteen years ago.[23]

Again, as in the case of Palmiter's work, the attempt to restore an ecosystem led to a deeper understanding of it. The realization that it is not necessary to remove existing vegetation in order to replace it with prairie, that the prairie species can do this themselves by a kind of ecological infiltration or intussusception, is of more than practical importance. It apparently works so well because it builds the community on the existing ecosystem, rather than tearing it out and building from scratch. In taking this approach, the restorationist is taking part in—and taking advantage of—the natural process of community change, or succession. Hence the term "successional restoration."[24]

Fortunately, the value of this approach is not limited to prairies. In fact, restorationists have often attempted to identify trends of succession and the mechanisms underlying them and to take advantage of these in their work. A half a century ago, for example, John Curtis suggested that the best way to establish a stand of oaks on certain sites was to plant pines, which as they mature create conditions ideal for oaks, which can otherwise be difficult to establish. Similarly, David Mahler, who practices restoration in the Austin area, finds that the cover formed by low-growing cedars provides conditions favorable for the establishment of evergreen sumac and other shrubs that are difficult to introduce into the grasslands of central Texas.

The fact that these methods do work offers important insights into the dynamics of the ecosystems involved and raises fascinating questions about the processes by which they change over time as species colonize, become established, and replace other species. It also represents a quantum leap in the restorationist's ability to restore high-quality prairies on a large scale. Packard carried out his early informal experiments with successional restoration on a small scale, on plots of just a few square yards. During the past few years, however, he and others around the Midwest have been scaling up rapidly. Ed Collins, the restorationist who master-minded the remeandering of a stretch of Nippersink Creek in northern Illinois, is relying heavily on a version of successional restoration on his prairie sites. And successional restoration will play an important role in restoration efforts now under way at the Neal Smith National Wildlife Refuge near Prairie City in central Iowa, where restorationists plan to replace nearly 9,000 acres of corn and soybean fields with tallgrass prairie.[25]

Driving such work is a vision of a restored landscape—not just a few glittering patches here and there, but the whole sweep and reach, the wild profusion, the awesome expanse and rolling oceanic vistas of the old prairies. Real prairies, in some places, from horizon to horizon. Artificial wild places.

Until recently, such an idea would have seemed completely unreasonable. But the development of a technique such as successional restoration, together with the adaptation of various agricultural techniques, such as the use of combines to harvest prairie seed, and a growing awareness of the contribution volunteers can make to the restoration process, gives such visions a new plausibility. I recently realized that the scale of the largest intensive prairie restoration projects has increased logarithmically during the past three or four decades, from just a few acres at the Morton Arboretum in the 1960s to projects of some tens, and then hundreds of acres in the 1970s, to thousands of acres in the 1980s, and now, at places like McHenry County and the Neal Smith refuge, to projects approaching ten thousand acres. (Extrapolating backward from this plot, the early work at the UW Arboretum, carried out on a scale of tens of acres in the 1930s and 1940s, was about three decades ahead of its time, a fact that attests both to the vision of the Arboretum's founders and the peculiarly favorable circumstances in which they worked.)[26]

Enormous challenges remain. It is not clear, for example, how to reduce the fuel load in the ponderosa pine forests of the Southwest to reduce their vulnerability to the ecosystem-destroying crown fires that have become increasingly frequent in recent years. One way is to gather downed wood into piles, which can be burned separately, as managers are doing, with the help of volunteers, in a few areas in Yosemite National Park. This, however, is labor-intensive work and is probably impractical on a large scale, leaving the fate of vast landscapes in the Southwest desperately uncertain.

In any case, the growing technical efficiency of restorationists in many situations brings us to yet another ceiling limiting the scope of restoration efforts—the economic ceiling. There will always be a question concerning how much land a human community will be willing to allocate for classic ecosystems such as tallgrass prairies. I can think of two morally acceptable ways to tip the balance in favor of a more generous apportionment of land for such purposes, and both of them depend heavily on restoration. The first and most important of these is to find ways to enfranchise large numbers of people into genuine membership in these ecosystems. The second is to find ways in which the ecosystems can contribute to, or in some way intermesh with, the economy of the human community. To the extent that this can be done, economy and ecology will cease to be in opposition at the most fundamental, ecological level and will actually pull each other along.

An example of how such a synergy between natural and human economies might work is currently emerging from research being carried out by soil scientists on the restored prairie at Fermilab. Six decades ago, pioneer ecologist John Weaver, writing in the aftermath of the Dustbowl, suggested that prairie might eventually be used to rehabilitate soils degraded by crop production.[27] More recently, mycologist Mike Miller and ecologist Julie Jastrow at Argonne National Laboratory near Chicago have studied changes in the soil under the Fermilab prairie, parts of which are now more than a quarter of a century old. What they have found is that the prairie has indeed supported soil regeneration on this site. In fact, the coarse "crumb structure" that accounts for many of the properties that make prairie soils so valuable for agriculture is recovering more rapidly under the prairie than under any other kind of soil-regeneration system studied so far.[28]

This bit of news ought to be getting more attention than it is in an area whose economy depends heavily on agriculture. According to Kevin McSweeney, a soil scientist at the University of Wisconsin, while widely quoted estimates that up to half the soil in parts of the Midwest have been lost since the time of European settlement are overstated, it is certainly true that degradation of soils through depletion of nutrients and breakdown of crumb structure is a problem with serious economic implications in many areas.[29] Using prairies as a component in a low-frequency crop-rotation program may be a way—in fact, it may well be the *only* practical way—to rebuild these soils. Using prairie in this way would bring it into an essential relationship with the human economy, truly linking a regional economy with the larger ecology of which it is a part. If this were to happen, the economy would not threaten prairie restoration and conservation but would drive them. And this opens up the possibility of a future with lots of prairie—perhaps 10 or 20 percent of the Midwestern landscape—in a shifting mosaic in rotation with corn, wheat, soybeans, and other crops.

In the meantime other economic roles are being found for prairies. Managers of parks, preserves, and public hunting grounds are restoring prairies to control erosion and to create habitat for both game and nongame species. Municipalities and departments of transportation are planting prairies on roadsides and other rights-of-way, where in addition to contributing to local biodiversity and regional identity, they can substantially reduce maintenance costs. Building on the pioneering work of designers like Olmsted and Jensen, landscape architects are using prairies in residential and commercial landscapes. And in Kansas, geneticist Wes Jackson is carrying out research to learn how to make a farm that works like a prairie, using the prairie itself as a model for a new sustainable form of agriculture.[30] Also on the Great Plains, in what may be the grandest restoration project and integration of natural and human economies yet conceived, geographer Deborah Popper at Rutgers University and Frank Popper, a land-use planner and political scientist at City College of New York, have proposed the restoration of vast areas on the Great Plains, complete with bison herds, in an attempt to replace a declining economy based on traditional forms of agriculture with one more in tune with the ecology of the region.[31]

Similar developments are taking place in other bioregions as well. In the Pacific Northwest, restoration of spawning habitat for dwindling populations of salmon has become a priority for conservationists, who are undertaking sophisticated projects aimed at the restoration not only of streams but, necessarily, of their entire watersheds. In this way a single species (in this case actually a genus) can become not just the basis for an economy, but a totem for an entire region, guiding and inspiring the work necessary to ensure its well-being.[32] Bison serve the same role on the plains. One reason why some find the Poppers' vision of a Buffalo Commons so compelling is that it resonates with the beliefs of Plains Indians, for whom the bison is a sacred animal, and also with the mythology of the American frontier and its role in the shaping of American character and identity.

Like fishing, forestry provides excellent opportunities to integrate human economies with local ecologies, in part because both actually involve forms of hunting and gathering—economies based on direct exploitation of a natural ecosystem and therefore dependent on its well-being. Despite the crimes against nature that have been committed in its name, forestry has always included a tradition of caring for the forest, and indeed some forms of forestry come closer to restoration in the modern sense than any other form of land husbandry. In recent years a school of forestry has emerged that espouses forest management based on the restorationist's principle of taking, giving back, and finding ways to let nature do most of the work—again borrowing from and paying tribute to some of the more ecologically sensitive forms of traditional agriculture.[33]

The same is true of wetlands, long regarded as throwaway ecosystems and economic liabilities. The great example here is CalFed, a $12 billion federal and state program to restore wetlands and waterways in central California as part of an effort to improve wildlife habitat and water quality in the Sacramento River watershed. In another large-scale project, the Army Corps of Engineers is restoring a channelized stretch of the Kissimmee River in south Florida to improve water quality and wildlife habitat, and similar projects on a small scale are underway in many areas in connection with efforts at flood control, habitat improvement, and—less romantically—wastewater treatment.[34]

Developments such as these both reflect and promote a growing awareness that the conservation of classic ecosystems is not merely a matter of noblesse oblige, or even of economic importance only in an indirect long-term sense but is often a vital and immediate economic concern—a fact that bodes well for their future.

Overall, the picture that emerges from this broad overview of the prospects for restoration is certainly no reason for complacency. Yet there are grounds here for a measure of optimism, and these will become more secure as we learn to take restoration seriously and take full advantage of its possibilities. For one thing, since the craft of restoration is still in its infancy, it is not unreasonable to suppose that restoration techniques will improve rapidly during the next few decades. For another, in the very act of carrying out restoration work, we are likely to find ourselves raising the one ceiling that will ultimately limit natural-area conservation in any landscape inhabited by human beings—that is, the depth and extent of human regard for the natural landscape.

This, then, is the first part of the restorationist's gift to nature—this new way of conserving the old amid the rising tide of the new. It is nature itself in its conservative mode, the offering back to the origin that Robert Frost called the tribute of the current to the source.[35]

So far, however, I have dealt only with the objective value of the gift the restorationist offers nature—the restored ecosystem itself considered in purely objective, or ecological, terms. Beyond this, there are other, subjective values such as authenticity or "realness," meaning, and beauty. These are exclusively human concerns, and they are internal and invisible. Yet even in purely ecological terms they are as important as objective values—and ultimately inseparable from them—because they underlie attitudes and feelings that to a considerable extent determine the behavior of the species that increasingly dominates the landscape and shapes its ecology. Here the question for the restorationist is whether these more elusive, transcendent values can be restored along with the "hardware" (or greenware) of the ecosystem itself.

Several years ago, the British naturalist and gardener Chris Barnes raised these questions in an especially vivid way by bringing in the idea of ghosts. "We may make the forest look as good as the original," he said, commenting on the restorationist's work. "But it won't sound as good, and it won't smell as good, and it won't have the ghosts in it."[36] By "ghosts," of course, Barnes means the appearance, the beauty, and the meaning of the forest or prairie or coral reef, the spirit it evokes and the feeling that arises from our sense that it is other than us and has a long history independent of humans—qualities that, he suggests, are not present in a restored forest.

Here then is a question. Suppose that restorationists have the ability to reproduce a particular ecosystem so accurately that the restored or artificial system is ecologically indistinguishable from the "original" or model system. Is this the equivalent of the model system, worthy of being accepted as a substitute or replacement for it?

One way to approach this question is to ask what kinds of values might be involved, then to consider how each of them might be affected by the process of restoration. Here two sets of values are of paramount importance. The first has to do with the meaning of the landscape—in particular the meaning of the "natural" landscape as "other" or "original," the outcome of a process of self-organization that owes nothing to humans. The second has to do with its authenticity—that is, how real or sacred we take it to be.

The question of the realness or authenticity—what philosophers call the ontological value—of the restored ecosystem may seem an arcane one. Of course it's real, some will say, meaning by this simply that it is really there, that it really exists. It may not be exactly the same *kind* of thing as the "original," but of course it's real—Let's get on with it. In fact, a colleague who happens to be a professor of philosophy has questioned the relevance of this question to the practice of restoration, suggesting that questions of ontology, or being, are of little interest to most people. On this point, however, I find that I disagree for two reasons. First, while it is true that most of us take our ontology for granted, we nevertheless have one, and it profoundly conditions the way we see and evaluate the world around us. Words such as "fake," "phony," "copy," "derivative," and "applied"—not to mention "authentic," "genuine," and even "real" itself—all imply a judgment of value based on a usually implicit ontology, and they come up continually in discussions of restoration, as in other areas of life. In any event, the question of the authenticity of the restored landscape is crucial because the way we resolve it will to a considerable extent determine the spirit in which we undertake this work and the values that emerge from it.

Environmentalists generally take it for granted that a restored ecosystem is not only less natural but in this higher sense also less *real* than its natural counterpart. But the question is not whether the restored ecosystem is real or authentic in some ultimate sense. It is rather, what do we *mean* by terms such as "real" or "authentic"? Several notions of authenticity that have been profoundly influential in the West imply a deep skepticism regarding representation of any kind, and lead inevitably to the devaluation of anything like a restored ecosystem that is intended to be a reproduction or re-creation of something else.

How, then, are we to rescue the restored ecosystem from second-class status as a mere *representation* of nature, a museum reconstruction that lacks many of the values we find in a pristine landscape? The easy way to do this would be to reject the distinction between natural and artificial and to insist, on the warrant of both ecology and evolutionary science, that, since human beings are part of nature, even a sloppily restored ecosystem is as natural as any other. But to assert this here would be to beg the question, and even to deny the value of what the restorationist is trying to do, since his attempt to recreate a natural landscape is in part a tribute to nature-as-given. While the conception of nature as "given" is not the only aspect of the many-sided concept of "nature," it is an important one. For one thing, while I take it as axiomatic that humans are not in any sense outside nature but are, in fact, wholly part of it and even its epitome, representing (at least at the moment) the terrible leading edge of nature in its great project of creation and emerging self-awareness, we do need to distinguish between ourselves and the *rest* of nature in order to make sense out of the world and define our place in it. Meaning depends on distinctions and boundaries, the primary one being the distinction between the self and others, and one way to articulate this distinction is in terms of "nature" and "culture."

The task here, then, is to consider how the process of restoration affects the value of an ecosystem or landscape, without dismissing the value we find in nature precisely because, even if it is not radically "other" than us, it is nevertheless in an important sense something *else*.

This sense of otherness, or givenness—of a world that owes nothing to our ingenuity—is one of the qualities we value in nature, and it is a quality that the process of restoration obviously compromises. In fact, this was one of the first questions that occurred to me when I began thinking about the UW Arboretum's restored ecosystems and what to make of them: did they embody the otherness we value in a "truly natural" landscape, or had that quality been eliminated or irreversibly compromised in the process of restoration? Of course, I was not alone in wondering about this. And in recent years concern about the loss of otherness in the process of restoration has been articulated in great detail and with considerable sophistication by two environmental philosophers, American Eric Katz and Australian Robert Elliott. Elliott raised the subject early on, in a 1982 article provocatively titled "Faking Nature," and he has since followed this up with a number of other articles and, most recently, a book with the same title as the original article.[37] In the meantime Katz has offered a similar, highly skeptical critique of restoration work in Chicago and other places in the United States.[38]

What Elliott and Katz argue is that a "natural" landscape has special value precisely because it owes nothing to humans, so that, once compromised by human influence (or, more specifically, by *intentional* human influence), this value cannot be recovered by any kind of human effort, including restoration. Both philosophers place great emphasis on the idea that the value of a thing depends on its origin. Drawing an analogy with a work of art such as a painting or sculpture, Elliott argues that a natural landscape is an "original," that its value derives in part from its purely natural origin, and that that value is irretrievably lost or diminished by any kind of deliberate manipulation, including the restorationist's attempts at "reproduction."

Basically, what both Elliott and Katz object to is the humanization, or "domestication" of the natural landscape. They point out that one of the meanings of the word "natural" is "not human" or "not influenced by or dependent on humans"—what I have called nature-as-other, or nature-as-given—and they argue that any deliberate manipulation by humans, including even the best-intentioned, compromises the landscape's "natural" value. The logic here is unassailable. Whenever we restore something—a prairie, an old car, or a medieval castle in France—we change its meaning. This new meaning arises both from the history of the thing, which we have altered, and from its new circumstances. There is a loss here, but loss is inseparable from creation and change. In any event, since the preservation—that is, the long-term survival of actual ecosystems—*ultimately depends on restoration,* the choice is not whether to preserve the old meanings or create new ones. It is, rather, whether we will find ways for the old species and ecosystems to survive and take on new meanings, or whether we will sacrifice them to the mistaken idea that we can preserve the old meanings.

Recently, environmental philosopher Andrew Light has offered a defense of restoration against the criticisms of Elliott and Katz. Concentrating his attention on Katz's broader attack, Light notes that it rests on a radical, ontological distinction between nature and culture—on the idea that these are ultimately different kinds of things. However, even if one accepts Katz's radical distinction between culture and nature (Light rejects it) and his argument that restoration compromises nature by humanizing it, restoration still has value as a way of developing what Light calls "the culture of nature"—that is, human caring for nature, which, he asserts, has value for nature, regardless of its ontological status. In developing this point, Light compares the development of a relationship with nature to the development of a relationship with another person. He points out that such a relationship may be based merely on duty, but that it can be deepened and given increased moral value through activities such as working or playing together or engaging in activities that involve an exchange of services or—implicitly—gifts and favors.[39]

Light's argument strongly supports the argument I am developing in this book—that relationship is crucial, and that restoration is the key to the development of our relationship with nature-as-given. In pointing out the value of restoration as a way of strengthening our relationship with nature by working—or playing—in the natural landscape, Light basically takes restoration to the second stage in the model of relationship-development I am exploring here—what I explored in the previous chapter under the heading of "restoration as work and play." Here, however, we are in a position to add to this a consideration of the value of the restored ecosystem (and, more broadly, the practice of restoration itself) in the economy of gift exchange. This places the question of value in a rather different light because what we find in this dimension is a very different kind of economy, one that is related to the "hard" economy of work and commerce rather as "soft" mathematics, which allows for near-equalities in equations, is related to ordinary mathematics, which insists on absolute equality. In this dimension, we admit that the gift the restorationist offers back to nature may not be commensurate in value with what we have taken from it. But we go beyond this to confront the impossibility of accurate accounting of the value of any kind of exchanges among subjects. From this point we can then go on to consider the means humans have used to deal with this problem, not by arguing about the value of the gift, but by finding ways of consecrating it.

For both Elliott and Katz, the value at issue in restoration is the autonomy of nature, or its freedom from human influence. But this idea of value is essentially *anti*ecological, since it insists on the value of autonomous subjects, independent of their relationships with others. At the same time, it is antievolutionary because it locates the value of a thing in its origin rather than in its process of becoming, and also because it insists on a radical distinction between humans and other species. The position they take—especially Katz's, with its rejection of even the best-intended forms of restoration—is radically inconsistent with any philosophy of nature based either on ecology or on organic evolution. And, as Light shows, it is inconsistent with the deeper kinds of relationship between ourselves and the rest of nature: denying our right or obligation to participate in the economy of nature, their position disallows the exchanges of goods and services and of gifts that are the basis for relationships generally. The result can only be a tragic alienation from the rest of nature.

Fortunately, there are alternatives to the idea that the authenticity or value of a thing lies in its autonomy. One of these, the diametrically opposed idea that a thing's value lies in its relationships with other things, has a long history that includes contributions from philosophers Edmund Husserl, Maurice Merleau-Ponty, and Martin Heidegger.[40] My own introduction to these ideas was principally through the work of Fred Turner, anthropologist Roy Rappaport, and comparative religionist Mircea Eliade; and, both for this reason and also because their emphasis on ritual has proved essential to my own thinking, I rely on their work to make this point here.

In his book *The Myth of the Eternal Return*, Eliade argues that what he calls "archaic" peoples have no concept of an isolated or autonomous individual, or of intrinsic value. For them, value, realness, and the sacred arise from relationships mediated by ritual. From the perspective of this "archaic ontology," Eliade writes, neither objects of the external world nor human acts have any autonomous value. "Objects or acts acquire a value, and in doing so become real, because they participate . . . in a reality that transcends them." In particular, he writes, an object such as a stone becomes sacred—and hence instantly becomes saturated with being—because it constitutes a hierophany [a revelation of the sacred], or possesses mana [supernatural force], or again because it commemorates a mythical act. . . . The object appears as the receptacle of an exterior force that differentiates it from its milieu and gives it meaning and value. . . . The crude product of nature, the object fashioned by the industry of man, acquire this reality, their identity, only to the extent of their participation in a transcendent reality.[41]

Especially interesting for us, within this ontology the value of acts such as eating and procreation acquire meaning and value only because and to the extent that they reenact a primordial event such as the creation. Eliade suggests that the archaic mind views unexplored, unknown, or unstoried areas not merely as "wild" areas in the modern sense, but actually as areas in a condition of *precreation*. They are *chaos* (formless) and remain so until brought within the world and made real, or *cosmos*, through rites that repeat—and in a ritual sense effect or constitute—the creation. The settlement of a new territory or a territorial conquest, for example, is conceived as the transformation of chaos into cosmos through the ritual reenactment of an original creation in acts such as cultivation, erection of an altar, or placement of a marker.

Similarly, Rappaport argues at length that the ideas of the sacred and the divine or numinous, both of which I take to be inflections of the authentic, are implicit in and arise directly—and uniquely—from the ritual process: the sacred from the invariant form of the ritual, which enacts and conveys a sense of ultimate certainty, and the numinous from the experience of unity with the world that the sacred provides. While questioning some aspects of Eliade's thinking, Rappaport endorses his argument—highly relevant to the practice of restoration and to the "reading" of restoration as performance or ritual—that "ritual may transform mere extent into ordered cosmos."[42] And Turner, drawing from his parents' work on the role of ritual and performance in human societies and his own work in literary criticism and performance theory, puts forward the idea of what he calls "performed being"—the idea that things exist and are real, not in and of themselves, but only through their interactions with and mutual registration on other things—that is, on the way they *perform* to each other.[43] In many respects Turner's idea is similar to Eliade's "archaic ontology" or Rappaport's idea of ritual as the source of the sacred, but in his development and use of this idea he brings in two additional elements that are of special importance here. One is an explicit and thoroughgoing commitment to the idea of the evolutionary continuity of nature. The other is an emphasis on the principle of limit, on evolution itself as the emergence and elaboration of limit, and on the feeling of shame as the natural response to that limit as experienced at the level of reflexivity characteristic of humans and other higher animals. I mentioned the continuity of universal shame in chapter 3 and pursue the point here because I am arguing that it is the experience of existential shame in the face of difference and change—both forms of limitation—that makes the actual achievement of community and other higher values so difficult. As I pointed out, we encounter this shame in the exchange of gifts. We also encounter it in the making of representations—such as restored landscapes—both because representations are always imperfect, and also because they represent a kind of immortality that highlights the transience of the original.

For all these reasons, the "performative ontology" has profound implications for environmental management generally, and for the practice of restoration and the value of the restored ecosystem in particular, and these are the exact opposite of those of the ontology of "autonomy" and self-sufficiency taken for granted by Elliott and Katz. From the perspective of this ontology, it is not nature as an autonomous "other" that is the ground and touchstone of being and authenticity, but rather nature in reflexive interaction with all its elements, including ourselves. Thus the authenticity of a thing depends not on its origins, its ontological pedigree, but on the intensity and reflexivity of its interactions with other subjects. Restoration and other modes of reproduction, in this view, do not compromise nature but actually fulfill or enact it, since it is the very essence of nature to reproduce itself, and to do so imperfectly, and at ever higher levels of self-awareness (the word "nature" derives from the same root as the Latin *natus,* birth, which is, after all, the creation of an imperfect copy of an "original"). If we in some sense transcend the rest of nature it is not because we are outside nature, but because it is the nature of nature to transcend itself in the process of creation, and we happen to be, as far as we know, nature's most reflexive species. In fact, we are nature at its *most* natural, the cutting edge of its own self-transcendence, with all the violence and pain and discrimination and loss that metaphor implies. And the restored ecosystem, to the extent that it has been implicated in the frontier of creation through engagement with humans, is not less but actually *more* natural, more real in this sense than its less self-aware, "original" counterpart. It is more real in the precise sense that it is more fully realized. And it is more natural (in the narrower sense of this word) because it has been realized, to the extent possible, on its own terms.

In contrast with the modernist ontology, which regards nature as given and deals with it as an object, the performative ontology regards nature as something that is earned and constructed and deals with it as a subject. Though this may seem strange to us, it is the way most human cultures have seen the world. It is what the Australian Aborigines mean, for example, when they speak of singing the world into being. This is not anthrocentrism. It merely reflects an awareness of the role humans play in the construction of their own reality. It construes the human as an actor among other subjects, and it is a way of seeing the world that has gained currency in the West during the past two or three generations, as critics, scientists, and philosophers have come to appreciate the extent to which the construction of our view of the world—all we can know about "reality"—is the result of deliberate effort carried out in the course of performative interaction with the world. It is only for the modernist that the notion of nature-as-given, represented by the *data* (from the Latin *datum,* given) "given" us by nature, has much currency. For the postmodern as for the premodern person, the real is not merely discovered but emerges from chaos through dialogue with other entities experienced as what Albert Borgmann calls "eloquent objects," and through rituals created to deal with the shame of this encounter with the other.[44] In this view, the idea of *data*—the merely given—is suspect. Our knowledge of the world is based not on data but on facts (from the Latin *factum,* made), which we do not simply receive or collect but actively create through the process of self-conscious, performative interaction with the world.[45] Restoration in this view is merely a phase in the dialectical process by which we collaborate with other species to build the world, not only in an ecological sense, but in an ontological sense as well. The restored community is such a fact, since *all* facts are, strictly speaking, *artifacts.* Thus the act of restoration, far from diminishing realness, actually promotes an object or *datum*—the merely given—to *factum,* or *artifact,* the deliberately made and more fully realized.

The performative ontology, then, in contrast with ontologies that stress autonomy, confers authenticity on the restored ecosystem: it may be of high ecological quality if the work has been done well, and if the project is successful in a purely technical sense; but it will also be *authentic* if the work is done properly in a performative sense. And while restoration necessarily entails the manipulation of the landscape and other species, this is, at best, not so much the imposition of a plan on nature, as it is the basis for a conversation with it. The best restoration work does not so much impose on the landscape as *propose* to it, opening a dialogue of which the practice of restoration represents only the technical and restoration ecology only the formally scientific component.

Conceived in this way, as a performative interaction with other species, restoration does not diminish authenticity but expands and deepens it. The restorationist begins by respecting the other—not its "autonomy," certainly, not its "intrinsic" value, and not necessarily its rights, but rather its integrity as a self-organizing subject, a respect he expresses in a radical way by attempting to act in such a way as to disappear from the landscape in an ecological sense. Like the preservationist, in other words, the restorationist aims for the *ideal* of a self-sufficient ecosystem, doing everything possible to let the system be, to turn it back into itself. Unlike the preservationist, however, the restorationist recognizes that the ideal of nature separate from humans is a fiction. It has value as a thought-experiment, but if taken literally, has tragic consequences both for the landscape and for its human inhabitants. Recognizing this, the restorationist undertakes the task of compensating for "his" influence on the landscape, and what emerges from this exercise in self-abnegation is not only a clearer idea of who "he" is in an ecological sense, but also a larger authenticity involving the self-authorization, not of "nature" apart from humans, but of nature whole, including humans.

From this perspective, Elliott's analogy between an ecosystem and a work of art misses the point, not because the analogy lacks value, but because Elliott misconstrues art as the creation of a product. In terms of the performative ontology art is best seen not as a process for creating products but as a performance—an expression of the reflexive interaction that defines the world and the things in it and makes them real. This ontology places less emphasis on works of art as objects, and more emphasis on art as a performative interaction between the artist, his subject, his materials and his audience. While the analogy with art is helpful, Elliott's choice of painting as exemplary was unfortunate. He might have done better to have chosen an art such as theater or dance that is explicitly performative and mimetic, and in which authenticity is explicitly located in the performance rather than in objects—props, sets, and costumes—that are explicitly inauthentic, a condition that itself dramatizes the process by which we generate authenticity out of the inauthentic and downright fake.

Ultimately, as we shall see in the next chapter, what this suggests is the importance of undertaking the work of restoration in a spirit of performance. What the performative ontology provides is a basis for the deliberate *creation* of the authentic, grounded in both archaic experience and in an ecological sensibility. On these grounds, the forest *is* restorable. Indeed, it is our responsibility to restore it and, by restoring it properly, to make it authentic. Forests without ghosts have simply been incompletely restored. When properly restored, they will be full of ghosts—the old ghosts, and perhaps some new ones, too.[46]

Here, in our search for ways of entering into a communal relationship with others, we encounter more evidence of the fundamental tension that lies at the heart of community. In chapter 3 we encountered it in the ambivalence and uncertainty that is inseparable from the act of gift exchange. Here, we recognize it in the sacrifice of autonomy, self-sufficiency, or purity that brings us into relationship. As Octavio Paz has pointed out, purity precludes communion, which at the deepest level is contamination or adulteration (that is, etymologically, a mixing with the other, from the Latin *alter*), and a violation of the individual self. We always have to choose between the purity of the "pristine," "unsullied," or "untrammeled" self—or landscape—on the one hand, and community and communion with it on the other. Here we face a dilemma that is at the heart of environmentalism, with its appeals both to community and to the value of wilderness. We may idealize nature as autonomous and independent of us, and we may yearn for communion with it, but we cannot, by the very nature of community, have both at once. Joining the land community need not mean taming or domesticating it, but it will always mean contaminating it with human intentionality.

The crucial issue here is what British anthropologist Mary Douglas calls the violation of categories. In her book *Purity and Danger,* Douglas notes that the categories such as bird and fish, nature and culture, person and nonperson, ruler and subject, good and evil and so forth, in which humans think, though necessary as a way of making sense of the world, are also inventions or fictions. They are not inherent in the world, but are invented and, while they connect us with the world in one way, they separate us from it in others. To achieve a deep relationship, or communion with the other, we need to rise above words and the categories they represent. And that, Douglas argues, is precisely why those things or objects or actions that violate the categories of a culture in an especially telling or dramatic way commonly become the basis for the rituals by which the culture gains access to the experience of oneness and the sacred.

To illustrate the point Douglas takes the example of the pangolin, or scaly anteater, and its role in the rituals of the Lele people of Zaire. The pangolin is an anomalous creature, with attributes that violate many of the common animal categories. It is scaly like a fish yet climbs trees; an oddly reptilelike creature that suckles its young; a nonhuman animal that, humanlike, bears only one offspring at a time, and so forth. And it is for just this reason, Douglas argues, that it plays a critical role in the process by which young men are initiated into the tribe, introducing them to the failings of the categories in which they think, and so to the epistemological frontiers of Lele experience.

Throughout their daily, and especially their ritual life, the Lele are preoccupied with form. Endlessly they enact the discriminations by which their society and its cultural environment exist, and methodically they punish or attribute misfortune to breaches of avoidance rules. . . .

Then comes the inner cult of all their ritual life, in which the initiates of the pangolin, immune to dangers that would kill uninitiated men, approach, hold, kill and eat the animal which in its own existence combines all the elements which Lele culture keeps apart. . . . By the mystery of that rite they recognize something of the fortuitous and conventional nature of the categories in whose mould they have their experience. If they consistently shunned ambiguity they would commit themselves to division between ideal and reality. But they confront ambiguity in an extreme and concentrated form. They dare to grasp the pangolin and put it to ritual use, proclaiming that this has more power than any other rites.[47]

Douglas also notes that the Leles' descriptions and interpretations of the pangolin cult "uncannily recall passages of the Old Testament, interpreted in the Christian tradition." They see the pangolin as a willing and kingly victim, and its death as a sorrowful mystery that brings about "a union of opposites which is a source of power for good."

Douglas's interpretation of the pangolin cult, and indeed her whole discussion of what she calls the metaphysics of dirt—the anomalous, ambiguous, or out of place—has important implications for our interpretation of the restored ecosystem and the act of restoration. Critics of restoration argue that the restored ecosystem is less worthy or valuable, or that it is radically different from its "natural" counterpart precisely because, like the pangolin for the Lele, it violates the categories—in this case "nature" and "culture"—we use to make sense of the world. Like the Lele confronting the pangolin, they apprehend this with deep misgivings, rightly seeing it as a danger threatening the very order of the world. Unlike the Lele, however, they lack the means to deal with this productively, to use it as an occasion to confront the categories, and to push through and past them to an apprehension of a transcendent unity.[48]

Perhaps for this reason, they fail to see that it is precisely because restoration violates the conventional categories of "nature" and "culture" that it has value as a way not merely of negotiating our relationship with the rest of nature, but of coming to terms with, and ultimately transcending, the distinction we make between ourselves and nature as other.

The tendency to avoid or deny recognition of the existential ambiguity inherent in language has deep roots in the West. Douglas speaks of "dirt-affirming" cultures that have means for confronting existential ambiguity creatively, and "dirt-denying" cultures that do not. The contrast is evident, for example, in the differences between the biblical and Winnebago Indian accounts of the experience of good and evil as interpreted by anthropologist Paul Radin. In his classic account of the myth of the trickster among the Winnebago people (now known as the Ho-Chunk) of southern Wisconsin, Radin shows how the trickster comes to terms with "the Besetting One," who "sits on the back of every one of us"—and how Job in his travails cannot do this.[49] In an introductory essay in Radin's book, anthropologist Stanley Diamond notes the same inability to deal with ambiguity in Plato's *Republic,* where it underlies the monstrous certainty of Plato's ideal fascist state. Like the book of Job, he argues, the *Republic* reflects a sensibility that "is bent upon denying human ambivalence and social ambiguity" in a world that ultimately offers no remedy for injustice.

As heirs to an attenuated, sentimentalized conception of values such as community, meaning, beauty, hope, and the sacred, we have often supposed that we may trust our feelings or our instincts to guide us toward these values. But if the argument I am developing here has any validity, our immediate feelings may not be an adequate guide to the higher values, all of which are inextricably linked not only to positive feelings such as love, affection, the sensually pleasant, or the esthetically attractive but also to *negative* feelings such as fear, ambiguity, and shame.

But what about the other values we look for in the natural landscape—the scientific, for example, the historic, or the esthetic? Here again, as in the case of authenticity, the performative ontology leads to answers very different from those based on a nonrelational idea of the real. In the case of scientific value, we can often learn more by attempting to restore or manage an ecosystem than by merely standing back and describing it, or even by carrying out analytic experiments on it. And if we replace the Cartesian idea of the experiment as a voyeuristic probing of the other with the idea of the experiment as a performative interaction with it, it ceases to be mere manipulation and the extraction of information and becomes a conversation. And this represents a crucial step toward the sacralization of research. Just as the first farmers invented ritual sacrifice as a way of dealing productively with the intensification of shame they encountered in the acts of domestication and cultivation, a similar step into the dimension of performance will be needed to make science an occasion for sacrament and the creation of higher values.

Like the issue of authenticity, the issue of beauty in the restored landscape is complex. In the next chapter I consider the experience of beauty in a fundamental sense, arguing that beauty is a product of performance, the creation of artists and designers, shamans and priests. Once conventionalized in the shared taste of a culture, however, the creation or reproduction of particular esthetic elements in a landscape, though it raises interesting questions, seems to me less problematic. At least to the extent that restorationists are able to create an ecologically faithful version of a model landscape, it seems to me that, with some sensitivity to its esthetic attributes, they ought to be able to reproduce those qualities too.

I realize that some will find this a bit cavalier. Some have questioned the idea of an esthetically authentic replica of a natural ecosystem, arguing that reproductions of works of art are rarely if ever regarded as the esthetic equivalents of the originals and that since an ecosystem is even more complex than a work of art, it must be even more difficult to reproduce. This analogy has at least two weaknesses. First, what ecological restoration requires is not a meticulous, plant-by-plant and insect-by-insect copy of a particular landscape but rather an esthetically true representation of a particular kind of system—a tallgrass prairie, say, or a tidal marsh. Second, once the ecosystem exists, to a considerable extent it takes over, managing for itself details such as the form of particular plants, even their position and distribution—the esthetic equivalent of brushstrokes in painting. In this way nature adds an element of both accuracy and spontaneity that can rescue an otherwise merely competent restoration from woodenness or banality.

A good example is the UW Arboretum's Henry Greene Prairie, which is said to reflect its creator's unusual sensitivity to patterns and combinations of color and texture, as well as his exhaustive knowledge of the habitat preferences of the various plants and the associations in which they ordinarily grow. Greene apparently thought esthetically as well as ecologically, botanically, and horticulturally as he assembled his prairie, and, partly because of this, Greene Prairie achieved at an early stage of its development a fairly high degree of visual authenticity. Curtis Prairie, where the restorers paid little or no attention to esthetic considerations, has also achieved this quality, but it has achieved it much more slowly. Despite their ecological flaws and deficiencies, both prairies are now generally regarded as fairly successful esthetic reproductions of natural tallgrass prairies. Indeed, the one esthetic deficiency in the vegetation that has been pointed out to me—a certain patchiness or coarseness in texture in some areas, presumably reflecting small-scale inaccuracies in the distribution and mingling of species—is actually more a technical than an esthetic problem. In any event, it will probably correct itself in time.

What about historic value? When we say that a landscape has historic value, we mean that it evokes the past or that it contains information about the past. A commonsense view is that a landscape of special historic interest should be left strictly alone in order to preserve that value. Ian Frazer, in *The Great Plains,* comments on the futility of reclamation as a way of recapturing the historic value and associations of a landscape disrupted by surface mining.

Like other arid but inhabited parts of the world, the plains sometimes hold pieces of the past intact and out of time, so that a romantic or curious person can walk into an abandoned house and get a whiff of June, 1933, or can look at a sagebrush ridge and imagine dinosaurs wading through a marsh. In the presence of strip-mined land, these humble flights fall to the ground. Scrambled in the waste heaps, the dinosaur vertebrae drift in chaos with the sandstone metate, the .45–70 rifle cartridge, the plastic-foam cup. It is impossible to imagine a Cheyenne war party coming out of the canyon, because the canyon is gone. . . . Even after "reclamation," land that has been stripped gives you no year to think about but the year when the stripping happened.[50]

It is true that some features in a historic landscape are irretrievably lost when it is disturbed, and obviously this reduces its historic value in certain respects. But this is only part of the story. The other part is the role restoration has in maintaining the site while at the same time both adding to its history and bringing that history to life. Not only is restoration likely to be required, as we have seen, to *maintain* a landscape in its historic condition, but restoration provides an incentive to explore and learn about that landscape. One of the very important intellectual—and I would say even spiritual—benefits of restoration is that it forces the botanist or the ecologist to become a historian. In many cases the process of restoration entails a kind of reenactment of the history of a place as the restorationist attempts to reverse ongoing change, or reproduce conditions that created the model landscape in the first place.[51]

Restoration is performed or applied history. Burning a prairie, for example, reenacts the burning of the prairies by Indians in pre-contact times and dramatically revives their history, making it part of the consciousness of a community. And, as Frazer himself clearly realizes, this process requires imagination. The curious thing about his reading of the reclaimed landscape is the boundaries he places on change and imagination. Cattle, for example, which have devastated vast areas in the West by grazing and trampling, he finds acceptable, but not strip-mining, which, though locally devastating, affects comparatively small areas. Frazer can imagine the vanished war party, but not the canyon. His use of imagination seems curiously, even arbitrarily, limited. More important, though, what he overlooks is the value of the act of restoration as a part of the history of a place and as a context for the exercise of historic imagination.

The point Frazer makes is an important one. The loss caused by activities such as surface mining *is* tragic. At the same time, it is a mistake to overdramatize such devastation as the obliteration of history. It is not that or need not be. Though he is not explicit about this, the "reclamation" Frazer is deploring probably falls far short of restoration, even in a technical or ecological sense. Almost certainly it lacks the element of ritual and storymaking that would enrich the history of the land by making the mining and restoration part of that history, even if the mining is a Calvary of the land. Conceivably it is this, rather than the mining itself, that leads Frazer to read the mining as radically different from the cattle ranching, railroad building, water diversion, and irrigation that also shaped the landscape of the plains: it is different because it is outside the story, and Frazer, a storyteller, is naturally troubled by this, and sees nothing but chaos in the mined landscape—a chaos that he argues cannot be redeemed, even in his imagination, by reclamation.[52]

Though not to be dismissed, Frazer's critique of reclamation has the same weakness as Elliott's. Approaching the landscape as a visitor, he sees it as a museum rather than an arena or theater. As a result his imagination is effectively engaged only by items that are, as it were, properly labeled, securely attached in some way to the preexisting stories they can be made to evoke, which place them in a context and give them meaning. Because reclamation has not been incorporated into the prevailing story of the Western landscape, Frazer finds only chaos at the reclamation site. But in a deep sense Frazer is right: it is story we need, not pristine landscape, as is clearly illustrated by his response to the ongoing attempt to carve a mountain in South Dakota into a statue of Crazy Horse. This is, objectively speaking, the ecological equivalent of a strip mine—and arguably a dubious memorial to Native Americans in general, much less to an individual who refused even to be photographed. Yet it is contained in a cycle of stories, and Frazer's account of it is upbeat.

Finally, a word about economic value. One reason environmentalists have been wary of restoration is that they have seen it as a dangerous step toward putting a price on nature, turning it into a commodity. The task of placing a monetary value on a natural ecosystem is a tricky one and raises some troubling questions, especially now that courts accept the cost of restoration as one way to determine economic value in litigation over environmental damage. This challenges the idea of nature as priceless. But we might ask whether the notion that nature is without price is actually a very good idea since it is really a version of the old error of separating economy from ecology. If, as environmentalists insist, economics should not be separated from ecology, why should ecology be free of economics? And in purely practical terms simply claiming that a thing is priceless without undertaking the psychological and spiritual work required to give it value to actual people, is dangerously close to giving it no value at all. If nature is taken in principle to be priceless, then the price that will be paid for it when the time comes to sell it will be determined by market value, or even arbitrarily, the way prices were placed on land in the homesteading era. Such prices have nothing to do with the network of ecologies and economies associated with the ecosystem itself. A price based on the cost of restoration at least reflects important attributes of the ecosystem.

Yet economic value is only part of the story, and possibly the least important part. More important ultimately are the relationships that develop in the course of restoration when it is properly carried out, and that are actually the basis of value—the real bottom line. Here again, as earlier when we considered the analogy between restored ecosystems and works of art, the performative ontology takes us beyond objects to consider the network of relationships that actually gives them value. It draws our attention to the work itself, and to the importance of the spirit in which we carry it out. If it is carried out in a purely commercial spirit, then indeed it may contribute little or nothing to the value of the landscape and may actually cheapen it, setting the stage for the sort of checkerboard conservation, the facile trading off and shifting around of natural landscapes to suit human convenience that environmentalists have rightly decried. If, on the other hand, we undertake this work (and play) in a spirit of respect, as part of a search for engagement and meaning, then restoration becomes a way of generating real value. In this way the community may gradually come to see the ecosystem not only as valuable, but as worth paying for. Having engaged the ecosystem by helping to restore it, people are going to care about it more than they care about a "natural" ecosystem, which they may be inclined to take for granted. The experience of restorationists supports this bit of common sense. I first became aware of this some years ago when a group of volunteers at the Arboretum protested a plan to adjust an outfall in one of the Arboretum's desilting ponds, a process that would have disrupted a prairie the volunteers had been helping to restore.

That was a minor incident, but a suggestive one. More recently Karen Rodriguez, a friend who works as a volunteer with the North Branch Prairie Restoration Project in Chicago, told me that a group of volunteers persuaded engineers to relocate an access port in the Deep Tunnel, a multibillion-dollar project to increase the capacity of the area's stormwater drainage system, in order to prevent the disruption of a patch of prairie they had been restoring. And the California restorationist John Steere recounts a similar experience in connection with a project in a neighborhood in Berkeley, commenting, "I sense that, without realizing it, all of us involved in making Halcyon Commons have been planting more than tree roots in our neighborhood."[53]

Experiences like these convey an important lesson. In the end, the ecosystems that survive will be the ones we have learned through the processes of engagement, participation, and gift exchange to value, care about, and take responsibility for. One way to achieve this is through the experience of restoration. As Derek Walcott once wrote, if you break a vase, "the love that reassembles the fragments is stronger than the love that took its symmetry for granted when it was whole."[54]

So far, in considering the value of the gift the restorationist offers back to nature, we have considered only the restored ecosystem itself, and the value we find in it. Restoration does allow us to give back bits and pieces of "nature" in the form of the restored landscape. But this by itself is an inadequate exchange because, taken by itself, the "restored" landscape contains so little that is distinctive of ourselves, so little of what we can do better than the rest of nature.

At least as important as the ecosystems the restorationist gives back to nature is the deepening of understanding, awareness, and caring that is the direct result of this work, when it is carried out thoughtfully and attentively. These values comprise our essential and distinctive gift to nature, values that only we can provide, and for which nature depends on us. In offering them we resolve, for the moment and in a provisional sense, the problem of difference inherent in nature itself.

Nature *is* creation, a continual, evolutionary flowering out into higher levels of reflexivity or self-awareness. But creation is shamefully destructive and becomes even more so as evolution accelerates, as nature, becoming increasingly reflexive, increasingly aware of itself, devises new mechanisms for evolutionary change. The evolutionary "invention" of sex, for example, represented a threshold in evolutionary change because it altered the hardware of evolution, providing a way of shuffling and reshuffling genetic material that accelerated enormously the process of creating and trying out new combinations of genes. Evolution itself, though chaotic in texture, reveals a long-term trend toward increasing reflexivity, from nonliving matter to microorganisms and plants and most recently to animals, including birds and mammals capable of technical innovation, communication, and ritual behavior. With the emergence of our own species, nature crossed yet another evolutionary threshold into the domain of self-consciousness and cultural evolution, through which the slow process of chemical-based change and natural selection is superseded by what amounts to an electronic, computerized system—culture and the human brain—that can generate, sort, and select mutations at a rate many orders of magnitude greater than any chemical-based system.

The result is yet another new mode of evolution, which has introduced novelty into the world at an ever-accelerating rate for roughly the past forty thousand years. The problem is that, as human culture—the "software" that perpetuates the new electronic mode of evolution—has come to dominate the planet, it has tended to displace species that are still dependent on the old, chemical-based mode of evolution. This is not because humans are malevolent or outside nature. It is rather that they are *so* natural, and "naturally" generate novelty so rapidly that, with the exception of the fast-evolving microorganisms, other species, being stuck, as it were, in the old, slow lane of Darwinian evolution cannot adapt fast enough and are in danger of being driven into extinction.

What restoration offers is a way of rescuing the classic ecosystems and the species they comprise by catching them up in the spiral of cultural evolution through a radical evolutionary uploading—the transcription of genetic information from the classic chemical-based Darwinian/Mendelian system to an electronic system of information storage, selection, transmission, and retrieval. This gives the classic system an alternative mode of reproduction—one that is capable, if not of handling it to perfection, at least of making it compatible with the speeded-up pace of the new evolution. In the process the classic system achieves what we might call relative, or ecological, immortality—the ability to survive in a landscape dominated by the processes of cultural evolution. This immortality, then, and the higher level of self-awareness it represents is the restorationist's real gift to nature.

A dramatic example of this has emerged in recent years from attempts to restore oak savannas in the area around Chicago. These orchardlike communities were abundant in many parts of the upper Midwest at the time of European contact but were profoundly affected by postsettlement changes in land use. By the beginning of the twentieth century, when ecologists began studying savannas, few remained undisturbed, and it remains an open question whether *any* remained in their pre-contact condition. By the early 1980s the Nature Conservancy had listed these savannas as among the most endangered ecosystems on earth and for all practical purposes had written them off as extinct.[55] As a result, when restorationists started working with oak savannas during the 1970s, they had to work without existing models or reliable descriptions of the pre-contact savannas. The most authoritative description of the Midwestern savannas available was in *The Vegetation of Wisconsin,* a fat volume by UW-Madison ecologist John Curtis that has been a basic reference for ecologists and restorationists in the Midwest since it was published in 1959. Curtis, acknowledging the degraded quality of the remnants of savanna on which his work was based, described the savannas as prairies with scattered trees, lacking a significant complement of distinctive species.

This description seemed like a reasonable blueprint for savanna restoration. But in the early 1980s, when Steven Packard, then a steward with the Illinois Nature Conservancy, began attempting to restore savannas, clearing the brush from beneath the surviving oaks and trying to reestablish the ground-layer vegetation using Curtis's description as a guide, he found that it didn't work. Prairie species seeded in under the old savanna oaks failed to flourish, leaving open areas, which quickly filled in with weedy exotics. Puzzled, Packard began poking around in out-of-the-way corners of Chicago's vast Forest Preserve system, searching out odd bits of vegetation he thought might be relics of oak savanna, putting together his own list of the species he thought might belong in the savanna. Eventually, his list included more than a hundred species, many of which were common neither on prairies nor in woodlands, and some of which were extremely rare. A number of these, such as savanna blazing star, purple milkweed, poke milkweed, and purple giant hyssop, though included in lists of native plants of the area, had no known habitat and—not being present in the better documented plant communities such as mature prairies or sandy savannas—had come to be regarded as ecologically miscellaneous.[56] Mixing the seeds of these plants together, Packard raked them into the bare soil on a few of his restoration sites and awaited the results. What he found was that, in contrast with prairie species, which had performed feebly in the dappled shade under the oaks, his putative savanna species grew vigorously, quickly occupying the planted areas and pushing out the exotics. He had plugged a hole in the plant community and at the same time discovered what amounted to an entire ecosystem that, he wrote in an early account of his work, "was gone before ecology was born."[57]

Scientists were skeptical of this unorthodox way of refining the description of an ecological community. But when a colleague directed Packard's attention to a long-forgotten list of savanna plants compiled by a pioneer doctor in western Illinois, he checked it and found that it corresponded closely to his list of savanna species. Even more dramatically, managers soon discovered a surviving remnant of savanna in Lake Forest, north of Chicago, that closely matched Packard's new, rapidly developing search-image for the savanna. Since then, the controversy Packard's work aroused has stimulated a dramatic growth in interest in the savannas and their conservation. A number of ecologists have undertaken experiments to test the new description of the oak savanna that has grown out of Packard's work, and it is beginning to seem that Packard and his fellow restorationists may have given new life to an ecosystem many believed to have vanished forever. To the extent that their new ideas about the savanna are corroborated by further research, their work demonstrates the value of restoration as a way of testing ideas about an ecosystem, even when the ecosystem, so far as is known, no longer exists, pushing the concept of restoration ecology to a new limit.[58] In any event, what we are seeing here is an example of the restorationist not only restoring an ecosystem to health, but bringing it back from the dead, beginning the process of transcribing it into cultural understanding and caring, and in fact conferring on it a kind of immortality.[59]

Restoration is, broadly speaking, a crucial step in the exploration and discovery of a landscape. What Columbus did with the old idea of a spherical earth, reducing it to practice, actually *doing* something with it, the restorationist does with the old idea of the ecological community or ecosystem. The result now, as then, is discovery in two senses. For one thing, the act of reduction to practice is a crucial step in the complex process of discovery—the act by which an idea is tested and realized as fact. For another, in taking this step the discoverer or inventor not only realizes the idea he had in mind, he also discovers new things, encountering, as Columbus did, unexpected islands, archipelagoes, and continents of fact and value.

CHAPTER 6

Value and Make-Believe

A Primer on Performance

We like to say, borrowing the idea from premodern cultures, that nature is cyclical, its processes of life and death, growth and decay always circular, but we tend to forget that this is true only when imagination closes the circle. Nature and time, change and difference, giving and taking are always tragically asymmetrical, and we achieve symmetry—the closing of the circle—only in the realm of make-believe, where we can resolve in imagination inequities and uncertainties that cannot be resolved in literal terms.

One occasion on which we encounter this troubling asymmetry is in the exchange of gifts, and indeed, this is why gift exchange is intrinsically ritualistic. As I noted in chapter 3, the exchange of gifts is an intimate encounter with the shame of difference and of dependence, one of many experiences that dramatize the distance between souls. It is always fraught with misgiving and anxiety, and the gift the restorationist offers nature is no exception. However we argue for its value, as I did in the previous chapter, the restorationist's gift dramatizes our shameful dependence on nature, and—even worse—its shameful dependence on us. Besides that, it leaves us in unresolvable doubt as to its worthiness: whether what we offer back to nature through the process of restoration is commensurate in value with what we have taken from it. We cannot solve this problem by noting that this gift is a gift in kind. Indeed, the fact that the restorationist's gift is so clearly an attempt to make recompense in a literal way only highlights the difficulty and increases the poignancy of our irremediable existential uncertainty. This is a barrier to communion. And the only way past it is through the spiritual and psychological technologies of performance, ritual, and the arts.

By performance here I mean simply self-consciously expressive action, or actions deliberately intended to convey ideas or feelings; and by ritual I mean, generally following Roy Rappaport, a performance that is to some extent stereotyped—not entirely encoded, or scripted, by the participants—and that is serious in tone. To this I add that ritual is generally concerned with the tensions and paradoxes of human existence.[1]

While this is conventional enough, it is important to be clear that the idea of the *function* of performance and ritual I am using here is different from the idea that most modern Westerners take for granted. Over the past few centuries, the West has gradually demoted and marginalized performance, so that most now both regard and experience performance in its various modes—as game, as sport, as art, as theater, and so forth—as entertainment, or merely as a way of recognizing and celebrating circumstances or events—the change of the seasons, for example, or a child's coming of age—regarded in an essentially positive light.

What I have in mind is quite different. This is the idea that while performance may culminate in celebration, it begins, in its toughest and most important uses, not in recognition of the positive aspects of experience but quite the opposite, in those aspects of experience that we find most troubling. In the case of the gift, for example, this entails first offering the gift and then inventing ways of dealing in a productive way with the shame and ambiguity we encounter in the act of gift exchange.

Since the inequities, asymmetries, and uncertainties involved here are inseparable from life itself, the discovery of ritual and the odd logic by which it works are so important that it is often recorded in mythology. The biblical story of Abraham who, commanded to sacrifice his son, Isaac, sacrifices a ram instead, is an account of the discovery of ritual, the realization that the divinity can be satisfied by a lesser gift if it is offered in the right spirit. The gift then becomes, as Fred Turner has said, *a way of not saying no* to the demand of the god. Some people, I have noticed, find this story incomprehensible and, considering the monstrousness of Yahweh's demand, even outrageous. But they are missing the essential points that give the story its power: first, the recognition that Yahweh makes his demands justly, since Abraham owes everything, including Isaac, to Him; but second—and just as important—that this crisis is ultimately resolved through the mercy of ritual substitution.

Similarly, Greek myth tells how Prometheus, who provoked the gods by giving humans the gift of fire, also learned to trick them by offering to

Zeus only the skin and bones of the sacrificed animal.[2] Euripides' story of Iphigenia dramatizes the same discovery through the mysterious replacement of a deer for Iphigenia on the sacrificial altar. Like the story of Abraham and Isaac, these Greek tales are mythic accounts of the discovery of the mysterious process by which we get, in effect, something—not for nothing, but for less than we owe.

In the case of the gift we offer back to nature, this means confronting our ineradicable uncertainty regarding the value of the gift, as hunting peoples do when they make offerings to propitiate the slain animal and to ensure its return in a new fleshly "garment," or as farming peoples do when they sacrifice part of their crop. In either case, what is offered back—a bit of tobacco or a sheaf of wheat—is obviously not commensurate in value with what has been taken. Yet it need not be if it is made in the context of a ritual that expresses the hunter's *desire* and *intention* to give back all he owes.

In the case of restoration, this might mean ritually consecrating the restored ecosystem, making it sacred, and therefore worthy. (This is why it such a bad idea to insist that the value of the restored ecosystem is irredeemably inferior to that of the "original" ecosystem: doing this forecloses the economy of the gift and so precludes community.) This sacralization might, as in traditional sacrificial ritual, entail the development of the whole cycle of our engagement with the landscape—restoration *and* destruction—as a context for the creation of rituals of exchange and recompense.

But gift exchange is not the only occasion on which we encounter existential shame in our interaction with others. We also encounter shame merely in confronting the other across the boundaries that define—and separate—us. We encounter it in the recognition of the differences between us. And we encounter it in the experience of change, which is difference in the dimension of time. Since all of these are directly related to the values espoused by environmentalists, with their emphasis on diversity (or difference), on change, and on the acceptance of limits, it is important to consider how humans (and other species) have used performance to deal productively with these experiences.

To begin with the experience of boundaries, I have already noted the problematic nature of the categories humans use to make sense of the world, and Mary Douglas's idea that it is precisely in violating these categories that humans gain access to the sacred. An important point here is that this is true whatever the categories happen to be. Consider, for example, two categories that are especially relevant here, the categories of "nature" and "culture." Westerners have construed the world in terms of these categories at least since the time of the ancient Greeks, creating a distinction that is naturally imbued with shame.

One response to this is to suppose that, since the distinction entails shame—and in a sense creates it—the sensible thing to do is simply to reject the distinction, perhaps on the grounds that it is, after all, "merely" a mental construct. But this misses the point, which is that shame is inherent in *any* categorization, *any* distinction, *anything at all* that defines or divides or discriminates, creating boundaries, and so making us aware of limits. Thus if you eliminate one set of categories in order to make sense of the world, you have to create new ones, and these then become a new locus of shame. Slicing through the world in different ways, different systems of classification merely provide different ways of confronting the shame of creation and of our own participation in creation through the invention of categories.

The various cultures described by anthropologist Philippe Descola and his colleagues in several recent books clearly illustrate this point. As interpreted by these anthropologists, these are cultures that do not share the nature/culture categories characteristic of the Western worldview. Some, for example, distinguish between "person" and "nonperson" in a way that cuts across the categories of "nature" and "culture." Yet reading the anthropologists' interpretations of these cultures, we find that all of them have institutionalized, often elaborate, and psychologically demanding ways of confronting and dealing with the negative aspects of life encountered along the boundaries between *whatever* categories they use to make sense of the world.

The Desana people of the northwestern Amazon provide an example. In Desana cosmology humans and animals are in a fundamental sense interchangeable. Some (though not all) animals are regarded as persons, and the souls of recently deceased humans are offered in exchange for the souls of animals killed by hunters.[3] In this way, the Desana achieve a kind of parity with what we would call nature in the usual way, through recourse to the realm of the imagination. Yet the theology behind this, and the institutions based on it are not ones that seem terribly attractive from a liberal perspective. They place great—in fact, ultimate—authority in the hands of the shamans who negotiate the fates of individual souls, and they are, according to anthropologist Gerardo Reichel-Dolmatoff, a source of profound anxiety, which, he suggests, may underlie various "psychological problems," including patterns of aggressive behavior that he found to be common among the Desana.[4]

Other cultures have made other situations occasions for confronting shame and naturally deal with it in different ways. According to Signe Howell, the Chewong of Malaysia do not oppose nature to culture in a fundamental way, but they do see the world in anthropocentric terms and make a radical distinction between their world and the outside world, which is inhabited by "other"—and feared—humans. For the Chewong, Howell suggests, the basic distinction is not between "nature" and "society," but between creatures that are "personages" and those that are not, adding "It is in this sense that they resolve what I take to be a human predilection, namely to lay down premises for distinguishing between self and others."[5] Such distinctions always entail existential tensions, and dealing with these invariably involves prescriptions and proscriptions regarding behavior. These may involve the choice of weapons used to take game, for example, imagined retaliation by other species for the killing involved in the hunt, or even, in a few cases, head-hunting.[6]

Africa provides another striking example of both the shame of distinctions and the value that arises from them. In his 1994 book *Earth's Insights,* environmental philosopher J. Baird Callicott notes that the philosophies and theologies of a wide array of religious and cultural traditions are consistent with the principles of nonanthropocentrism, favoring a kind of egalitarianism among species.[7] He notes, however, one major exception in the cultures of sub-Saharan Africa, where the worldview of society after society is explicitly anthropocentric, positing a high god who created the world and the creatures in it for the sake of humans. (The Lele people of Douglas's study are an example of this, since for them the pangolin is a metaphysical scandal in part because it violates the categories of "human" and "nonhuman.") Since humans have lived in Africa longer than anywhere else on earth, and with less impact on the landscape than in many other places, this constitutes an enormous body of data that is inconsistent with the idea that a nonanthropocentric worldview is crucial to a healthy relationship with nature. What it shows is that how a culture defines its categories, where it draws the lines that distinguish kinds of things—us from them, self from other—is less important than what it *does* with the shame and tension created by those boundaries it does use to organize the world.

This, however, is not an ethical or philosophical problem. It is a mystery. As Victor Turner comments, acknowledging the impossibility of accounting for aspects of Ndembu ritual in philosophical terms, "these assaults on the head were not assaults on cerebration or reason; rather, they were attempts to say the unsayable."[8] What is called for here, Turner is saying, is not philosophy, with its endless ordering and reordering of categories, but what theologian Catherine Pickstock calls "the liturgical consummation of philosophy," the shift from abstract articulation to concrete, expressive action that humans (and other social species) use to finesse what Pickstock calls the "impossibility" of liturgy in its attempt to achieve communion.[9]

Viewed from this perspective, African anthrocentrism is important, not as a puzzling exception to an environmentally friendly ecocentrism, but because it represents a forthright acknowledgment of the most troubling aspects of difference, including the natural self-centeredness that is necessary for the survival of the individual or the species, and the violent hegemony of a heterotrophic species over those species that serve as its prey.[10] What it suggests is that the categories of "nature" and "culture" characteristic of Western thought are as good a basis for the formation of relationship and the creation of the higher values as any—a hopeful possibility, since it is not likely that society is going to change these categories in response to any amount of shame-denying insistence on the "equality" of all creatures.

This is also true of another kind of boundary—those geographic boundaries, political in nature, that define personal space, territory, or, more generally, the rules of behavior. In his classic *Rites of Passage,* French anthropologist Arnold van Gennep made the crossing of territorial boundaries a paradigm for existential crisis and the creation of value.[11] And in many cultures, boundaries are crucial in defining the sacred and setting it apart from the profane.[12]

Some object to this spiritual and psychological dualism, urging instead a kind of spiritual egalitarianism that makes either the whole world sacred or denies a special quality of sacredness to anything. The idea here seems to be that categories—in this case, the sacred and the profane—are arbitrary and peculiarly human and therefore dispensable. But nature subsists on boundaries, from the membranes that define cells to the psychological and political boundaries that people everywhere use to organize their world. Boundaries and categories are essential to both identity and meaning. And the making and respecting of boundaries is by no means a peculiarly human trait.

Consider, for example, ethologist Konrad Lorenz's interpretation of the mating behavior of the greylag goose, a territorial species in which the drive to mate conflicts with the equally fundamental need to defend a territory from other members of the species.[13] Torn between these conflicting drives, courting geese adopt the remarkable strategy of *inventing* a third, *imaginary* goose toward which each directs its hostile energy in the courtship ritual. In the ritual the two rivals join forces to drive away the imaginary third goose, and this exercise—or performance—apparently serves as a way of resolving inner tensions that cannot be resolved in purely literal terms.

What this mating ritual reveals—or at least can plausibly be interpreted as revealing—is a tension inherent in the relationship between the two geese; and the ritual itself, with its measure of dissembling and make-believe, reminds us of the dissembling associated with the ritual of gift exchange as interpreted by Mauss. But what is especially remarkable here is the relationship between imagined and factual reality that this illustrates. The third, trespassing or "enemy," goose exists only in the imagination of the courting geese, but, as Fred Turner points out, the ritual actually creates two literal entities: the pair bond between the courting geese, and new individuals of the species. Moreover, Lorenz pointed out that the territoriality involved here, and the inner and outer conflicts it creates, are actually a *precondition* of the qualities of individuality, personal recognition, and love and do not exist in species such as herring, which lack both territoriality and aggressive drives. Both personality and personal love apparently evolved as a ritualized response to the xenophobic hostility characteristic of territorial species. They are actually a way past this hostility, and around its alienating and self-destructive consequences, and would not exist without it. "Without the resistance to strangers," Turner concludes, "there could be no individuality and love." In other words, even the most positive relationships, such as love and friendship, are inseparable from tensions that can be resolved only in the dimension of performance. Love itself, the cardinal virtue, is in this view actually the outcome or product of a ritual by which territorial and aggressive species single out one individual as an exception to the rule of territoriality, saying in effect "No one is welcome here. But you are different. You are OK. You can cross the line." Lorenz goes so far as to insist that love and ritual are identical or at least operationally indistinguishable, and that what we call love "actually" *is,* at the most fundamental level, the ritual that resolves the existential crisis created by territoriality. He writes, in connection with another, similar mating ritual in several species of ducks,

It would be misleading to call the ritualized movement patterns of inciting in the Mallard, or even in most diving ducks, the "expression" of love, or of affinity to the mate. The independent instinctive movement is not a by-product, not an "epiphenomenon" of the bond holding the two animals together, it is itself the bond. The constant repetition of these ceremonies which hold the pair together gives a good measure of the strength of the autonomous drive which sets them in motion.[14]

Another illustration of the process by which value and relationship emerge from tensions associated with difference and identity—in this case race and social status—is provided by Mark Twain's novel *Adventures of Huckleberry Finn*. Rereading this novel not long ago, I realized that it explores a succession of modes of performance from prayer and masquerade, poetry and theater, play and make-believe, to lying and feud (a negative form of gift exchange). I also realized that the plot, which follows the developing relationship between Huck and the runaway slave, Jim, closely resembles the scheme I am exploring here as a model for the deepening of relationship, and that the concluding sequence, often criticized as implausible and even cruel, may be read as an exploration of the crucial role of performance in relationships that offers, even in its defects, a brilliant reflection on the racially divided American society of Mark Twain's time.[15]

The reader will recall that at first Huck, preoccupied with his own loneliness and fear of his father, sees Jim simply as Miss Watson's "big nigger." Introduced as a kind of watchdog in the darkness of Miss Watson's garden, he is merely an obstacle to be overcome, and Huck takes this more or less for granted. Very early in their experience on the river, however, Huck begins to become aware of Jim as a human being, in part through pranks he plays on him as a figure of fun. Beyond this, Jim and Huck find themselves "economically" dependent on each other, and this dependency soon progresses to an exchange of gifts (or favors), which Huck later catalogs as he considers whether to turn Jim in (chapter 31), and ultimately to the ritualized "evasion" of Jim in the controversial concluding chapters.

This conclusion, in which Tom Sawyer improbably reappears and stage-manages Jim's escape through a childish reenactment of escape sequences from romantic novels, does feel, on a first reading, discontinuous from the earlier parts of the novel, as though Twain has lost control of his story. But from the perspective I am suggesting, Tom's make-believe liberation of Jim may be read as the climax of a series of emancipations: first personal (Huck's acceptance of Jim as a friend, which culminates in the liminal experience on the raft), then social (through Tom's make-believe), and only then—and almost as an afterthought—legally and economically through the provisions of Miss Watson's will.

Others in the novel, who, like the critics who read the ending in purely literal terms, miss—or dismiss—its value as a liberation through performance, find the evasion escapade both implausible and reprehensible. Thus Huck, whose matter-of-fact reading of events is held in tension against Tom's romantic make-believe throughout the novel, remains skeptical, and his reintegration into society is inconclusive as he famously declares at the end of the novel his intention to "light out for the Territory." Perhaps what the "evasion" episode suggests is the need for a ritual that is both self-consciously performed and shared with others or with a third party (in this case Tom) to carry the process of liberation beyond the purely personal liberation that Huck achieves through his experience with Jim on the raft.[16]

If the concluding episode, read this way, still comes across as childish, that is simply because, in a puritan society, the work of liberation through performance is left undone by adults and must be carried out by a child. Yet Twain seems to be suggesting that performance is crucial to emancipation, achieving in the novel (itself a performance) what the Civil War and formal emancipation had so clearly failed to achieve. Perhaps it is the failure of our society to provide means of carrying out this work that accounts in part for our continuing difficulties in the areas of racism, sexism, and civil rights. All this has important implications for our reading of the "act" of ecological restoration, as we shall see.

This perspective on the phenomena of territoriality and relationship is radically different from the one that environmental thinkers have generally taken for granted. In keeping with the tendency of liberalism to celebrate diversity while downplaying difference, environmental thinkers have consistently overlooked the shame of difference, precluding access to the values that lie within and behind this shame. Thus biologist E. O. Wilson, in an indictment not just of human bad behavior but of human nature itself, has suggested that it was a great misfortune for the planet that a tribal, aggressively territorial primate, rather than some "more benign" species made the breatkthrough to the level of consciousness represented by humans. Arguing that "we have become a geophysical force" "unlike any creature that lived before," and curiously combining the idea of an innocent nature and the human Fall figured in Genesis with the Calvinist's assumption of predestination and the prospect of a damnation we have no power to avert, Wilson writes that "The human species is . . . an environmental abnormality. It is possible that intelligence in the wrong kind of species was foreordained to be a fatal combination for the biosphere. Perhaps a law of evolution is that intelligence usually extinguishes itself."[17]

Oddly, in rejecting what he calls "exceptionalism"—the idea that humans somehow stand outside of nature—Wilson insists on an exceptionalism of his own in the idea that, as he repeats elsewhere, "by every conceivable measure, humanity is ecologically abnormal."[18] But every new species begins as an abnormality. And what is unfortunate about this form of exceptionalism is the implication that it is not just human bad behavior but human nature and indeed *nature itself* that has somehow to be corrected or fixed if we are to save ourselves from environmental catastrophe. This is a truly hopeless message, and this hopelessness is the logical consequence of the failure to acknowledge the shame of creation and to grasp the link between shame and the higher values—in this case, the link Lorenz proposed between territoriality and love.

Finally, consider another kind of encounter with shame—the shame of change—and that most radical kind of change—creation. If difference is shameful because it entails limits, change is shameful for the same reason—it is difference in the dimension of time. Thus death is shameful, but so are origin and birth because both represent a limit in time and both involve a clearing away of the old to make way for the new: before my birth I did not exist, as I will not exist after my death, and both my birth and my death are a loss to something or someone else—death obviously; birth because it is a beginning (that is, a limit), because of the inescapable differences and deficiencies encoded in the genes, and because of the discrimination and destruction that are inseparable from life.[19]

This is why, as I noted in chapter 3, myths commonly treat origin as shameful, depicting the beginning of the world as a violent division—the separation of earth from sky, for example, in the Babylonian myth of Enuma Elish—and locating the creation of humans in the murder and sundering of a primordial being that is androgynous, complete, and therefore without shame.[20] The classic example of this in Western tradition is the story of Adam and Eve. But as I pointed out earlier, the biblical story is peculiar in disconnecting shame from creation, suggesting a time, in the Garden, when creatures lived free of shame. In contrast, Fred Turner points out, most myths of origin locate the shame at the very beginning, often making it inherent in the process of creation itself, and he notes examples of this in Eskimo, Shinto, Greek, Australian Aboriginal, and Amerindian myth. "Take for instance," he writes, "the Eskimo story of Sedna and her father Anguta. Sedna, against her father's wishes, marries a dog. Enraged, the father kills Sedna's dog-husband; on the way back a storm rises and Anguta, to lighten the boat, throws his daughter overboard; she clings to the boat and he, to get rid of her, cuts off her fingers, which later reemerge as the beautiful marine mammals on which the people depend."[21]

In the story of Sedna and Anguta, as in the Genesis story, shame is conflated with guilt, the origin commencing in an act of disobedience that incurs guilt, but that also dramatizes the shame of difference and the limits of relationship—the recognition that even in a culture that regards animals as persons with souls, a dog is not regarded as an appropriate husband for a woman. Other origin stories involve no moral wrongdoing, but merely shameful experiences and encounters, and in this way distinguish the shame that radiates from guilt from the existential shame that arises from the experience of limits. In the creation story of the Joshua Indians of the Pacific Northwest, for example, no one does wrong. Rather, an appealingly inept maker, represented as fully aware of his limitations and anxious about their consequences, twice fails in attempts to create humans, his efforts yielding only water monsters and snakes. Finally, with the help of an aboriginal "companion," he succeeds in creating the first woman, but her union with the companion to produce the first child is then accomplished through a complex process of secrecy and indirection, clearly reflecting the sense of shame that human procreation shares with creation itself.[22]

It is this idea of the world's being conceived in a shameful act, whether this is figured as destructive violence or merely in the misguided gropings and false starts of an inept maker, that is reflected in the sacrificial killing, the reenactment of the primordial murder, that is a common element in rites of world renewal, as we will see in the next chapter.[23]

What such cosmogonic myths reveal, Turner argues, is the human awareness of a fundamental inadequacy or incompleteness—what at one point he calls an "amateurishness"—inherent in nature itself. This is evident in the incompleteness and inadequacy of things as they currently exist, in the process of evolution, through which nature continually generates a whole expanding ecology of differences, limitations, and unresolvable tensions and contradictions, and in the realization that, even in everyday experience, creation always entails destruction. In order for a person or a culture to live deeply in the world, it is necessary to encounter and in some way come to terms with these contradictions and the feeling of shame that arises from awareness of them.

A modern society such as ours, having relegated ritual to a position of marginal importance, has no way of doing this. As a result its members either come to advocate the removal of boundaries and distinctions at the expense of difference and meaning, or they continually find themselves crossing existential frontiers with little but self-help books to guide them, and so they lose touch with their circumstances and their surroundings, and the "landscape" they inhabit loses its meaning.

These disparate examples of the uses of performance all have two things in common. All of them begin in an existential crisis of some kind, each of which is distinctive, but which in each case is arguably related to the experience of shame or, in the case of Konrad Lorenz's geese, to an ambivalence that, in our own species, we might suppose would entail the experience of shame. And in each case the result is not the resolution of the problem but rather the *creation of transcendent value*. Thus the crossing of a boundary or the violation of a category leads to an encounter with the sacred—that aspect of experience that transcends categories. In the case of the geese, the experience of ambiguity is, in Lorenz's interpretation, resolved through a dramatic ritual, which not only establishes the pair bond between the two geese—the personal and exclusive relationship that in our own species we call love—but actually constitutes it. In *Huckleberry Finn,* the relationship between a white boy and a black slave in a slave society develops, under conditions of mutual dependence, in a literary experiment that closely parallels the four-step process of community-creation I outlined above, concluding in an elaborate performance that is, in its very cartoonish character and stylistic discontinuity from the rest of the book, a commentary on the failure of Huck and Jim's culture to provide the performative tools needed for this work.

Others point to the essential role of performance in generating or providing access to the higher values. In an exhaustive study that complements Douglas's account of the generation of the sacred through rituals related to the violation of categories, Rappaport has argued that the sacred and the closely related values of the numinous and the holy are all exclusively the products of ritual.[24] Fred Turner argues that meaning is the result of what he calls ritual commutation—the substitution of a symbol for the literal exemplified by Abraham's sacrificing of the ram in place of Isaac. Meaning, in this view, is precisely the difference between what literally is and what is intended: the ram *means* Isaac, precisely because it is *not* Isaac but is designated to stand for him. An object or an act takes on meaning to the extent it is made to substitute for the merely literal and is used to convey those meanings imparted to it by performance. Thus Catherine Pickstock argues that the logic of the Mass, insisting on a change in the substance of the Host, and allowing the thing to exceed its appearance, is the necessary condition not only for communion, but also for meaning.[25] And Fred Turner and James Hans have explored the link between shame and beauty, as we have seen.

So far as community is concerned, the importance of ritual is perhaps more obvious, since rituals and expressive acts of various kinds, from weddings and initiations to the rules of etiquette and conventions regarding gesture, eye contact, and tone of voice are an integral part of everyone's social experience. Such rituals and expressive gestures serve in part as signals, subtle means of conveying information about matters such as status and intent that are crucial in any relationship. As Rappaport points out, these rituals both establish conventions and insulate them from the vagaries of personal conduct, maintaining the boundary between private and public processes, and for these essentially political reasons alone he describes ritual as "*the* basic social act."[26] But as the examples of Lorenz's geese and *Huckleberry Finn* suggest, they serve other functions as well. Specifically, they provide means of dealing with the presence of the other and, most fundamentally, the realization that the self emerges from performative interaction with the other and so depends on the other for its very identity. This is an encounter with limit so radical and so deeply shameful that we are driven to recognize it only by necessity and will do almost anything to avoid it. The usual way of doing this is to replace the shameful organic bonds of personal relationship, obligation, and mutual dependence with more abstract relationships of a commercial nature. In doing this we downgrade the relationship by taking a step back, from the level of gift exchange to an exchange on a quid-pro-quo basis, which is why religions commonly regard wealth as a danger to the soul.

It is the basic function of ritual and the arts to provide an alternative, productive way of dealing with this problem—in Victor Turner's phrase, by making the obligatory desirable.[27] Using terms introduced by van Gennep, and reflecting his interpretation of the rites of territorial passage, Turner interpreted ritual as taking place in three stages, which serve to deconstruct elements of the self and then to reconstruct them in order to negotiate the inner changes demanded by changes in status or relationship. In the crucial middle phase, which van Gennep termed the "liminal" phase (from the Latin *limen,* threshold) Turner writes, the participant stands on the threshold between two conditions and belongs fully to neither. He or she is in a kind of psychological or ontological adolescence, "betwixt and between" the old and the new. Only in this liminal phase, Turner believed, do people achieve the deepest *experience* of community. To distinguish this experience from the factual, physical, and economic dimensions of community, he called it *communitas*.

Communitas is the essential *experience* of community, the sense, not just of fellowship but of a kind of unity with others. He stresses, however, that *communitas* is a subjective state, and typically a fleeting one, noting that "the spontaneity and immediacy of *communitas*—as opposed to the jural-political character of structure—can seldom be maintained for very long."[28] The relationship between *communitas* and community is complex. *Communitas* exists outside the mundane structures of community yet in a context or container—ritual—that is in every way a product of the community, and indeed perhaps its greatest and most distinctive achievement. Partly because it exists outside structure, it gives value to structure. Turner referred to it as "an essential and generic bond, without which there could be *no* society." In other words, it is not community but one of community's reasons for being. Community exists, in this view, at least in part to create the rituals needed to provide access to *communitas*. *Communitas,* on the other hand, though a fleeting experience, is the psychological core of community.[29] Community itself may be defined operationally as an association of subjects that provides access to *communitas* through institutionalized performance and uses it to form bonds, establish obligations, and inform the consciences of the members.

Turner's work suggests that ritual is essential to community not only because it provides access to the experience of *communitas,* but also, and more generally, because it is the means by which individuals or groups bring about the inner changes needed to make transitions such as those from individual to member or from child to adult. This is psychologically demanding work. And this is why feelings alone are an inadequate guide to the formation of relationships, and why it is difficult to achieve the deepest kinds of relationship through experience alone, unaided by performance. Thus, reflecting on the monastic practice of communal prayer, poet and essayist Kathleen Norris writes of "the tyranny of personal experience," suggesting that the performance, rather than the mere reading, reciting, or "saying" of prayer "counters our tendency to see individual experience as sufficient for formulating a vision of the world."[30]

What this all adds up to is an argument that performance and ritual are the essential technologies by which humans (like geese) create or achieve or gain access to the higher values. They do this, moreover, at the most fundamental level, by providing psychologically productive ways of dealing with shame—of passing, as Fred Turner says, through shame to beauty. In doing so, they elevate fact to truth, establishing, Rappaport argues, the ground of morality. They also form the conscience, providing the essential link between what actually is and what we think ought to be that has always eluded philosophy.

Contrary to what a puritan society encourages us to believe, this process is not essentially conservative or noncreative. Indeed, Victor Turner, who is often credited with rescuing ritual from this misconception, regarded it as the crucible of creativity, the technology a community or an individual uses to examine, criticize, and change the deepest structures of its worldview and system of values and relationships. Nor is it essentially authoritarian. Indeed, at the most fundamental level, ritual is the means a community uses to *transcend* authority. Ritual, Rappaport suggests, does not require authority because it generates its own authority out of the voices and assent of the participants and so, he suggests, must have been "the primordial means by which men, divested of genetically determined order, established the conventions by which they order themselves."[31]

Modernism has been unfriendly, even hostile, toward ritual from the beginning. For one thing, because it links inner experience with overt action, ritual makes little sense from the perspective of the Cartesian dualism that became an integral part of the philosophical underpinning of modernism. For another, as theologian Tom Driver points out, the Enlightenment, with its emphasis on reason and its wariness of numinous experience, had little use for ritual.[32] Liberalism, with its emphasis on the self-interested atomic individual, inevitably undermined both commitment to ritual and faith in its efficacy. And emerging nation-states, having good reason to be apprehensive about experiences such as liminality and *communitas,* which represented the ultimate meltdown and questioning of social structures at the community and personal levels, were quick to appropriate ritual for their own use.[33]

Another factor was Protestantism, with its tendency toward iconoclasm and its explicit program for the demotion of ritual. In a recent essay titled *John Muir and the Roots of American Environmentalism* historian Donald Worster argues that the emergence of an environmental ethic that deemphasizes human dominion over nature and accords other species a more nearly equal footing with ourselves is a distinctively American development and is in many ways an outgrowth of the liberal brand of Protestantism that played an important role in the shaping of the American moral imagination.[34] In particular, Worster cites four characteristics of liberal Protestantism that strongly influenced the thinking of early environmental thinkers, notably Muir. These, which he identifies as moral activism, ascetic discipline, egalitarian individualism, and esthetic spirituality, all played key roles in the shaping of environmental thought and are clearly reflected in the environmentalism of our own time. While Muir has often been portrayed as having rejected his father's severe Calvinism in favor of a kind of pantheism wholly at odds with Calvinism and with Christianity generally, his individualistic approach to the problem of achieving communion with nature is clearly a reflection of his religious background and is in this crucial respect completely unlike paganism, with its reliance on community-based ritual to mediate relationships, including the relationship between humans and the natural world. Worster notes that Muir's thinking about humans and nature reflects Calvinist thought in other ways as well. Thus, while Muir replaces the God of Calvinism with nature, he sees nature in idealized terms. Like the Calvinists, I would add, he also sees humans as peculiarly fallen creatures and, being ill equipped to deal with shame, consistently confuses shame with guilt, overlooking the shameful aspects of experience and defining the relationship between humans and the rest of nature in terms of good and evil.[35] Overall, Worster makes a convincing case for the idea that American environmentalism owes a great deal to Protestant traditions of thought. He sees this in a positive light, as a development that partly offsets what he sees as Christianity's contribution to a sensibility and an ethos that have legitimatized the despoliation of nature.

But if environmentalism is built partly on Protestant foundations, it seems reasonable to suppose that elements of Protestant thought might well account for some of its weaknesses and limitations as well as its strengths. One of these is the diminished conception of the value of ritual that lies at the core of Protestantism, which essentially denies the ontological power of performance—its power to make real and to transform reality, as exemplified by the pre-Reformation doctrine of transubstantiation—and so deprives it of the power to deal with existential shame.

In view of the crucial role ritual plays in community and the formation of relationships, this demotion of ritual is obviously an important matter. It underlies several additional attributes of Protestantism, which are also reflected in American environmental thinking, and which may help us to understand, and perhaps to remedy, some of environmentalism's shortcomings.[36] These include a sense of radical separation between God and humankind, an idealization of purity rather than the violation and contamination of the self in communion, and an either-or sensibility that cannot deal productively with ambiguity and the violation of categories.

They also include the idea that humans are fallen, unworthy, and incapable of redemption through personal effort; an emphasis on faith rather than "works" as the key to salvation; a mistrust of hierarchy and institutions, associated with a radical individualism and an extreme conception of spiritual self-reliance that leaves the individual alone to achieve a relationship with God unmediated by a priesthood or by sacrament.

All these characteristics reflect the reaction against certain elements of Catholicism that was the defining feature of the Reformation. They vary in expression from denomination to denomination but were pronounced features of the beliefs of the Puritans, who strongly influenced the development of mainstream "Yankee" American culture. The Puritans, then, contributed to the American sensibility a complex of assumptions, feelings, and ideas about relationships with God, and so about relationships in general that, like those Worster discusses, helped shape American thinking about nature and the environment and are clearly reflected in modern environmental thinking.[37]

Taken together with Worster's summary of the contributions that liberal Protestantism has made to environmental thinking, these conservative, puritan attributes may help us gain a clearer understanding of both the achievements and the limitations of environmentalism, and—most important—of how these limitations might be overcome. It may be that ideas and attitudes encouraged by Protestantism, such as moral activism, egalitarianism, a work ethic, and other elements described by Worster, in conjunction with the faith in reason and the ability of humans to identify the causes of problems and to correct them that was characteristic of Enlightenment thought, were preconditions for the development of a modern movement aimed at identifying and solving environmental problems. At the same time it is hard to believe that some of the limitations of modern environmentalism are not in some way related to its distinctively puritan "take" on the very technologies of performance and ritual that humans (and other social animals) have always used to build community and negotiate and maintain relationships. From this point of view, the limitations of environmentalism may ultimately be due to its failure to provide ways of dealing productively with the problem of shame, a weakness it inherits from puritanism.

To gain a clearer sense of the various ideas of performance, their implications for relationship, and the way the skeptical, puritan conception of ritual entered and influenced environmentalism, it will be helpful to consider two seminal environmental thinkers, John Muir and Henry

Thoreau, from the point of view of their ideas of performance and their relationship to it. What we find here is a profound contrast in attitudes. We find, first of all, that both men (like Aldo Leopold almost a century later) broke with puritan literalism to the extent of making a deliberate, self-conscious use of imagination in negotiating their own relationship with nature. Think for example of Thoreau playing muskrat, as I mentioned earlier, or imagining himself to be a coyote or wolf, capturing a woodchuck and devouring it raw; or of Muir's imaginative identification with the elements, even dressing in the colors of granite to express his sympathetic identification with boulders, or working out the glacial geology of the Sierra by imagining himself to be a glacier. What is involved here, however, is merely the use of imagination to achieve a sympathetic identification with nature. This is by no means the same thing as "actually" coming to terms with one's relationship with nature as a predator, for example, or as exceptionally self-aware, as capable of abstract thought, as mortal, and so forth. The use of imagination in the context of ritual to deal with these more problematic aspects of the relationship between ourselves and the rest of nature demands a faith in the *ontological* power of imagination—that is, in the power of imagination, aided by ritual, to actually bring about change—a transubstantiation of sorts—that is a far greater challenge to the puritan sensibility.

Of the two men, only Thoreau achieved this insight. We can see this clearly if we compare the means by which each man carried out his search for communion with nature. For Muir, this took the form of the lifelong quest for a pristine landscape, unsullied by human influence, that led him further and further afield, first on his famous thousand-mile walk from Kentucky to the Gulf Coast, then to the Sierra, and eventually to Alaska. This quest may be seen as the environmentalist's version of the puritan's search for redemption through unmediated communion. But this means leaving out the more troubling aspects of relationship, and in his writing Muir rarely touches on either the economic or the political, power-related aspects of his relationship with nature, marginalizing these shame-laden aspects of relationship, just as he marginalized indigenous people in his constant search for the ideal of perfect harmony with unsullied nature. Repelled by domestication and generally indifferent to domestic animals, he never even tried in his writing to integrate his work as a prosperous orchardist with his commitments to wild nature and its conservation. Indeed, his neglect of the murderous and violent aspects of nature has led Michael Cohen, in his sympathetic biography of Muir, to suggest that "there is something deeply and seriously flawed in Muir's vision. . . . He seemed essentially frightened of looking too closely into the hunter in Nature or the hunter in himself. He believed that meat soiled. Indeed, he did not want to think of any struggle in Nature at all."[38]

In this important respect, Thoreau stands in striking contrast with Muir. This is evident in the manner in which he sought communion with nature—not through a search for nature in the form of the pure and unsullied wilderness Muir sought in the West, but in a self-consciously performative relationship with whatever landscape happened to be at hand. Just at the time when many enterprising young New Englanders were going west to seek their fortunes, Thoreau defiantly proclaimed his intention to conduct his own business close to home. Despite his ironic portrayal of Walden Pond as a wilderness, offering "no path to the civilized world," the area around Walden Pond was no wilderness when Thoreau took up residence there, but in fact a rural landscape that had been under cultivation for nearly two centuries. In Thoreau's time it was just beginning a process of natural recovery as farmers pulled up stakes, abandoning their stony New England farms for richer land in the West.[39] Moreover in 1844, barely a year before Thoreau took up residence in Walden Woods, the Fitchburg Railroad completed track that passed just a few rods from the pond, and during his two years there loggers cut a stand of timber on the shore of the pond across from his cabin.[40] Walden Woods, then, was not a real wilderness, but a make-believe wilderness— a bit of countryside in the suburbs of Boston that retained just enough of the flavor of wilderness to sustain Thoreau's exploration of the wild, an exploration that was carried out in imaginative as much as in literal terms. Thoreau was not living in the wilderness at Walden Pond. He was playing house in the woods. But it was the essence of his achievement to show that, in the last analysis, communion with nature is achieved in exactly this way—not merely by immersion and sympathetic identification, but through an act of the imagination that reconciles in make-believe terms what is irreconcilable in literal terms.[41]

Similarly, Thoreau's writing is filled with accounts of the politics and economics of his relationship with the landscape and with other species. The great example is *Walden* itself, which deals, in its first and longest chapter with "Economy," and which in several respects follows the progression from economic values to higher values that I am exploring in this book. In chapter 7, "The Beanfield," an account of his experiment in agriculture, Thoreau develops this theme in miniature, progressing from a somewhat ironic accounting for the project in economic terms, and reflections on the killing and discrimination—the "invidious distinctions" he makes with his hoe—to the conclusion that the real value of farming lies not in the crops it produces but in the meanings it creates, and that "some must work in fields if only to serve a parable maker one day."[42] Here, at least for an experimental moment, Thoreau read his work in his beanfield as a transforming ritual, which he describes in terms strongly reminiscent of the formula of consecration in the Mass, including even the ringing of the bell: "My hoe tinkled against the stones," he writes, "and that music echoed to the woods and sky and was an accompaniment to my labor which yielded an instant and immeasurable crop, *so that it was no longer beans that I hoed, nor I that hoed beans*" (emphasis added). Here even the rhythm of the prose suggests the incantatory words of the consecration—think of the concluding phrase, with its succession of monosyllables, set to Gregorian chant: "So that it was no longer beans that I hoed, nor I that hoed beans." Thoreau's declaration of his own transformation and that of his beans differs significantly from the transubstantiation of the Mass only in that it is expressed in negative terms: telling us not what the thing now is but only what it no longer is, he leaves us, characteristically, guessing at the precise nature of the transformation, the flowering of meaning out of fact, that has been achieved.[43]

This transcendental (or sacramental) manner of confronting shame and transmuting lower into higher value reaches its fullest expression in Thoreau's account (in "Spring," the last chapter of *Walden* before the "Conclusion") of the thawing of the embankment of the railroad that skirted the pond. This passage is of special interest here because of its strongly metaphoric, or performative character, and also because of its uncanny resonance with the work of restoration. As the bank thawed in the spring, Thoreau found, water carried sand and clay down the slopes, depositing them at the base of the embankment in elaborate shapes that he saw as suggestive of organic forms.

Few phenomena gave me more delight than to observe the forms which thawing sand and clay assume in flowing down the sides of a deep cut on the railroad through which I passed on my way to the village, a phenomenon not very common on so large a scale, though the number of freshly exposed banks of the right material must have been greatly multiplied since railroads were invented. The material was sand of every degree of fineness and of various colors, commonly mixed with a little clay. When the frost comes out in the spring, and even in a thawing day in the winter, the sand begins to flow down the slopes like lava, sometimes bursting out through the snow and overflowing it where no sand was to be seen before. Innumerable little streams overlap and interlace one with another, exhibiting a sort of hybrid product, which obeys half way the law of currents, and half way that of vegetation. As it flows it takes the forms of sappy leaves or vines, making heaps of pulpy sprays a foot or more in depth, and resembling, as you look down on them the laciniated, lobed and imbricated thalluses of some lichens; or you are reminded of coral, of leopards' paws or birds' feet, of brains or lungs or bowels, and excrements of all kinds.[44]

What is striking here, as literary scholar Leo Marx has pointed out, is the figure Thoreau chooses to make his point and the way he handles it.[45] The thawing bank was not pristine nature but its antithesis. It was, in fact, a harsh, freshly made scar across the landscape, which must have seemed to Thoreau very much as a strip mine or an oil spill seems to us today — an extreme form of degradation and disruption of the landscape. Even worse in a way is the erosion itself, since it represents the ongoing break-down of the ecosystem following disruption, the unraveling of land, and the fouling of the pond — for Thoreau a symbol of the pure character of pristine nature — by silt-laden water.

Literally, then, the thawing bank is an ecosystem unraveling under as-sault. Yet in his account of the thaw Thoreau barely acknowledges this. Though he does not himself deliberately perpetrate the destructive act — this alone distinguishes his account here from the practice of sacrifice in the fullest, classic sense — he makes no complaint about the railroad, does no hand-wringing, and offers no dirge or jeremiad over the violation of nature. What he presents, rather, is an extended, almost hallucinatory re-flection on the creative power of nature, figured both in the organic shapes of the silt, which Thoreau sees as a kind of primitive vegetation, anticipating the return of actual vegetation and organized on the same creative principle; and also in human language, which Thoreau sees ris-ing from these shapes. Nature is falling apart as a result of human influ-ence, yet Thoreau describes all this in positive, even rhapsodic terms and finds in the suppurating sandbank evidence of the very principle of cre-ation and renewal.

When I see on the one side the inert bank, — for the sun acts on one side first, — and on the other this luxuriant foliage, the creation of an hour, I am affected as if in a peculiar sense I stood in the laboratory of the Artist who made the world and me, — had come to where he was still at work, sporting on this bank, and with ex-cess of energy strewing his fresh designs about. I feel as if I were nearer to the vi-tals of the globe, for this sandy overflow is something such a foliaceous mass as the vitals of the animal body. You find thus in the very sands an anticipation of the vegetable leaf. No wonder that the earth expresses itself outwardly in leaves, it so labors with the idea inwardly.[46]

Marx points out that this crucial passage (like the mating ceremony of Lorenz's geese) owes much of its force to its relentless counterfactuality. The sandbank in Thoreau's account is not being revegetated in any literal sense. In fact, the forms in sand and clay he celebrates are the direct result of erosion, a destructive force that a restorationist attempting the literal revegetation of the sandbank would work hard to counteract. Yet Thoreau looks beyond this to see in the figurative thalluses of lichens, the "pulpy sprays" and forms of vegetation at the base of the bank, an expression of the creative power of nature that underlies not only the actual growth of plants and vegetation, but the redeeming work of imagination itself. In this way, Marx writes, "order, form and meaning are restored, but it is a blatantly, unequivocally figurative restoration. The whole force of the passage arises from its extravagantly metaphoric, poetic, literary character."[47]

Or, we might say, from its religious and sacramental character. For here again, as in his reflections on the work of hoeing beans, Thoreau's act of redemption amounts to an act of transubstantiation, the conversion of what is merely humdrum or even, as in the case of the sandbank, downright destructive, into something charged with a higher, deeper, richer form of life. This is a resurrection, and indeed critic Andrew Delbanco has suggested that what Thoreau achieved at Walden was a kind of catholicism in which communion and redemption could be achieved through the work of imagination aided by ritual.[48] It was this faith in what Frederick Garber has called the redemptive imagination—the discovery that redemption is, in fact, a creative act, an imaginative revisioning and re-creation of the world—that underlay what, even if it fell short of hope in the fullest sense, was at least a kind of defiant optimism in Thoreau's thinking.[49] Indeed, the cycle of loss and redemption is a prevalent motif in Thoreau's writing, culminating in the exuberant "The sun is but a morning star" at the end of *Walden*.

Muir's take on performance was very different, and it led him to a very different conception of the importance of actual wilderness. While both Muir and Thoreau approached nature in a religious spirit, seeking redemption through communion with it, for Muir redemption depended ultimately on immersion in literal wilderness. Thoreau, in contrast, had discovered and was exploring the phenomenon of performative commutation, the fact that an initial, or "primary," experience or act can be scaled down, simplified, and stylized without losing—and in fact even gaining—sacramental efficacy. If Walden Woods was a qualified ritually commuted wilderness—closer in this sense to a cathedral than was the literal wilderness Muir sought—Thoreau himself was aware of the value of commutation as a way of creating meaning, and he was prepared to push the process even further. "If I were confined to a corner of a garret all my days, like a spider," he wrote in the "Conclusion" of *Walden*, "the world would be just as large to me while I had my thoughts about me."[50]

While it is important not to overlook Thoreau's celebration of the wild, what is even more important is the way he went about immersing himself in "wilderness," not through excursions into truly unsettled country, but through his experiments in the commuted, symbolic wilderness of the countryside around Concord. Nature, Thoreau's experiment shows, is available everywhere and so, at least implicitly, to everyone, not just to the relative few who have access to remote wilderness areas. This is a message of great importance today, when millions, following Muir and a succession of leading environmental thinkers in their search for salvation through contact with a too-literal wilderness, have adopted the economically alienated relationship to the land represented by the suburbs, the house or second "home" in the country, or the wilderness retreat—all at grievous cost to both the country and the city. This colonization of country is now arguably one of our gravest environmental problems—not least because it is so often carried out in the name of environmental values. What it reveals is the inadequacy of the rituals of engagement and communion modeled by environmental thinkers from Muir to Leopold, Gary Snyder, Barry Lopez, and Ed Abbey. These typically entail withdrawal from society rather than engagement with it. And they are essentially consumptive and so in a fundamental sense elitist, as becomes clear when the numbers reach democratic proportions, millions of us fleeing to the countryside seeking the redemption of our souls and raising the question of what to do with a thousand Thoreaus.

The solution to this problem is suggested by Thoreau's experiment— less in the distance he ironically and poetically claimed to have put between himself and the city than in his literal proximity to it, but even more in his celebration of the power of commuted or symbolic experience.

The solution is, first of all, to live in the city unless your work—that is, your economy—takes you elsewhere, and to learn to "do" nature there. The solution is also to learn to deal with the ambiguities of our relationship with nature through the exercise of the imagination, carried out in community and in the context of ritual and the arts. Both of these are tasks for the restorationist, as I will show in the final two chapters.

CHAPTER 7

Sacrifice and Celebration

Restoration as a Performing Art

When the Walbiri of central Australia set out to renew the world, as they do annually, they do it through elaborate rituals that have no direct effect on the landscape or its ecology yet have ensured its renewal and well-being through thousands of years of human inhabitation. For us in the West it's the other way around. We go out and inventory the vegetation. We take soil samples and plant trees. We look for results in terms of survival rates and recovering soil profiles. We call what we are doing "restoration" rather than "world renewal," and ritual is the last thing we think about.

It was certainly the last thing I thought about. When I started thinking about restoration I thought first about what my culture taught me to think about—the restored ecosystem itself, the tangible product of the restoration effort. When it occurred to me that the process of restoration had value in and of itself, as a way of studying the landscape or ecosystem being restored, that struck me as a small revelation. It was several years before I got past thinking about restoration in purely "objective" terms and began to consider the value it might have as an experience. And it was another half-dozen years before I made the turn into what I came to regard as a "fourth dimension" of value and began to think seriously about restoration as a performance.

Then in the space of about a year I came across two articles that led me to reexamine some of my own ideas and to begin thinking seriously about performance and the idea of restoration as a performing art. The first was an essay by Frederick Turner titled "Cultivating the American

Garden," in which Turner explored the idea of gardening as a performing art. Since I was already thinking about restoration as a kind of gardening, I found this idea intriguing, so I got in touch with Turner and began a conversation with him that eventually led to the ideas I explore in this chapter.

The other article was a report prepared for the National Park Service by an advisory board chaired, interestingly, by Aldo Leopold's son, Starker Leopold.[1] Published in 1963, the report summarized the board's recommendations on the management of wildlife in the national parks and had played an important role in the development of policy for managing the parks in the years since. Having been told about it by a friend, I was eager to read it because the issues it deals with were not unlike those raised so clearly by the restoration effort at the Arboretum. Besides that, I wondered whether Leopold's experience growing up in Madison during the years when his father was playing a leading role in the Arboretum's development might have influenced his ideas on the management of wilderness areas.

What I found in the report was a philosophy of management that might very well have been informed by the Arboretum experiment. Acknowledging the need for more or less continual management to compensate for "constant changes due to natural or man-caused processes," Leopold and his colleagues prescribed what looked to me like a program of ongoing restorative management for the parks. "As a primary goal," they wrote, "we would recommend that the biotic associations within each park be maintained, or where necessary recreated, as nearly as possible in the condition that prevailed when the area was first visited by the white man."

To me, immersed in my reflections on the historic work at the Arboretum, this seemed like a call to extend the idea of restoration beyond the odd tract in an arboretum or ornamental landscape and into the national parks. That made sense to me. But two things about the Leopold committee's development of this idea bothered me: its view of the parks; and the manner in which it proposed the actual work of restoration should be carried out. Treating the parks rather like exhibits in a museum, the committee suggested that each park should be managed as "a vignette of primitive America," providing "a reasonable illusion" of the pre-contact landscape. "This," they concluded, "in our opinion should be the objective of every national park and monument." Thus they conceived of the parks in theatrical terms, as an illusion, like a stage set. But the stage they imagined was a proscenium stage, and the work of creating the illusion was to be carried out discretely backstage by a corps of professional specialists. They noted specifically that "observable artificiality in any form must be minimized and obscured in every possible way. . . . Management may at times call for the use of the tractor, chain-saw, rifle or flame-thrower but the signs and sounds of such activity should be hidden from visitors insofar as possible."

What troubled me about this was not the idea of nature conceived in theatrical terms. That is where my own thinking was taking me. What troubled me was the *idea* of theater implicit in the Leopold report, and in particular the idea of the relationship between the public and the natural landscape the Leopold committee seemed to take for granted. By keeping the work of restoration backstage, as it were, the committee not only turned nature into an "illusion" for all but a few insiders, it cut the vast majority of people out of the very work that, I was beginning to realize, not only defines what the natural landscape will be but literally *constitutes* our relationship with it. It wasn't the idea of nature as theater that was wrong. That, I now realized, was a powerful metaphor that led into a vast area of human experience that could help me think more clearly about the work of restoration. What seemed somehow off key was the idea of theater as mere illusion, and the idea of the audience—in this case the public—as mere unself-conscious consumers of that illusion. This, I felt, turned the natural landscape into a mere show—a sort of Disneyland.

This was a minor theme of the Leopold report, but I found it provocative, in part because it touched on my own, at the time rather vague, ideas about the value of restoration as a kind of performance, forcing me to think them through more carefully. It was in doing this that I found Fred Turner's ideas and those of his parents Victor and Edith Turner, indispensable.[2] Beginning with their pioneering research in Africa in the 1950s, Victor and Edith Turner had extended their work into other cultures and performance traditions and, by the time of Victor's death in 1983, their work was widely regarded as constituting what their colleague Ronald Grimes has called a kind of reinvention of ritual. It had become the foundation for a whole school of research on ritual, with implications far beyond anthropology in areas such as theater, criticism, history, and the social sciences. Fred has built on his parents' work in his own highly interdisciplinary research in literature and cultural criticism. Reading the work of the Turners and, eventually, other students and practitioners of performance and ritual such as Grimes, Roy Rappaport, Richard Schechner, and Tom Driver, I began to develop a clearer idea of the nature of performance and ritual and the crucial role they play in dealing with the tensions and ambiguities inherent in relationships.

I also realized that the act of restoration represented such a point of tension and ambiguity in the relationship between nature and culture and that, far from devaluing restoration, this actually opened up a whole dimension of value that I had so far overlooked. While the Turners' work was concerned mainly with relationships among humans, I was struck by its relevance to the "practice" of relationships in a more general sense, and also by how restoration fits neatly into the pattern by which Victor Turner came to believe ritual, and ultimately theater, arise out of the inevitable tensions of social life. Life in any society, Turner wrote, naturally gives rise to disagreements and disputes. These lead to what Turner called *social dramas,* which he saw as working themselves out in four stages: crisis, breach, redress, and resolution, which may be either the restoration of a relationship or the formal recognition of a permanent breach between the parties involved. Ritual, Turner suggested, emerges from the third stage in the process, the stage of redress in which the argument is brought into court, so to speak, where a third party acts as an arbiter, and the issues are to some extent objectified and dealt with performatively and reflexively. He writes, "ritual and its progeny, the performing arts among them, derive from the subjunctive, liminal, reflexive, exploratory heart of the social drama, its third phase, where the contents of group experiences . . . are replicated, dismembered, remembered, refashioned, and mutely or vocally made meaningful."[3]

Turner and his students applied this idea to the interpretation of a wide range of social phenomena and historical events. For our purposes, the important point is that the work of ecological restoration represents precisely that third stage in the social drama of relations between nature and culture, the stage of redress, that gives rise to ritual. Besides this, our ideas and experiences of nature certainly are reflexively "replicated, dismembered, remembered, refashioned, and . . . made meaningful" in the process of restoration, as I have tried to show. Thus Turner's concept of social drama and its relationship to performance and ritual lends support to the idea that the work of restoration offers a suitable occasion for the invention of rituals of relationship with nature. Indeed, in a concluding comment Turner links this pattern explicitly with the work of restoration, understood as world making: "The cosmology has always been destabilized, and society has always had to make efforts, through both social dramas and esthetic dramas, to restabilize and actually *produce* cosmos."[4]

Encouraged by these ideas, and also by Rappaport's suggestion that ritual, because it entails both word and object, combining form and substance, contains a "paradigm of creation," I began to think seriously about the development of restoration as a performing art—not the alienated theater of illusion implicit in the Leopold report, but a theater in which the audience is not only fully aware of what is going on backstage but also participates in the performance and even in the writing of the script. What I eventually came to envision was not a shift from one form of theater to another—from classical to experimental theater, for example—but a shift from theater to ritual, and from the conception of the public as an audience to a conception of the public as making up a *congregation* that actively participates in the performance and is not merely informed or even edified, but is "actually" transformed by it. Stepping back in this way to consider restoration as a performance takes us beyond technical, scientific, and even merely personal considerations to ask fascinating questions about what the *act* of restoration expresses or means, or—more accurately—what meanings might emerge from it if we were to take it seriously as an expressive act and to develop it as a context for the exploration and creation of meaning and other values. One way to approach these questions is simply to ask what the work is about and what sort of relationship with nature it implies.

I have already pointed out several such meanings. Restoration expresses caring for nature by deferring to it, by nurturing it, and by giving back to it. It is a form of reenactment and an experiment in the reversibility of time and of change. It turns technology back against itself, since it is carried out for the explicit purpose of making the signs of technology disappear from the landscape. It is a way of achieving intimacy with ecosystems and with the plants and animals and objects and processes that make them up and it enacts a positive relationship with the landscape being restored. They are by and large positive experiences through which the restorationist achieves both familiarity and intimacy with nature at the level of the low-key rituals of etiquette and courtesy.[5] Restoration, however, is also problematic, involving a wholehearted attempt to defer to nature while at the same time accepting a measure of responsibility for and—inseparable from that—dominion over the land. This ambiguity is at the heart of the environmentalist's wariness about restoration. Yet it is precisely because of this ambiguity that restoration provides an occasion for the higher rituals of reparation, initiation, and communion.

Coming at restoration as performance from another direction, we can explore performative traditions and genres that might be expected to resonate with the work of restoration in various ways, and that might provide useful comparisons and contrasts with it. These, it turns out, are easy to find. Restoration is elemental work, related in various ways to the work of reconciliation, for example, or to redemption, and to a wide array of performative traditions. Here I consider four performative or artistic genres that offer especially useful or suggestive parallels with the work of ecological restoration: festival and comedy; initiation into community; rituals of world renewal through sacrifice (and the closely related artistic genre of tragedy); and finally, stepping outside the domain of ritual proper into the closely related domain of the arts, the art of literary pastoral.

Restoration is an occasion for comedy and festival simply because it brings people together in work—or play—that has positive value and seems to call for celebration. Comedy has been traced in the West to celebrations of fertility, and indeed the word "comedy" is thought to derive from the name of the god Comus, a god of fertility in the Greek pantheon, and a symbol of eternal life achieved through perpetual rebirth. Philosopher Susanne Langer writes,

Comedy is an art form that arises naturally wherever people are gathered to celebrate life, in spring festivals, triumphs, birthdays, weddings or initiations. For it expresses the elementary strains and resolutions of animate nature, the animal drives that persist even in human nature, the delight man takes in his special mental gifts that make him the lord of creation; it is an image of human vitality holding its own in the world amid the surprises of unplanned coincidence.[6]

Restoration is "comic," we may say, because it entails reproduction and engagement and all the uncertainty, ambiguity, and opportunity for misunderstanding that naturally accompany these life processes. It also lends itself to festival and feasting because it brings—or can bring—people together to celebrate life and even, without taking it too seriously, their role as lords of creation, as Langer notes. Community-oriented restoration projects have in fact given rise to festivals and, in at least one case, even to outright comedy, in the form of a musical comedy, *Queen Salmon,* that restorationists working in the watershed of the Mattole River in northern California created a few years ago, first to celebrate and then to draw attention to their work.[7]

Such experiences and events are invaluable because they provide something that has been rare in environmentalism, especially the environmentalism of the past few decades—an occasion for celebrating our participation in the ecology of a classic landscape. Besides this, they add a social and communal dimension to the more or less solitary and personal experience of the naturalist or observer. For both these reasons they are an indispensable first step toward a healthy relationship with the classic landscape.

But one of the benefits of taking restoration seriously as a performing art is the critical perspective this provides. Seeing comedy as both universal and unpretentious, writer Joseph Meeker suggests that comedy provides a basis for an environmental ethic and a relationship between nature and culture generally. In particular, Meeker is attracted by the figure of the picaresque character who, like Thomas Mann's confidence man, Felix Krull, makes his way by trickery and by appealing to the vanities of others but does not—in contrast with the tragic hero—take himself too seriously. The picaresque hero is an opportunist who acknowledges wickedness and whose politics are "machiavellian," but who is motivated by love as well as self-interest, and whose ultimate objective is to accommodate himself to the world.[8] Underplayed in Meeker's account, however, is the dark side of comedy and its close relationship to its theatrical counterpart, tragedy. Meeker notes that, unlike comedy, tragedy is not a widespread genre, as comedy is, but is peculiar to a few Western cultures, notably those of ancient Greece and Elizabethan England. He sees it as the expression of a peculiarly alienated sensibility, rather than as a high artistic expression of the experience of alienation and difference that is part of the human condition. But, as Langer points out, if comedy is the image of fortune, then tragedy is the image of fate; the two together make up destiny. While one celebrates the truth of human oneness with the world, the other explores, without rejecting or downplaying it, the tragedy of human otherness. Taken together, they represent, Joseph Campbell notes,

the terms of a single mythological theme and experience which includes them both and which they bound: the down-going and the up-coming . . . , which together constitute the totality of the revelation that is life, and which the individual must know and love if he is to be purged . . . of the contagion of sin (disobedience to the divine will) and death (identification with the mortal form).[9]

This is achieved, he points out, not by denying evil but by achieving an "all-sustaining love" that sees "an immanent, imperishable eternity," even in the "dreadful mutilations" of violence and death. Thus, the way down is the way up. Death and pain and the knowledge of shame must precede resurrection and the delights of comedy with its promise of eternity. Before the festival and the feast must come the killing. And, Campbell writes, "it is the business of mythology proper"—and, we may add, of performance generally—"to reveal the specific dangers and techniques of the dark interior way from tragedy to comedy."[10]

Here again we encounter the realization that the knowledge of shame is the pathway to communion. In the end (like those in Lewis's party of Hope) the picaresque hero is alone and isolated, succeeding in his quest for individual advantage only at the expense of intimacy and community. The hero, for both Meeker and Campbell, is best and most fully represented by the figure of Dante, who passes through the pain and alienation of Hell to achieve the bliss and transcendence of Paradise. In its way restoration can be redemptive too, but only if it is tightly linked to the acts of destruction that make restoration necessary—the movement downward that both necessitates the movement upward and makes it possible.[11]

An important point here is that, while the pattern of redemption, the movement of the soul through "the worst" in order to achieve "the best," may be universal, the conditions and terms of this journey change in the course of cultural evolution. The idea of progress is currently unfashionable because, being part of creation, progress always comes at a price and entails an intensification of shame. One way of dealing with this is simply to deny the reality of radical change: if there are no metaphysical frontiers, then there is no need for means of dealing with the metaphysical crisis of crossing them. This is psychologically convenient: if nothing has changed, then the psychological/spiritual tools that allowed, say, the Australian Aborigines or the Plains Indians to achieve a more or less satisfactory relationship with their environment should prove adequate for an industrial or postindustrial society.

In this spirit Meeker proposes the rejection of the tragic in favor of the picaresque hero. And similarly, Gary Snyder notes that landscape poetry is an invention of civilized peoples, implying that if we lived properly we could do without it; Paul Shepard idealizes the rituals of the hunt and rejects sacrifice (and along with it agriculture and history); and the trickster figure of myth gains popularity as an appealing alternative to such troubling figures as Job, Oedipus, Lear, and the crucified Christ.

What these observations and proposals have in common is what I referred to earlier as a kind of creationism—a belief that the world is, or ought to be, as we found it. Implicit here is a rejection of radical change, of an evolution that entails real loss and generates real novelty, greater difference, and deeper shame but at the same time opens up possibilities for deeper levels of communion. Going hand in hand with this is a diminished conception of ritual, which is seen as a way of dealing with the old, comfortable shame of the hunt or of coming of age, say, but not with the new shame of agriculture and genetic engineering. Sacrifice, tragedy, and pastoral art may indeed be absent in archaic societies: agricultural and urban culture invented them to deal with psychological crises associated with new technologies and new ways of life. But what these new modes of performance reveal is not the failure or decline of culture, but the power of the imagination to generate values such as beauty and community out of the deepening shame of creation. What is called for, then, is not a return to the old ways, but, as before, the invention of new ways of dealing productively with the new frontiers of shame opened up by the deeper alienation of science and the new technologies and economies it makes possible. The failure to do this can have catastrophic consequences. Consider, for example, the consequences we face as a result of having treated pesticides and antibiotics as mere tools, rather than having dealt with them sacramentally.

Initiation is the ritual process by which a community admits new members, provides instruction in the knowledge and ways of the community, engages initiates in the social contract, and provides passage across the psychological barriers between childhood and adulthood. Significantly, the process of coming of age and of joining the human community has often been problematic in America. In a study that picks up where Lewis's *American Adam* leaves off, the literary critic Ihab Hassan identifies a characteristic feature of the American sensibility as "radical innocence," which he defines as a neurosis of arrested development and "a regressive force that prevents the self from participating fully in the world," leaving the hero trapped between the backward-looking ideal of Eden and the forward-looking one of Utopia. The result is an unresolved view of one's place in the world that, Hassan argues, both puritanism and the transcendentalism of the Emersonians failed to resolve.[12]

Radical innocence finds expression in fables of initiation that more often that not fail, leading to victimhood and alienation. As a result, in American literature figures like Huckleberry Finn, Henry Fleming in Crane's *Red Badge of Courage,* Jay Gatsby in Fitzgerald's *Great Gatsby,* or the young characters in Sherwood Anderson's *Winesburg, Ohio,* who fail at integration of the self into some version of the human community, far outnumber characters like Hemingway's Nick Adams or Faulkner's Ike McCaslin, who more or less succeed.

Hassan's interpretation of literature is supported by the experience of the millions of young persons who, left to shift for themselves in this crucial matter, invent bizarre and often dangerous rituals of initiation for themselves. Considering our society's failure to provide means of initiating people into the human community, it is hardly surprising that it has failed at the task of providing means for initiation into the larger community that includes nonhuman species. Only recently have psychologists, teachers, guidance counselors, and scholars begun to take steps to remedy this situation by working with young people to invent coming-of-age and initiation rituals. These frequently involve experiences in the natural landscape, often modeled on the traditional vision quests of Native American peoples, and it seems likely that the work of restoration might easily be incorporated into efforts of this kind.[13]

In his book on reinventing rites of passage, Ronald Grimes offers a list of elements that appear in rituals of initiation in various cultures.[14] Perhaps not surprisingly, many of these—for example, instruction, ritual humiliation and displays of subservience, ordeal, the revision of values, and the assumption of new responsibilities—are a commonplace of initiation into any kind of community, as when a person enters a military unit or joins a profession or trade, a fraternal society or service club, a religious community, a gang, or any form of association that functions as a community in the tougher sense, as distinct from a neighborhood, say, a club, or even a society. What is striking here, if we think of restoration as a context for initiation into the land community, is the opportunities it offers for the kinds of experience Grimes and other anthropologists identify as common elements in rituals of initiation in traditional societies. Perhaps the most obvious of these is the self-abnegation, the setting aside of the will in deference to the interests of the group, that is implicit in the work of restoration. In traditional initiation rituals this is dramatized (and ritually effected, or realized) by acts of self-abasement imposed on the initiate. I see this as similar in a way to what the restorationist does by accepting the responsibility of copying—not imitating, but copying—the model system.

Also on Grimes's list are ordeals—demanding tasks, routines or vigils, often involving fasting and other kinds of deprivation, which, together with tattooing and ritual mutilation, dramatize the authority of the group over the individual. These in effect domesticate the initiate and also bring about physiological and psychological conditions conducive to the experience of *communitas,* and they do this in part by simulating what we might call necessity—the often demanding encounter with the basic facts and demands of life in a "state of nature." Since such experiences must originally have been what drove humans through the barrier of shame into community, it may well be that *communitas* itself is part of the hard-wired reward evolution has provided for this effort, as Fred Turner has suggested is the case for beauty.

Another key element of many initiation rites is acceptance of responsibility, and the recognition of the role humans play in the ordering of the world. Among the Walbiri of Australia, for example, children are taught to believe that the well-being of the community and the environment depends on spirits, and the initiation rites themselves include elaborate effects attributed to these spirits and designed to terrify the naive initiates. Their discovery, in the course of the ritual, that these effects are actually stage managed by the adults is a dramatic introduction to human responsibility for the ordering of the world. This is what Géza Róheim means when he writes that, for the Aborigines, "this is a man-made world."[15] It is, of course, precisely this kind of radical responsibility for the classic landscape that environmentalists have found so difficult to accept.

As Grimes points out, it is dangerous to generalize across cultures when discussing initiation practices; he notes that even the three-part pattern many scholars have used in interpreting ritual is a theoretical construct that fails to take into account the complexity and variety of initiation as it is actually practiced. He would be pleased with the work of Ed Collins and his colleagues at the McHenry County (Illinois) Conservation District. This group has systematically and self-consciously developed its large-scale prairie, wetland, and river restoration projects as contexts for initiation both into the group and into the landscape. In fact Ed has developed his own van Gennepian system of stages in this process — in this case seven, which he calls epiphany, struggle, annealing, transformation, recollection, triumph, and transmittal.

Some cultures, Grimes notes, do not initiate members at all, and some readers will object that in emphasizing the more harrowing aspects of initiation I am exaggerating the emotional difficulties involved in entry into community. These, they might say, reflect a high level of tension between the individual and the community, and it would be more appropriate to seek models of community in situations that reflect something closer to harmony. This, however, is a mistake. As I noted earlier, different cultures find different occasions for confronting shame, and if we are serious about the task of building community or achieving communion with the rest of nature, the place to look for ways to do this is not in situations where tension is absent, or where it has been dealt with so successfully as to have become more or less invisible, but in less harmonious situations where underlying tensions reveal themselves most clearly, either directly or in practices designed to resolve them.

In any event, the relevance of all this to restoration and its role in the task of building community and joining the land community is obvious. As my friend Walter Rosen has pointed out, restoration entails the loss of innocence, and it is for just this reason that its acceptance as *the* paradigm for the conservation of classic landscapes represents nothing less than the coming of age of environmentalism.[16]

Here, though, the question is whether community and adulthood provide plausible or even relevant models of relationship for a postindustrial society such as that of the modern (or postmodern) West. Adulthood may be obsolete in a society that worships youth, one in which, I sometimes feel, children no longer really aspire to grow up. Society in general provides few rites of passage of any kind, and those that adolescents create for themselves are commonly—and understandably—curiously inverted—expressions of defiance of adult authority rather than of submission to it.

Perhaps this is yet another threshold of radical change in the trajectory of cultural evolution suggested by the neoteny, or delayed development, characteristic of humans and also by the "juventocracy," the revolt of the young men against the authority of the old that Fred Turner suggests occurred at some point in the course of cultural evolution. If so, then the sooner we face up to this and start figuring out how to derive value from it, the better.[17]

Of all the performative traditions and genres, restoration is perhaps most obviously related to ancient institutions of world-renewal, or fixing the world. These reflect an awareness that the conceptual and psychological ordering of the world achieved by culture is always running down and requires periodic renewal by a deliberate human effort. Being directed at the soul, this effort is not literal but figurative, involving rituals that do not affect the landscape directly, but do renew the conceptual, psychological, and spiritual structures on which the health of the landscape quite literally depends.

Thus, in archaic and premodern tradition these rituals commonly involve a sacrifice that reenacts the violent act of creation, providing a passage through the shame of creation to communion with it.[18] Eliade notes that many American Indian groups commemorate a mythical deluge that, like the biblical flood, put an end to all human beings except a mythical ancestor. Similarly, the New Year rites of the ancient Babylonians included a reading of the account of creation and a reenactment of the combat between the god Marduk and the sea monster Tiamat, from whose torn body the god ultimately created the cosmos. And in Christian belief the sin of Adam and Eve is expiated and humanity is redeemed through the sacrificial killing of Christ, often identified with Adam. As is the case with any ritual, sacrifice can mean many things and can be read in many ways. Most pertinent here, however, is the idea suggested by Turner that in the art of sacrifice we reenact the primal murder and in doing so declare our solidarity in crime with the rest of nature.[19]

Looking at the act of restoration in light of these traditions, we can see striking parallels and resonances, suggesting the value of restoration as a context for confronting and dealing with the contradictions at the heart of creation. Like rituals of world renewal, restoration reenacts history. Like them, it also commonly begins with a killing—first, the killing and destruction of the ecosystem, an act of violence that implicates the restorationist in the very act of attempting to reverse it; and second, the killing associated with restoration itself, to clear exotic vegetation, for example, or eliminate or control populations of exotic animals. Not surprisingly, people often find this troubling. Public objections to such activities, especially when they involve killing animals such as deer or burros, often block restoration projects, and restorationists themselves often feel conflicting emotions about this phase of their work. This is no doubt why the use of fire as a tool for restoring ecological communities such as prairies and forests has often been controversial, fire being an archetypal emblem of destructive chaos.[20] Yet like the epic floods, murders, and battles of myth, fire can prepare the way for renewal—a resurrection of the kind symbolized by the phoenix or, for the Christian, by the pentecostal tongues of flame. There is a striking resonance here with classic modes of sacrifice, as Jerry Escher, a restorationist in Tacoma, Washington, remarks: like the innocent victim of traditional sacrifice, the weeds and exotic plants the restorationist kills die for our sins. This may be painful, but, we must remind ourselves, the victim must be innocent because what is involved here is not a punishment for sin, but an acknowledgment of existential shame.

Perhaps it is the restorationist's responsibility, then, to take advantage of this link with myth, to ritualize the process of restoration in order to turn it into an occasion for figurative and subjective—as well as literal and objective—world renewal. An example of how this might work is provided by a project carried out at the UW Arboretum several years ago by Barbara Westfall, an ecological artist from Mt. Horeb, a small town 15 miles west of Madison. Exploring the Arboretum's restoration projects for opportunities to create art that would draw attention to the prairies and their history, Westfall was attracted to a project being carried out to remove a grove of mature aspen trees that was encroaching on a patch of prairie adjacent to Curtis Prairie. The trees would be killed by girdling. To turn this more or less routine project into a work of art, Westfall directed her attention to the girdle itself, a ragged wound a foot or so wide, made by stripping a band of bark from the trunk, all the way around and several feet above the ground. Ordinarily this is done, and the tree is simply left to die. To draw attention to what was going on, however, Westfall painstakingly removed the dark surface of the bark on the yard or so of trunk between the girdle and the ground on more than two hundred trees, exposing the rust-orange layer beneath. This she treated with vegetable oil, deepening the color and enhancing its striking contrast with the smoother, greenish-gray bark above the wound. She then highlighted the ragged edges of the bark above and below this wound with black paint, rather, I thought, like mascara. This created a sharp contrast in color and texture with the bone-smooth white of the exposed wood.

In this way, Westfall used the classic technique of sacrificial ritual—not only performing the shameful act but intensifying the shame by highlighting it, drawing attention to it, and making it public. In doing so she turned what might have been a routine, clinical procedure into a sacrificial act and an occasion for the creation of beauty. The result was a population of dying trees standing among other, flourishing trees at the edge of the prairie—a contrast that became especially vivid and poignant at the time of leaf-out in the spring. Westfall, borrowing a phrase from the Arboretum crew, titled the project "Daylighting the Woods." Easily visible from a nearby trail, it was an affecting visual testimony to the discrimination and respectful death-dealing that are an integral part of the act of restoration.[21]

Westfall's project dealt with killing at the population level—a grove of trees—and represents a step beyond more traditional sacrifices, which typically deal with killing at the level of the individual organism. The next step would be to the level of the entire ecosystem or ecological community. This would entail, first, the consecration of the ecosystem, possibly by restoring it, and then, eventually, the destruction of at least part of it. This might involve a ceremonial plowing down, for example, in the case of a prairie, or a timber harvest in the case of a forest. On the prairies, this ceremonial cycle of consecration and destruction could coincide with the cycle of shifting agriculture suggested by Mike Miller and Julie Jastrow's studies of soil regeneration under prairie.

This cycle of ritual renewal offers a way to counter the problem Aldo Leonard described in an often-quoted sentence in "The Round River." "One of the penalties of an ecological education," Leopold wrote, "is that one lives alone in a world of wounds."[22] We can read this with an emphasis on "wounds" and aspire to a world without wounds, but this would be unrealistic, sentimental—even antiecological since the world as we know it is constructed in such a way that life depends on killing and death. A better reading is with the emphasis on "alone." Read this way, Leopold's formulation of this problem is beautifully apt: in the absence of ritual to transmute the violence and shame of killing into an occasion for communion, we do indeed live alone in a world of wounds. But our task is not to end killing or eliminate all wounds but, through ritual, to turn the act of killing from impure violence—mere casual or unreflexive killing in a clinical or matter-of-fact spirit—into the purifying violence that is a source of grace. As Turner points out, the word "blessing" actually derives from the Old English word *bletsian,* which means to consecrate with blood, to wound, or make bleed.[23] This is the wisdom implicit in the tradition of ritual sacrifice: the realization that communion is achieved in the act of eating, in which we encounter in an especially immediate and vivid way the inextricable link between life and death, and in doing so achieve a state of grace.

Some skeptics may still ask, what good does ritual actually do for the environment? Granting that restoration is worthwhile in a practical sense, how does ritualizing it or turning it into a work of art add to its value? What is the relationship between the literal act of restoration and the process of world renewal or redemption through ritual? Clearly, fussing over a girdled tree, scraping off its bark and dabbing paint on it, has no immediate ecological effect on the landscape. Similarly, the practices of the Hupa Indians, the Australian Aborigines, or the Babylonian priest—renewing the world through ritual reenactment of the creation—have no literal effect on the landscape. The results of such acts are entirely internal and subjective.

As materialists, we see more value in "real," literal work, such as restoration, in which the effects on the landscape are obvious. Indeed, we ignore or at least fastidiously exclude from official accounts of the work its other, inner results. From our modernist perspective this is a sensible move. What the Hupa or the Aborigines merely *pretend* to do, we *really* do—or so we like to think. But is this really the way it works? Of course not. As environmentalists frequently point out, the ecosystems we inhabit are not merely dependent upon us but are ecologically dominated by us, their quality and even their survival depending to a considerable extent on the contents of our hearts and minds. Thus to overlook the effects of the work on those involved in restoration, either as participants or as part of an audience, is to overlook what is, even in purely ecological and "practical" terms, quite simply its most important result.

The importance of the subjective results of restoration is clearly expressed in an account of a restoration project of sorts in the novel *Winter in the Blood,* by the Native American writer James Welch:

> The sugar beet factory up by Chinok had died seven years before. Everybody had thought the factory caused the river to be milky but the water never cleared. The white men from the fish department came in their green truck and stocked the river with pike. They were enthusiastic and dumped thousands of pike of all sizes into the river. But the river ignored the fish and the fish ignored the river; they refused even to die there. They simply vanished. The white men made tests; they stuck electric rods into the water; they scraped mud from the bottom; they even collected bugs from the fields next to the river; they dumped other kinds of fish in the river. Nothing worked. The fish disappeared.[24]

"The analytic science of Welch's fish department fails," the critic Chris Norden comments, "because its strategy for restoring the river consists in doing things *to* the river rather than doing things *with* the river. By excising the human participant from the ecosystem proper, Welch suggests, such analytical, nonritualized restoration may simply reinforce the fragmentation of ecosystems which instrumental (industrial) use has initiated. Restoration fails, Welch implies, so long as it is regarded and carried out merely as a form of technology. To succeed it must be carried out by members of a human community sustained by ritual."[25]

Perhaps Welch's account proves nothing, since fiction is just another form of make-believe. But we should recall here Victor Turner's suggestion that make-believe is a way of making *belief,* which is the key issue here. And the experience of restorationists makes it pretty clear that Welch is right. This really is the way the world works—not in an abstract or mystical sense, but in actual fact. The best restoration projects, those that result in the highest-quality ecosystems with the best chance of surviving over a long period of time, are those that are carried out by people who have had a chance to develop a close attachment to and an intimate understanding of the landscape through direct participation in the work. Best and most promising of all are those projects in which this work has been ritualized to some extent. The worst ones, the ones restorationists deplore, are projects carried out as mere technical procedures to meet regulatory requirements, excluding as irrelevant the subjective element, not to mention its expression and development through ritualization of the work.

Such projects *do* fail because they fail to achieve the reordering of ideas and values required to make the *restorationist* and other members of his or her community effective, knowledgeable, loyal, and responsible members of the biotic community. Crucially, what really has to be renewed is not the landscape at all, but the human community's *idea* of the landscape, on which the well-being of the landscape ultimately depends. These are not, we must remind ourselves, separate things. The link between them is nicely reflected in an uncertainty about the meaning of the word *Intichiuma,* which the Arunta people of Australia use to refer to their world-renewal rituals.[26] This word has been variously translated as meaning to put into good condition or to instruct, but the uncertainty of translation is surely misplaced. Clearly *Intichiuma* does both. It ensures the maintenance of the totemic species *by providing the instruction and means of transformation needed to bring the human community into communion with it.* In any event, the distinction between subject and object is a modern one. In the archaic mind, as in the virtual space created by ritual, the two realms are inseparable. The world *is* what we make of it through performative interaction with it, redeeming it from chaos into cosmos by rituals that renew our ability to order the world, make sense out of it, and experience beauty in it.

In the end, then, we are led to conclude that Welch is right. Ritual without restoration may work. But to undertake restoration projects without ritualization is to overlook and waste what is perhaps most valuable about them. Possibly the single most striking example of this, recently pointed out by California restorationist Freeman House, was the work of the Civilian Conservation Corps back in the 1930s.[27] The young men of the CCC planted billions of trees and carried out projects to control erosion and improve watersheds and habitats at thousands of sites throughout the nation. In many areas they did a vast amount of good, halting and reversing degradation of the landscape on a truly vast scale. Many of them learned something from the experience. Yet they were, by and large, nonresidents of project areas and therefore lacked a close association with the projects. And the work was not ritualized. As a result, it was easy, two or three decades later, for society to lose interest in the old CCC sites and to neglect or exploit them.

If, on the other hand, CCC enrollees had been recruited from local communities, and if the work had been ritualized, with project planners and crew supervisors calling in artists and ritualists, and taking their advice as seriously as that of the scientists and technical experts involved in the work, my guess is that the results would have been very different.

Pastoral, as described by literary critic Leo Marx in his classic study of the genre, is one of the several great artistic modes that arise from and provide ways of exploring the deepest tensions in human experience.[28] If tragedy is the exploration of the tension between what is and what ought to be, and comedy is the exploration of the tension between what is and what seems to be, then pastoral is the exploration of the tension between nature and culture. Pastoral explores this tension in the same way tragedy and comedy explore their themes, by moving the characters through the field of tension involved. In the American version of pastoral, this is accomplished through a combination of symbols and patterns of action that Marx refers to as the pastoral design.

This typically takes place in three "acts" or movements that, like the three-part structure of classical drama, correspond to the three phases scholars like Victor Turner use to interpret and describe the ritual process: separation, liminality, and reaggregation. In the first phase, separation, the protagonist, motivated by dissatisfaction with civilization, withdraws from civilized life, typically represented by a city, a factory, experience in battle, or the like, and seeks renewal through contact with nature in a more natural setting—what Marx calls a "middle landscape"—that combines elements of nature and civilization. There he ultimately achieves some kind of heightened experience, often including a moment of epiphany or a feeling of oneness with the world. This, however, is only the middle of the story, the second of the three "acts," and Marx outlines two quite different ways for the story to end. In the first, which he calls "sentimental" pastoral, the story concludes with an implied promise of redemption, in the sort of happily-ever-after ending we find in escapist art: good examples are the films *Mr. Blandings Builds His Dream House* and *Baby Boom*. This, however, is defective, incomplete pastoral. Like any sentimental art, it falsifies experience and is artistically dishonest, or at any rate superficial. In contrast, what Marx calls "complex" pastoral denies both protagonist and reader any such easy conclusion. Here, something—a reminder of death, or of civilization—breaks into the protagonist's epiphany, revealing the limitations of the pastoral retreat and motivating him or her to return to civilization, presumably with a deeper understanding of the ambiguous and troubling relationship between himself and the world.

A crucial feature of complex, as opposed to sentimental, pastoral is that complex pastoral confronts the irreducible tensions inherent in the relationship between nature and culture, or in relationship generally. As the "evasion" episode in *Huckleberry Finn* suggests, this can be done only in the domain of make-believe and performance. The resolution, in other words, is not literal (like the resolution of *Baby Boom* in which J. C. Wyatt, the "Tiger Lady" of the early scenes in Manhattan, winds up having it all: baby, husband, cottage in rural Vermont *and* the directorship of a multimillion-dollar corporation) but figurative, offering what Marx calls a "virtual resolution." Being, like tragedy or comedy, a major artistic mode, pastoral is ubiquitous. It is a major element in the work of canonic writers such as Herman Melville, Emily Dickinson, Willa Cather, Sara Orne Jewett, Robert Frost, Ernest Hemingway, John Steinbeck, William Faulkner, F. Scott Fitzgerald, and Mark Twain. It is a common element in advertising and in popular art forms such as the western, crime, and adventure genres, and even in sports. Michael Gershman and Scott Schiamberg, both students of Leo Marx, have noted that baseball incorporates elements typical of pastoral art, such as the suspension of time and the choice of a pastoral landscape, the "ballpark," as the setting for the action.[29]

As in the case of traditional rituals of initiation and world renewal, there are striking parallels between pastoral art and the act of ecological restoration. For one thing, the basic movement or "plot" is the same: like the pastoral figure, the restorationist is motivated by disaffection or disappointment with civilization and attempts to resolve it through a return to nature. For another, both take place at least partly in a landscape that combines elements of nature and culture—Marx's "middle landscape"—creating the field of tension between nature and culture in which the pastoral experiment is carried out. In traditional pastoral art this landscape is usually defined geographically, being located, like Thoreau's Walden Pond or Twain's Mississippi River, in some sense on the boundary between city and wild nature. The restored landscape also provides a middle ground, even if it is only a patch of green in an urban park that is betwixt and between, both in the sense that it represents "nature" physically juxtaposed with "culture" and in the sense that it is partly natural, partly artificial.

Viewed as a performance, then, restoration is a new way of carrying out the pastoral experiment, and for this reason the restorationist has much to learn from pastoral art, and also much to offer it.

One limitation of American pastoral literature is the action on which it commonly relies as the way of conducting the pastoral experiment—that three-part action of withdrawal, immersion, and return that Marx describes as the pastoral design. Both restoration and traditional artistic pastoral follow this basic pattern of action, but they do so in very different ways. While the protagonist in traditional literary pastoral withdraws from civilization by actually moving in space, leaving the city, for example, and seeking contact with nature in the country, the restorationist remains in place and, rather than leave the city for the country, attempts to remove the city or other marks of civilization from the landscape in order to reconstitute country or "nature" in place. In other words, instead of exploring the field of tension between nature and culture by moving in *space,* the restorationist explores it by moving in *time,* and this has important implications for the outcome—that is to say, for the meaning of the performance.

As I noted earlier in discussing John Muir, it is a mistake to take the search for the garden too literally. American history, for example, may be seen as a literal pastoral, a withdrawal from Old-World civilization and a search for a new and unspoiled world outside history. Columbus, skirting the coast of Venezuela during his third voyage to the Americas in 1498, recorded in his journal, apparently in all seriousness, that he believed he was approaching Eden.[30] The early explorers sought a fountain of youth and often assumed that the native people they encountered were living in a state of prelapsarian innocence.

The tragedy inherent in this, over and above the yearning after innocence it reflects, lies in the mistaken belief that Eden is a place to be found or rediscovered rather than a relationship to be achieved. This misconception has led to much fruitless searching, from Columbus's time down to our own, where it is evident in such futile—and environmentally destructive—practices as the construction of homes and vacation retreats in rural and remote wilderness areas. The restorationist, in contrast, is a pastoral figure who has taken what those in religious life call a vow of stability. Rather than withdraw from the city, abandoning it even temporarily, he attempts to redeem it by bringing the grace of nature back into it. This is harder than taking a vacation in the country or moving to the suburbs, but it is also, as restorationists are learning, deeply rewarding. And it opens up the possibility of actually residing in and reinhabiting the middle landscape rather than merely visiting it.

Another limitation of traditional American pastoral, expressed as much in ritualized activities as in formal works of art, is that its plot commonly hinges on actions that intrude on or consume the natural landscape. The obvious examples are overtly consumptive or intrusive pastoral activities such as hunting, fishing, motorboating, driving off-road vehicles, or moving to the country. But even activities such as hiking and birding, which usually involve a commitment to minimize "impact" on the landscape, are essentially consumptive. They take from the natural landscape, altering it (even if only in subtle ways), and they give nothing back. The restorationist, in contrast, does give back to nature by making a place more natural *both* in the conventional sense that it becomes more like its "natural" counterpart *and* in the sense that through the process of restoration the landscape becomes more fully realized, more aware of itself. In this way it provides a basis for a reciprocal relationship with nature, while at the same time allowing us to fulfill our obligations as a uniquely self-conscious species.

Yet another limitation of American pastoral art is its individualism, which reflects the radical spiritual individualism of puritanism, reinforced by the experiences of immigration and settlement on the frontier. The New England Puritans themselves were plagued by a separatist tendency and, as Marx points out, a logical outcome of Puritan separatism is the congregation of one, exemplified by the solitary figure of Thoreau sitting on his pumpkin at Walden Pond. He notes that the protagonists of our pastoral adventures and fables are commonly solitary figures, lonely, disaffected, or rebellious, Huck Finn being only one of the more conspicuous examples.

The reason for this is not simply a willful individualism, but rather the failure of culture to provide adequate means of connecting with the natural landscape in a social or communal manner. Other, less individualistic cultures characteristically place more emphasis on the individual as a member of a community, taking it for granted that both an individual's identity and his or her relationships to a considerable extent depend on the community and its institutions. As Chris Norden points out, in Native American cultures, even an apparently individual experience such as the vision quest, which entails personal isolation, sometimes for extended periods, is communal in orientation. It is a rite of initiation into community. It takes place through a ritual, which is itself a social institution, and its purpose is not withdrawal or escape but actually socialization. In the end the individual "resurfaces," as Chris Norden says, into the community to take his or her place in it. Other traditions offer examples of pastoral that involve a group rather than a purely solitary activity— think, for example, of *Robin Hood,* or of Shakespeare's pastoral plays, *As You Like It* and *A Midsummer Night's Dream.* All of these are pastorals, but they are *communal* pastorals, in which the characters, having withdrawn from civilization as a group, eventually return to it in the same way.

Modern pastoral, in contrast, offers few examples of pastoral retreats that either involve or achieve community.[31] It reflects the assumptions of a culture that encourages us to think of our relationship with nature—like the Puritan's relationship with God—as essentially a personal, even private affair. Left more or less to his own devices, the American is compelled to undertake the pastoral experiment alone, improvising as he goes along. And even if he is successful in carrying the project through to some kind of communion with nature, American society offers no way back in, no institutions or congenial, biologically enfranchised sensibilities within the culture that the successful initiate can connect with upon emerging from the transforming experience of the pastoral rite. As a result, the reciprocal movement of the ritual, first out, and then back in, is not completed, and the experience is one of outward movement only, a centrifugal movement away from community that results not in community but in separation, and ultimately in alienation. In this context, Marx suggests, the "inspiriting vision of a humane community" implicit in the pastoral experiment "has been reduced to a token of individual survival." And, he continues, "the outcome of *Walden, Moby Dick,* and *Huckleberry Finn* is repeated in the typical modern version of the fable; in the end the American hero is either dead or totally alienated from society, alone and powerless. . . . And if, at the same time, he pays a tribute to the image of a green landscape, it is likely to be ironic and bitter."[32]

The limitations of this sensibility for environmentalism are obvious. Human beings are a social species. For such a species, the relationship with nature is not a personal matter but is necessarily mediated by the community. The solitary individual, King Lear's "unaccommodated man," is an ecological and spiritual nonentity, as helpless and as ecologically irrelevant as a solitary honeybee, cut off not only from the human community, but from the larger community of other animals and plants as well. In the end, as important as personal and even solitary experience may be in the process of creating a relationship, the relationship between humans and the rest of nature is essentially a relationship between *communities.* To borrow a phrase from the legal profession, it is not the individual but the community that has standing with nature. This being the case, it is clear that the fate of the natural landscape depends not only on individual people, but on the coherence and vitality of the communities to which they belong and the means they develop for negotiating their relationship with the biotic community.[33]

One advantage of restoration as a way of conducting the pastoral experiment is that the work of restoration lends itself to community and group effort. It is not that restoration cannot be carried out by individuals working alone. Often it has been, especially in the early stages of its development, when it was a new idea that appealed to mavericks and loners such as Henry Greene at the UW Arboretum or, more recently, Dan Janzen in Costa Rica, or Bob Betz in Illinois. At the same time, restoration is *conducive* to group effort because of the variety of skills and interests it engages, and because it is by nature a constructive rather than consumptive (and therefore ultimately exclusive) activity—an environmentally oriented version of a barn raising or a quilting bee. In fact, group effort is commonly needed to carry out high-quality restoration work on an environmentally significant scale. As a result, restoration projects tend to become community projects and even, as we have seen, occasions for festival. In this way restoration carries the participants, not away from the human community but back into it and, through it, back into the biotic community, correcting one of the fundamental weaknesses of modern environmentalism and pastoral art.

A fourth limitation of modern pastoral is the language in which it is expressed. The task of pastoral, so far as we are concerned, is the same as that of classic rituals of initiation and world renewal—to provide the symbolic context we require to explore and define our relationship with the rest of nature. Ritual, we have seen, can provide this, but it does so partly because it is carried out in the language of nature itself, the language of action, which not only addresses nature on its own terms but engages us in dialogue with it at the deepest levels of our own nature. The arts, as we know them, are close relatives of ritual. Indeed, Victor Turner saw them as the descendants of ritual, which emerged as the various elements of ritual—poetry, music, dance, and gesture—were detached from their original ritual context.[34] To the extent this is true, arts such as literature have the same aim as ritual: reconciliation through make-believe in a metaphoric space. But even though the arts may retain the same aims and sometimes even the same basic structure as ritual, they are not exactly ritual. One reason for this is that in varying degrees they replace the natural language of action with more abstract, conventional human language. To the extent that they do this, the arts make possible a higher level of reflexive awareness and so a fuller realization of nature itself. But they also make it more difficult for us to establish communion with less reflexive creatures, confining us to communication with other humans.

To avoid isolation from other creatures, we need to find ways to communicate across various thresholds of reflexivity. Marx notes that

Thoreau sought communion through language: "If he could only connect the right words to the right facts, he could then transmit feeling, hence ideas, beauty, meaning, and value across the gap between minds."[35] In this way, through language, Thoreau sought to make mere fact "flower in a truth," linking the facts of nature with the higher reflexivity of the human mind." To do this, Marx suggests, Thoreau creates in his writing a series of links that together make a chain joining the fact, the observer (Thoreau himself), and the reader. When successful, Thoreau was able "to maintain the evanescent feeling . . . that we are on the verge of a thrilling revelation. Yet given his respect for fact, he was forced to accept the achievement of form, the aesthetic unity he so desperately sought, as a surrogate for what the Puritans had called justification."

In other words, words can go only so far as tools in the work of transmuting fact into truth. For that, another link in the chain may be necessary: to the act that converts data into facts must be added the ritual through which facts are *act*-ually transmuted into truth, beauty, and meaning. A process such as restoration, then, when developed as a performance, or act in the dramatic sense, offers a way to engage nature on its own terms and provides the missing link in the chain Thoreau sought to create between nature, himself, and his reader. What it offers is a context in which to take what Max Oelschlaeger calls "a hermeneutic step backward," from abstract human language to the more concrete language of action and performance. This, of course, reverses the step Emerson took when, having stepped down from the lowest rung of Christian ritual practice, he turned to poetry, as the context for redemption.[36]

Understood and practiced in this way, as a performing art, restoration provides a way of overcoming yet a fifth weakness of modern pastoral—its failure to provide what Marx calls an adequate symbol of reconciliation or possibility. In literary pastoral it is typically the pastoral or Arcadian middle landscape, harmoniously combining elements of nature and culture, that is the basic symbol of reconciliation between them. This middle landscape plays a key role in the pastoral experiment, and Marx attributes the failure of American writers to design "satisfactory resolutions for their pastoral fables" to the fact that this symbol is inadequate to bridge the widening gap between civilization and the primitive landscape. "The resolutions of our pastoral fables are unsatisfactory," Marx writes, "because the old symbol of reconciliation is obsolete."[37]

What Marx means by this is that the old ideal of the middle landscape is no longer convincing because it has been stripped of its meaning by forces, often represented by the machine, that act on the landscape instrumentally rather than sacramentally. For example, Huck Finn's famous decision to "light out for the Territory" is undercut by the fact that what was Indian territory in his time is now, as Marx has said, Kansas City. Much of the American landscape, which Fitzgerald, in *The Great Gatsby,* figures as Nick Carroway's vision of the Long Island that "flowered once for Dutch sailors' eyes—a fresh, green breast of the new world"—has been reduced by the machine to a wasteland figured by the valley of ashes along the road from New York to West Egg, a truly desolate, manmade wilderness, and an ironic allusion to the green, Arcadian landscape of pastoral reconciliation.

Here, Marx argues, our pastoral art fails to provide even the virtual resolution that art can achieve. "To change the situation," he suggests, "we need new symbols of possibility." Ecological restoration is such a symbol. In addition to creating the middle landscape of the restored ecosystem, restoration is itself a kind of middle *action.* Mixing elements of nature and culture, it explores the relationship between the two. When the pastoral experiment is carried out in this way, its success no longer depends on the condition of the landscape at the outset but rather on the skill, understanding, sensitivity, energy, and imagination of the restorationist. Undertaken in this manner, the pastoral experiment need not fail when encountering the valley of ashes. If the pastoral ideal is figured, not by the middle landscape of a tamed Kansas or an ecologically degraded Long Island, but by the middle action of ecological restoration, then the valley of ashes is not so much the bitter end of the story as a challenge to action. In fact, almost 300 square miles of land around Sudbury, Ontario, virtually sterilized by a century of mining and smelting, and possibly the largest valley of ashes ever created, has in recent years become the scene of a restoration effort that is renewing the human community of the area even as it restores its devastated landscape.[38]

If restoration has much to offer the pastoral tradition, it also has much to learn from it. Pastoral art, like classic traditions of ritual world-renewal, reminds us that perfect harmony between nature and culture is neither "natural" nor attainable in purely literal terms. Like other relationships, this relationship entails problematic elements that reflect contradictions inherent in nature itself. These can be resolved only in performative, or make-believe, terms, in the liminal state achieved through ritual, in the realm of dream, where Campbell locates the origin of myth, or in the momentary stay against confusion that Frost identified as the aim of a certain kind of poem.[39] Such resolutions are always virtual, not literal resolutions, and though they can inform our sensibilities and affect our relationships in lasting ways, they take place in the psychological "time outside time" experienced in the liminal state, and they may be short-lived. In other words, the experiences of harmony and communion may be achieved only within certain limits, and the attempt to achieve literal harmony where only a virtual harmony is possible inevitably does violence to the real differences between creatures. The crucial distinction here is that between complex pastoral, which deals with the irreducible contradictions in our relationship with nature, and sentimental pastoral, which does not and therefore falsifies the relationship. If restoration is a form of pastoral, then it must be judged in the same terms: whether, read as a performance, it depicts the complexity and ambiguity of our place in nature, or whether it does not.

A second lesson the restorationist-as-performer has to learn from the pastoral tradition is that history is real, and that events have consequences that are both irreversible and morally significant. Just as ecosystems have ecological Humpty Dumpties that may preclude restoration in the literal dimension, there are also psychological or spiritual Humpty Dumpties that preclude a literal retrieval of past experience. This, indeed, is one of the lessons of restoration—that restoration in the moral as well as the literal sense is impossible, that what is done cannot be undone, as Macbeth says—and that to disregard this is to court catastrophe. This is well illustrated by the character of Jay Gatsby, as interpreted by Marx. Reading *The Great Gatsby* as a pastoral fable, Marx sees Gatsby as the pastoral protagonist, a "modern primitive" who denies history and takes it for granted that he can step out of circumstances and return to the past, the idyll of his early relationship with Daisy. When Nick objects, Marx writes, "observing that one cannot undo the past, Gatsby is incredulous. Of course he can. 'I'm going to fix everything,' he says, 'just the way it was before.'" Nick, in contrast, though "drawn to images of pastoral felicity," learns how destructive they are when cherished in place of the literal.[40] In the same way, we can undertake the work of ecological restoration sentimentally, in a naive attempt to return to the past. Or it can become a way to explore change and learn to discriminate between those changes we can reverse and ones we can only expiate or atone for through ritual.

Keeping these suggestive precedents and parallels in mind, how can we apply them to the work of restoration? Before considering this question I should reiterate that I understand ritual to be a process that is fundamentally inventive and nonprescriptive. Ritual, in other words, is not ultimately a prescription but a grammar and a vocabulary. It is not, in the last analysis, a way of imposing meaning, but a way of discovering and inventing it. It is, at the deepest level, a process of personal and social self-creation and self-transformation.

It is recourse to ritual in this creative sense that I am proposing here—certainly not, preposterously, a program of ritual invented by one group and imposed on another. What I am suggesting is simply this. Here is an interesting experience, one that obviously has a lot to do with our relationship with nature. Let's try it out in a reflexive way and see what happens—to the landscape, and to us. Beyond that, let's try ritualizing it, in an attempt to select, focus, and articulate the feelings, values, and meanings associated with this work. We will do this, of course, in the expectation that the meanings that do emerge, though they may pertain to universal themes such as shame and redemption, will nevertheless vary in important ways from community to community.

As I noted earlier, what I have in mind is not an ethic but a way of creating, criticizing, refining, and reforming an ethic by generating and exploring the values, ideas, and feelings on which an ethic is based. I am under no illusion that this will be easy. It seems to me an open question whether the classic route through shame to the higher values is available in a society where most have escaped what might be called ecological and social necessity and can afford to replace the shame-laden bonds of personal obligation with the more abstract linkages mediated by money, civic duty, and legal obligation, trading, as Huxley's World Controller put it, beauty for happiness.

As Catherine Pickstock argues in her analysis of the medieval Mass, the new, post–Vatican II Mass no longer accomplishes the work the old Mass did because it is basically a creation of scholars that inevitably lacks the performative elements that made this work possible. To be effective, she writes, a new liturgy "would either have to overthrow our anti-ritual modernity, or, that being impossible, devise a liturgy that refused to be enculturated in our modern habits of thought and speech."[41] That is a tall order, suggesting that, if ritual is as important in the creation of value as scholars like Pickstock, Rappaport, Lorenz, and the Turners suggest, it may be necessary either to find some other way to do this work or reconcile ourselves to the loss of the old values, as in fact many of us seem to have done.

The danger here is that, whatever we make of it, ritual will not go away. It is, after all, the most powerful way we have of defining ourselves and communicating with each other, and when we don't deliberately and self-consciously make our own rituals, others do it for us and we become its products rather than its creators. Hence the dangerous and destructive confusion in our society between a thing like an automobile, and the symbol attached to it—Mustang, Yukon, Expedition—deploying the powerful technologies of performance traditionally used to generate the sacred and other higher values to generate the "realness" of brand names and celebrity. This is what critic George Trow is referring to when he suggests that television is a ritual that only works for the priests.[42] This is, of course, the confusion out of which political elections and innumerable other decisions are now made, and it is a direct result of performative dysfunction in a society that misunderstands performance and has lost control of its rituals. Perhaps the great questions are whether the classic economy of value can exist at all in the presence of wealth, and, if so, how it might work in a society dominated by more abstract forms of association such as the nation state.

That said, and the difficulty of exploring the highest elevations of ritual experience acknowledged, there are good reasons to suppose that we can at least begin by exploring the foothills. There are also good reasons to suppose that this will be delightful work. And there are several reasons to suppose that the work of restoration will provide a promising place to begin.

One of these is the many ritual traditions and genres with which the work of restoration resonates. Another is the essentially conventional nature of the work and its relationship with popular activities such as gardening, hunting, and nature exploration. A third is the field of tension and ambiguity this work generates. This is something we will want to keep in mind as we set about the task of ritualizing restoration. As I pointed out earlier, one danger to be avoided here is sentimentality. We will, of course, devise rituals to celebrate the positive outcomes of the restoration effort—the return of a rich assemblage of native plants to an old pasture in Iowa, or the first pair of rare clapper rails that nests in a restored wetland in California. But the toughest and most useful rituals will be those that emerge from tensions and contradictions generated or thrown into relief by the restoration effort. These will be the moments when the restorationist most clearly confronts shame—in the making of the copy; in the knowledge that the copy is imperfect; in the complicity in destruction implicit in restoration; and in the manipulation and killing that restoration always entails. It is these aspects of restoration that are most likely to be controversial, but they also underlie those strong moments that are inherently expressive and dramatic and that serve as the starting points for ritualization. Besides this, controversy itself is a bene-

fit if it is seen as the social and political expression of the shame and ambiguity inherent in the work.

Of these strong moments, perhaps the most obvious, and also the
most important, are those that involve the discrimination, destruction,
and killing involved in restoration, both in the act of restoration and
within the larger cycle of our taking from and giving back to nature. This
being the case, it is not surprising that ritual emerges naturally out of the
work of brush clearing, for example, which is a major part of the work of
restoring many ecosystems. Thinking about the "negative moment" of
clearing tamarisk from natural areas in southern California, and the lessons it conveys to participants and audience alike, restorationist John
Rodman questions the combative language that sometimes accompanies
this work—the references to "tamarisk bashing," for example.[43] But he
also anticipates with some concern the unlikely, far-off time when all the
tamarisk is gone and some other way has to be found to achieve this vig-
orous, violent, caretaking relationship with the landscape. Similarly, we
have seen how the first self-conscious attempt to create a work of art out
of the restoration effort at the UW Arboretum began with the killing of
trees to open up space for prairie. With an artist's instinct, Barbara Westfall picked this moment of shame out of the Arboretum's round of activities and transformed it from a routine procedure into an occasion for the
making of beauty, meaning, and community.

Psychologically, the acts of discrimination and killing exemplified by
the removal of invasive species are, like the hunter's death-dealing or the
farmer's calculated killing, both problematic and promising. They paral-
lel the ancient practice of clearing the sacred groves in order to maintain
them, the clearing of land for settlement and agriculture, and the work we
naturally do to place our mark on the landscape, possess it, and in the crucial, performative sense make it real. Literary critic Richard Garber has
shown how Thoreau used the creation of a clearing in the forest as a central metaphor for the redemption of nature.[44] We are creatures of the
clearing—the great clearing in the forest represented by the African savanna, where we perhaps emerged as a species; but also the clearings we
make in the Arcadian and Edenic landscapes of myth and the pastoral or
middle landscape of art; and those we make in creating our own habitat.
The danger is that the act of clearing easily becomes exploitation. But restoration provides a way to redress this problem. By clearing the under-
brush, opening up the forest insofar as we can on behalf of the forest itself, we create the clearing and, at the same time, turn nature back into
itself, realizing and freeing it at the same time.

In entering the forest or savanna to restore it, the restorationist goes back to the beginning of religion, to the act by which we engage nature, roughly perhaps, even violently, but then step back to question the meaning of that engagement and make it an occasion for the creation of value. The same argument applies, at an even higher level of intensity, to the killing of animals such as deer, donkeys, mongooses, nutrias, carp, or rabbits to control exotic species or to compensate for the absence of a natural predator from an ecosystem. Here the restorationist encounters a classic experience of shame, that of the hunter, who is aware that his life depends on his deliberate destruction of his fellow creatures. Here again the instinctive response is to deny the shame, to carry out the killing discreetly. But this is true violence, like murder or rape, since it is unredeemed by a shared public ritual that would make it an occasion for the creation of transcendent value. This makes the whole potentially beautiful enterprise vulnerable to the criticism it commonly receives when word of the killing leaks out.

Though it took me a long time to realize this, the animal-rights activists and others who object to this behind-the-scenes killing on behalf of restoration have a valid point. On purely ecological grounds, they are wrong to insist that we must not kill, because of course we must kill in order to maintain health, whether our own or that of the ecosystems we inhabit, and to deny this is to cut ourselves off from genuine relationship. But they are right to insist that we must not kill in a merely clinical or "scientific" spirit, attempting to hide the experience from others. And they would be right to insist that we must not kill without creating rituals to redeem the act of killing from mere violence. Though I can't recall ever hearing the matter discussed in these terms, I wonder whether this is really what the critics are objecting to—not to killing but to killing outside the context of ritual. This is a serious issue ecologically as well as morally, since public outcry over what is often euphemistically referred to as the "control" of plant and animal populations often curbs restoration efforts. If restorationists systematically—and publicly—ritualize the killing that is a part of all restoration efforts, might resistance to such killing fade away, revealing the genuine caring and the sense of shame behind it?

Similarly, we may expect to find rituals and liturgies emerging from other points of tension and contradiction encountered in the process of restoration. The burning of vegetation, essential for the restoration of many fire-dependent ecosystems, is an obvious example. Dramatic and evocative, the burning of prairies here in the Midwest has become an informal seasonal ritual for many, and I foresee the time when it will become the basis for real festival and liturgy, part of the repertory of rituals by which a community defines itself, exploring and celebrating the terms of its relationship with the landscape it inhabits. It is true that burns are dependent on the weather and can't be scheduled, but that is just the point: one of the many lessons implicit in the burning of the prairies is that some events in nature are unpredictable. Restorationists acknowledge that fact and not only accommodate it but willingly defer to it. So, to snow days, when we close schools and offices because the weather forces us to, creating a holiday that has the special charm and magic of the unexpected, we can add unscheduled burn days, called by local burn supervisors, when schools and offices close to allow people to witness and participate in the restorative burning of prairies and woodlands.

While some may suppose that ritualization would introduce a mushy, "subjective," nonrigorous, or unserious element into the practice of restoration, this reflects a misunderstanding of both the rigor of artistic and performative thought and what Victor Turner called the seriousness of play. In fact, ritualization demands rigorous attention to meanings because it is the process of meaning making. As I have noted, we can think of an experiment as a performance, and this adds to the merely intellectual rigor of science the more comprehensive and in some ways more demanding rigor of the artist. This, however, does not imply a turning away from sound technique based on the best available theory.

In fact, the relationship with practice and effective technique is crucial. Ritual or performance should grow out of the work—or play—of restoration and should remain in an organic relationship with it. A weakness of much contemporary environmental ritual is that it is carried out in connection with events such as the equinoxes that have little to do with practice of any kind, with the way most of us actually live or with the shameful experiences at the center of our economic lives. Rituals of this kind have an unconvincing, adventitious quality—they can decorate life but hardly come to terms with its more problematic aspects. Restoration, because it involves a good deal of robust, and even violent action, provides endless opportunities for a tougher kind of ritualization. An excellent example of a ritual arising from the practice of restoration is the annual Bagpipes and Bonfires festival in Lake Forest, Illinois. This event has developed naturally out of the brush clearing that is a major element of the restoration effort. The ceremonial burning of brush piles that mark the festival's climax are an effective as well as an expressive core for other activities that have grown up around this work.[45]

Even when commuted to a gesture, the ritual act should still include or "contain" the original, literal act. I have burned a few stalks of dried prairie grass standing in a bowl of sand for audiences with good effect. The point is that the essential, problematic act remains at the center of the ritual, and performative elements, such as words, dance, and music should be used to enhance the expressive value of the act, rather than merely to decorate it or to evoke feeling. We should be wary of attempts to use ritual techniques to achieve *communitas* without a solid base in community, for the same reason that we should resist the separation of ritual elements such as alcohol, tobacco or peyote from their ritual context. Ritual, Roy Rappaport often emphasized, is not just about feeling good. As much as anything it is about entering into obligations, including obligations of the most problematic and psychologically challenging kind, and we should be wary of rituals that overlook this—that offer the sweet pang of endorphin release detached from the obligations of relationship.

It will be important to consider carefully the role of leadership in the creation of ritual. While it is true that we are by nature a ritual-making species and that good ritual grows out of experience, it does not follow from this that effective ritual happens spontaneously. Like any art form, ritual follows certain principles, and the creation of effective ritual demands special talents combined with an understanding of these principles, a grasp of technique, and knowledge of relevant performative traditions. These are valuable and highly developed skills, and will have to be respected and rewarded accordingly. While it is important that rituals and ritual repertories remain flexible and responsive to changes in the community and its circumstances, some formalization and even institutionalization of the ritual tradition is important in order to provide a degree of structure and coherence. Since ritual often deals with sensitive and deeply problematic matters such as identity, shame and relationship, it can be difficult, sometimes even dangerous work, demanding skill and informed judgment. Thus adepts specially trained in the conduct of ritual are among the first specialists and authorities in any society. The emphasis on the personal and experiential that is characteristic of a secular and intensely individualistic society should be balanced with respect for the role of the leader and adept.

The ritualization of restoration will involve both invention out of the experience of the community and borrowing from the experience and ritual traditions of others. Allusions to other ritual traditions can deepen and enrich a ritual by adding to or enhancing its meanings. At the same time borrowing must be done with care, not only out of respect for the ritual traditions and cultural property of others, but also in order to avoid performative irrelevance. Generally speaking, ritualization should involve at least as much invention as borrowing—here is an important outlet for the restorationist's creative abilities. Yet the search for resonance with existing genres and occasions for performance (quite apart from borrowing from them) will surely prove fruitful. In addition to the performance genres of festival and comedy, initiation, world renewal, and pastoral, the work of restoration offers interesting parallels with other genres and traditions, including rites of passage, of healing and of reconciliation. To these we may add genres such as pilgrimage, vision quest, rituals of the hunt, and various agricultural and seasonal rituals, all of which are related in various ways to the work of restoration. When possible, it will be advantageous to build on rituals and ritual traditions already existing in a community. Of the traditional seven Christian sacraments, all offer interesting parallels with restoration. If Christianity has tended to underemphasize the natural world in favor of the transcendent and otherworldly, perhaps what is called for is a kind of greening of the sacraments, or a spinning off of new ones, to allow us to explore our relationship with the rest of creation.

Similarly, the restorationist can find useful links between the work of restoration and traditional holidays and public celebrations. Thanksgiving, Easter, New Year, and Christmas, for example, all enact meanings that resonate in various ways with the work of restoration and that provide opportunities for integrating it into other parts of our culture, as do other more or less ritualized activities such as hunting and fishing, picnicking, athletics and sporting events, reenactments of various kinds, and of course traditional rituals of engagement with nature such as hiking, backpacking, birding, botanizing and the like, all of which have ritual as well as merely recreational or intellectual value.

While the ritualization of restoration will depend on contributions from the arts—and will provide many opportunities to put the arts and humanities to work—it will be important to keep in mind the modernist tendency for the arts to separate themselves, often quite deliberately and self-consciously from ordinary life, repudiating both the values and the idioms of expression of the marketplace or the cultural commons. After a century of this, the fine arts today are often meaningless, even alienating to the vast majority of people, who simply—and often rightly—feel left out by them.[46] Elements of ritual, whether invented by performance artists trained in the modernist tradition or borrowed from other cultures, often come across as flaky, incomprehensible, highbrow, or otherwise off-putting. Obviously, this must be avoided. The aim here is to use the universal language of performance to open lines of communication, not only among people, but between people and other species as well, and this cannot be done through an esoteric idiom. What we need is populist art in the best sense. Both classic and folk-art genres are relevant here, as well as popular art and culture, the best of Hollywood, and even of Madison Avenue and the fashion industry.

The audience is crucial. If a performance isn't working for them, then it isn't working. Ultimately, the audience should be large and culturally diverse. A special attempt should be made to appeal to the mainstream and the middle class, as well as to minority groups, and any tendency toward the artiness and in-your-face quality characteristic of much modern art should be resisted. The place to begin will not in general be with theater or the more intensive forms of ritual, but rather with the low-key rituals of protocol and etiquette involving the handling of tools and the manner of relating to plants, animals, and other people on a project site. It may also involve a self-conscious attempt to find the rhythm and other expressive or emotionally engaging elements in the work in order to develop it as a kind of dance. Recently several colleagues and I experimented in a modest way with this idea as we participated as volunteers in restoration work being carried out at North Park Village Nature Center in Chicago. We found that the natural division of tasks involved in brush clearing—cutting, hauling, and stacking—lent the work a certain rhythm, and that the work became both more efficient and more enjoyable when we found that rhythm and worked with it. We also found that both brush cutting and seed gathering involve two kinds of performative interaction—an essentially personal one between the restorationist and the plants, and a more social one between the people in the group. Since these to some extent interfere with each other, even as they complement and reinforce one another, we tried "articulating" them, rather as in monastic practice, by agreeing on brief intervals of silence. Reactions to this experiment were mixed. Some thought it was just a distraction, but my own sense was that it was effective and suggested a way to increase the psychological benefits of the work.

As restoration develops into a performing art, a tradition of criticism of this work will emerge, borrowing from other traditions of criticism and expressing the self-critical component Victor Turner believed was inherent in the ritual process. As in other art forms and in work generally, evaluation and criticism are crucial. Standards must emerge, a discerning audience, capable of applying them must be developed, and superior work must be recognized and rewarded.[47]

And of course, while restoration, like any work, should always be carried out in a spirit of respect and attentiveness to the emergence of meaning, it will not always be explicitly ritualized. Or perhaps it is better to say that it will be ritualized in varying degrees of intensity. An ordinary meal is not the Eucharist; yet no meal should be taken without some sense of the communion generated by the Eucharist. The same applies to the work of restoration, even in its profane or everyday forms. Just as not all areas will be restored to some historic condition, but all areas will benefit from those that are, not all restoration work will be carried out as ritual, but all such work will gain meaning, validity, and political standing from the work that is.

CHAPTER 8

Conservation and Community

Restoration, the Environment, and Environmentalism

Egoists that we are, we like to think that even our problems are unique, and this is as true in environmentalism as anywhere else. We live, we keep insisting, in a time of unprecedented danger with respect to the environment, and this may be true. And yet the problem of living in a sustainable relationship with the rest of nature, and of achieving a state of grace in our relationship with our fellow creatures, is as old as our species. The real problem for us, perhaps, is that in the last analysis this is not so much a problem as a mystery and, for this reason, has proved difficult for modernism to deal with.

If, as Fred Turner and James Hans have argued, shame is the pathway to beauty, and beauty itself is the master value—the "value of values," as Turner puts it—we may begin to understand why a value like community eludes us; why we can espouse values and recommend virtues but have so little ability to do anything about them; why we can celebrate difference and diversity and change only by draining them of their shame and so trivializing them; and why our various environmentalisms have so far failed to provide a plausible, much less compelling vision for the long-term conservation of classic landscapes and wilderness areas.

Restoration, I believe, provides a way around this impasse because it offers, as other environmental paradigms do not, a context for confronting and dealing productively with the shame of our encounter with nature as other—or given—at the level of the landscape, the ecological community, or the ecosystem. This paradigm may not be ideal—in fact, it is explicitly *not* ideal—but for this very reason it offers the best possible prospect for the conservation of the classic landscape. It rests on the following premises:

first, that what we call "nature" *is* creation, a process figured in the act of giving birth, as the metaphor of birth in the word "nature" itself suggests

second, that creation is not orderly but chaotic and violent, involving the radical violation of rules represented by the genetic mutation

third, that, though chaotic, creation tends generally toward an increase in self-awareness

fourth, that because, like birth, creation generates difference and therefore limits, it is an occasion for the experience of shame, shame being the emotion that arises from a reflexive awareness of limits

fifth, that the human experience of shame does not represent a discontinuity with nature, or a peculiarly fallen condition, but is rather a natural response, at the human level of reflexivity, to nature's own shameful limitation and makeshift, trial-and-error amateurishness

sixth, that the experience of transcendent values such as community and value depends on a reflexive awareness of shame, which we deal with productively only in the realm of the imagination supported by the psychological and spiritual technologies of symbol, myth, and ritual

seventh, that the effectiveness of environmentalism has been limited by its skepticism regarding these technologies of the imagination, which it shares with modernism generally, and by the limited repertory of stories, myths, and rituals it has provided for dealing with the shame inherent in the relationship between humans and the rest of nature

eighth, that restoration is important not only because it provides a way of interacting with the natural landscape in a positive way, but also because it provides a context for confronting this shame and for the invention of rituals for dealing with it productively

Action, Lewis Mumford once wrote, often precedes and anticipates ideas, and this has certainly been true of restoration. Restoration was invented in the early decades of the twentieth century and had been around for three-quarters of a century before anyone took it seriously or gave any serious thought to its value as a conservation strategy. Now that has begun to change. During the past decade and a half, environmental practitioners have discovered in rapid succession the environmental, ecological, educational, psychological, and social value of restoration. As they have done so they have established the foundation for a new environmentalism, one that combines elements of earlier schools of environmental thought and practice but will prove to be psychologically more coherent and therefore more effective than any of them.

This change is already under way, a revolution of sorts, but a soft one, since it depends more on the synthesis and integration than on the rejection of old ideas. This is what I foresee taking place during the next generation.

First, restoration will emerge as the dominant paradigm for the conservation of natural and historic landscapes, not replacing preservation but properly construing it as an objective, with restoration serving as both the means for reaching this objective and as the link between human cultures and the rest of nature, the middle landscape in which we negotiate the relationship between nature and culture. As this happens, we will learn to think of natural areas quite differently—not as "preserves" but as landscapes that exist in a dynamic, working—that is, ecological— relationship with human beings. And we will think not only of protecting them from harm, but of expanding and upgrading them and integrating them with economic activities such as agriculture, forestry, fishing, and new forms of tourism. This is already happening in programs such as Earthwatch and Sierra Club work outings, which are based on participation in restoration efforts. At the same time we will think of agricultural lands and other working landscapes as existing in dynamic relationship with classic landscapes such as forests and grasslands, modeling these artificial systems on classic systems, and in some cases even cycling between them, using prairies, for example, as an intercrop in rotation with corn and soybeans in a version of the slash-and-burn agriculture practiced by humans for millennia. As this happens sizeable areas—half of Maine, say, or a fifth of Iowa—may be returned to natural ecosystems, which will be given a new economic as well as a new esthetic, spiritual, and ecological value by their working relationship with the human economy.

Equally important, environmentalists will continue to explore the value of restoration in its human dimensions—the dimensions of process, experience, and performance. Restoration will emerge as a paradigm for learning about the natural landscape and for our relationship with it. It will also emerge as a new way of experiencing the classic landscape, one that integrates the experiences of the hiker and the birder with those of the hunter, the gardener, the caregiver, and the artist. In the process, it will become a rapidly growing form of outdoor recreation, the paradigmatic way of "using" the natural landscape without using it up. This, too, is already happening in programs such as the highly successful Adopt-a-Stream program and the volunteer stewardship and watershed management programs now taking shape in many areas.

More slowly perhaps, working their way past the barriers of skepticism and misunderstanding, the dangers of flakiness and sentimentality, and the outright alienation of many of the arts from most of their potential audience, restorationists will also begin to develop their craft as a performing art and the basis for the rituals needed to move ahead in the search for communion with the rest of nature.

This will begin simply—not with the creation of the high rituals of theater and church, but with the self-conscious development of low-key rites, the protocols, etiquette, ritualized division of labor, and small celebrations that emerge from the practice of restoration, as from any work reflexively undertaken, and that reflect the rhythms and patterns of the work and the interests, prerogatives, values, and insights of those who carry it out. With these in place, the most adventurous restorationists will advance to more ambitious forms of ritualization, based on the deep performative exploration of the experience of restoration, and on ways in which this experience resonates with other experiences such as gardening and hunting, and with performative traditions such as world renewal and initiation. As in any art, the best of these efforts will avoid sentimentality, refusing to celebrate the practice of restoration without identifying simultaneously with the destruction that both complements and accompanies it. Ultimately, restorationists will celebrate not merely the positive but the negative as well—not just the restoration but the plowing down of the prairie, the harvesting as well as the regrowth of the forest—the taking and giving back, tightly linked in a ritual cycle that leads through shame to community, meaning, and beauty.

As this happens, restoration will develop as a way of linking people with the natural landscape through institutions such as the archaic rituals of world renewal, the Jewish Rosh Hashanah and the Christian Eucharist as well as weddings and funerals and other rites of passage. Weddings, for example, will come to include restoration activities through which a couple accepts responsibility for the care of a piece of landscape and in turn acquires special privileges of access and use. Families will bury their dead in neighborhood restoration parks, a practice now being advocated by an organization called Memorial Ecosystems, in South Carolina.

So far as recreation is concerned, we will no longer see "nature" as free, simply "there" for the taking, but rather as something we have to earn, just as a culture earns its idea of nature, the set of ideas and values by which it makes sense out of the world, through the hard work of invention, discovery, and ritualization. Young people will earn this privilege through rites of initiation that draw on the experience of restoration and involve initiation first into the human and then into the larger biotic community. And out of these rituals will emerge the myths and stories of humans and nature in interaction needed to sustain our sense of place.

For most, the deep engagement of restoration will replace escapist, destructive, and ultimately elitist activities—the trip to the mountains, the house or vacation home in the country, the off-road vehicle—as the most popular way of carrying out the pastoral experiment. Giving up, for most purposes, the consumptive use of pristine nature, the "crown jewels" of remote wilderness preserves, millions will participate in restoration, an environmental practice that everyone can carry out almost anywhere and that, because it benefits the natural landscape rather than detracting from it, provides opportunities for limitless participation. As this happens, problems of overuse of natural areas will decline as a new, constructive way of "using" the natural landscape becomes commonplace and the thousands who now vacation in remote wilderness areas or commute to rural homes and vacation retreats, consuming the natural landscape, will stay at home to participate in neighborhood restoration projects.

Restoration will become, in short, a popular outdoor sport and model for the public use of natural landscapes. Millions will participate—the more the better—and those who don't will come to feel that they are represented by those who do, establishing a new, positive, and hopeful model for the relationship between our species and the rest of nature. This will be especially valuable for those who move frequently, or whose work isolates them from daily contact with nature. In a recent article about the new "business class," writer Pico Iyer described an emerging culture of international entrepreneurs who live out of hotels in commercial capitals around the world, and who have little or no economic connection to any particular place. Iyer notes that he deals with his own sense of unrootedness and alienation by retreating to a monastery several times a year.[1] In the future we will learn to use restoration in this way, restoration programs in a person's "home" city providing not only a retreat but a measure of connectedness and environmental homemaking in the place where one is, perhaps, most likely to retire.

Wilderness areas will still exist. In fact, they will expand in size and improve in quality as the constituency for conservation grows and as people find that, for most purposes, they can experience nature more richly by participating in restoration projects near their homes than through occasional visits to remote, "pristine" areas. In this way, relieved of pressure to provide millions with the experience of nature, such areas will come to serve their highest and best human use, as places for special activities such as vision-quest, filmmaking, research, and of course the ongoing process of restoration. This may not only relieve but in many cases may actually solve the problem of overuse of natural areas that has been a dilemma for conservationists since the time of John Muir.[2]

At the same time wilderness will be different. Though it may include vast tracts, remote from cities and relatively free of their influence, such areas will never again be understood as an ontological frontier, radically other or separate from humans—like the California, depleted of Indians, that John Muir misunderstood as a paradise that had escaped human influence. They may not be gardens exactly, but they will be understood to be part of the global habitat, inhabited by all species, including humans, and subject to their influence, however subtle or indirect it may be. In the case of areas chosen to serve as "natural" areas, representing historic or classic landscapes, these will be the outcome of restoration efforts of a sort that, though often low-key, will nevertheless be discussed and celebrated as providing the ecological basis for our relationship with them— the shameful and beautiful enactment of mutual dependence.

Out of all this will emerge a constituency for the natural landscape that is thicker, broader, and tougher than the constituency built on preservationism and the rituals of limited engagement it provides. While environmentalists once worried that the promise of restoration would weaken arguments for the protection of "original" historic landscapes, the opposite will prove to be the case. That concern reflected the tendency to see the landscape as an environment, and to think about restoration and to evaluate restoration projects in the single dimension of the "product" or "object" of the restoration effort. This narrow view actually objectified the landscape, providing little opportunity for most to participate in its ecology or to take responsibility for its well-being. Seen whole, in all the dimensions of value, restoration will change that, extending to millions the opportunity to engage classic landscapes and the plants and animals that inhabit them as subjects, deepening their relationship with them, both increasing and toughening the constituency for their conservation beyond the imagination of a preservation-oriented environmentalism. The old environmentalism that insisted that classic landscapes were "irreplaceable" and could only be degraded ecologically and compromised in value by humans effectively precluded taking responsibility for them. As that alienated and exclusive sensibility yields to one that engages nature, accepting the shame of engagement, of imperfection, and of mutual dependence, the result will be the environmental equivalent of being given a chance to tend the garden or feed the baby — a new environmentalism, capable of creating a culture of restorationists who will fight hard to protect landscapes, whether restored or "preserved," that they feel connected with through the experience of restoration.[3]

This will profoundly influence the political balance between nature and culture, between the classic landscape and the settled or working landscape, placing us in a position to achieve goals that would otherwise be totally unrealistic in a democratic society. In recent years, for example, an organization called Wild Earth has developed a plan called the Wildlands Project that calls for setting aside vast areas — over a third of Florida, for example — essentially as wilderness and developing a system of corridors connecting existing preserves, making them, in effect, ecologically larger.[4] Such goals reflect extensive research and carefully thought out ideas about the ecology and design of preserves. But we stand little chance of achieving them through the various environmentalisms of the past, with their psychological and political limitations. They become far more plausible in the context of an environmentalism capable of creating rich links between humans and natural landscapes through activities such as restoration.

There will be philosophical consequences as well. Lately, environmentalists and environmental philosophers have been arguing about the implications of the observation that ideas such as "wilderness" and "natural" and even "nature" are "merely" a social "construct."[5] Some have been concerned that if people come to understand these ideas in this way, the result will be a diminished respect for the values they represent. But what this reflects is our loss of the sacramental sense that *all* value is constructed and is constructed most reliably and robustly through performance and the arts. Of *course* "wilderness" is a construct. So is the Eucharist, for the Christian the most real and valuable thing there is. And "wilderness" may acquire this kind of value too, in the context of a ritual-based environmentalism that has a firm grasp on the techniques of value creation. Restoration will play a key role here. Indeed, it is curious that, despite all the debate over the "construct" issue, few have noticed the relevance of the process of actually constructing pieces of nature as a context for constructing our idea of nature and giving it value.[6]

Solidly positioned in this way, equipped with a robust, shame-embracing practice for the construction of the real and the negotiation of relationships, and rejecting what Mircea Eliade called "nostalgia for Paradise," environmentalism will be in a position to contribute to the formation of beautiful relationships not only between humans and the rest of nature, but among humans as well, helping generate community and beauty out of the "new and sharper paradoxes, new tensions, and more painful disharmonies—the 'more intense demonism'" that Paul Tillich saw as an inevitable component of "New Being."[7]

Most important, as restorationists learn to derive full value from their work as a way of upgrading landscapes, learning, achieving intimacy, and creating community and other transcendent values, restoration will gradually become not merely a practice and a strategy, but a positive, self-sustaining force for environmental renewal. By this I mean that people will seek out restoration projects, participating in them and supporting them for the same reason people have always sought out and supported activities and institutions, from organized religions to the arts to professional sports, that offer them access to the values that give life its meaning and higher purpose. I foresee the formation of local and regional groups—or congregations—of people who will pay to support the leadership they need to carry out restoration work and to derive the greatest possible value from it. In this way, given a basis for a rich, shame-embracing engagement with nature that appeals neither to ethics nor to altruism alone but to the highest kind of self-interest, we may begin to approach the work of the reinhabitation of nature and the preservation of the world with a measure of optimism.

At the beginning of this book I quoted Loren Eiseley's evocation of a "third world" within which the needs of nature and those of humans might somehow be reconciled. Poignantly, Eiseley found his metaphor for this imagined world in the past, in the sunflower forest of his boyhood experience. Yet, as an anthropologist, Eiseley knew better than most that the answer to the problem of inhabitation is not to be found in an imagined "pristine" nature. Thus his sunflower forest, like Thoreau's Walden Pond, was not a natural area but a partly artificial one, existing not in a remote wilderness but in a neglected area on the edge of town.

Like Walden Pond and the woods around it, Eiseley's sunflower forest represents nature first compromised and then redeemed by the human imagination.

Like Thoreau, Eiseley had his own rituals for achieving this redemption. But, like Thoreau's, Eiseley's rituals were personal, not social or communal. What we need at this juncture is something more democratic, even more popular. What we need is a new *Intichiuma,* a way of linking the interests of the natural landscape with the interests and ambitions of human beings who are, as the Aborigines realize and express in their myths and rituals, responsible for its beauty and well-being. Any attempt to resolve environmental problems in the other way, by placing nature and culture in opposition, or by demoting human culture to mere equality with the rest of nature, denying its shameful transcendence over it, will inevitably fail. But I believe that if we accept this transcendence and the responsibility it entails and make the carrying out of this responsibility an occasion for confronting shame, for learning, and for celebration, we stand a fair chance of succeeding. This, surely, is the great lesson restorationists have learned on the prairies and oak savannas of the Midwest, where an entire ecosystem that had been virtually destroyed is now reviving in the hands of restorationists.

The great value of restoration is that it provides a basis for this new *Intichiuma,* with its double benefit of environmental healing and deepened understanding and caring. The importance of this struck me a number of years ago during a conversation after a talk Fred Turner gave in Madison. The talk had included readings from Fred's epic science-fiction poem *Genesis,* an account of the colonization and terraforming of Mars in the twenty-first century.[8] Some in the audience worried about the environmental implications of this vision, and during the discussion afterward someone asked whether the idea of creating a new, habitable biosphere on Mars wasn't merely a way of distracting ourselves from more immediate environmental and social problems here on earth. In response, Fred pointed out that in his poem it didn't work out that way. The ecosystem-makers in *Genesis* depended on existing ecosystems on earth both as models and inspiration and as sources of genetic material for their project. Indeed, the heroic enterprise of bringing life to a dead planet motivated deeper study of earthly ecosystems and greater caring for them. In other words, it was by taking on the task of creation that the heroes of the poem came to care about creation itself.

Of course, like James Welch's novel, Turner's *Genesis* is "just" a story, and doesn't exactly prove anything. Yet as I listened to this conversation

I realized that what Fred envisioned in his poem about the colonization of Mars was exactly what had actually happened at the UW Arboretum. There, an attempt to create a collection of historic ecosystems, undertaken with relatively little understanding of them, has led to a whole succession of insights into their ecology and their history. Indeed, it was this work that in part motivated John Curtis's pioneering study of the vegetation of Wisconsin, which led to a body of knowledge that not only in a sense "contains" the historic landscapes of Wisconsin but, as I noted earlier, is the key to their future as well. As in Fred's poem, it was the effort to recreate the system, motivated by the human traits of curiosity, esthetic sense, need for community, and even personal and professional ambition that drove the work, providing both its organizing principle and its ethical justification. The result was not only a new prairie but a deeper understanding of the prairie, and a greater caring for it. In the end it will be experiences like this that will lead to the cultural discovery—and so to the survival—of the classic landscape.

Notes

1. Weeding Key Biscayne

1. Dave Egan, "Historic Initiatives in Ecological Restoration," *Restoration & Management Notes* 8, no. 2 (1990): 83–90. At this point, no comprehensive history of restoration has been written, though several historians have undertaken initiatives in this area. See, for example, two studies by Marcus H. Hall: "American Nature, Italian Culture: Restoring the Land in Two Continents" (Ph.D. diss., University of Wisconsin-Madison, 1999); and "Co-workers with Nature: The Deeper Roots of Restoration," *Restoration & Management Notes* 15, no. 2 (1997): 173–78; and two by Tamara L. Whited: "The Struggle for the Forest in the French Alps and Pyrenees, 1860–1940" (Ph.D. diss., University of California, Berkeley, 1994); and "Restoration in 19th-Century France," *Restoration & Management Notes* 14, no. 1 (1996): 53–56.

2. Though this assertion would have been controversial a decade or so ago, most ecologists and environmental managers now agree on the need for some form of management to compensate for novel or "outside" (usually human) influences on "preserved" landscapes.

3. A noteworthy exception was the development of a program specializing in restoration in the UW's Department of Landscape Architecture under the leadership of Darrel Morrison. During the late 1970s he did pioneering work on the use of native plants in designed landscapes and on the use of prairie plants in reclamation efforts at mine sites in central Wisconsin. While there was a long history of land reclamation prior to this, it was the first attempt I had encountered to apply "the Arboretum idea"—the re-creation of an ecological community modeled on a "natural" or historic community—to such a project, and it made a strong impression on me.

4. For recent discussions of the problem of coming up with a satisfactory definition of the word "restoration," see Eric Higgs, "What Is Good Ecological Res-

toration?" *Conservation Biology* 11, no. 2 (1997): 338–48. See also Anthony D. Bradshaw, "What Do We Mean by Restoration?" in K. M. Urbauska, Nigel R. Webb, and Peter J. Edwards, *Restoration Ecology and Sustainable Development* (Cambridge: Cambridge University Press, 1997), 8–16; and Joan G. Ehrenfeld, "Defining the Limits of Restoration: The Need for Realistic Goals," *Restoration Ecology* 8, no. 1 (2000): 2–9. The Society for Ecological Restoration's current definition may be found on its website at www.ser.org.

5. *The American Heritage Dictionary of the English Language* (Boston: Houghton Mifflin, 1992), s.v. "restore." As the phrases themselves indicate, "ecological restoration" and "restoration ecology" are not the same thing, and it is a mistake to use these terms interchangeably. One is a kind of restoration, the other a technique for scientific research. When I coined the second term, "restoration ecology," sometime in the late 1970s, I initially used the phrase "synthetic ecology" but shifted to the softer—and, I later realized—less decisive term in response to complaints that the adjective mixed a "negative" (synthetic) with a "positive" (ecology). Common usage still blurs its meaning, one result being use of the ambiguous term "adaptive management" to refer to the idea Keith Wendt and I tried to identify and label. I believe the time has come to go back to "synthetic ecology" and I plan to do so in an upcoming book.

6. There are exceptions—at historic sites, for example, where an attempt may be made to restore and maintain specific features of the landscape such as the peach orchard at Gettysburg or the historic vegetation at Abraham Lincoln's boyhood farm in Kentucky. Though most restorationists regard "postcard" projects of this kind as incidental or irrelevant to the practice of *ecological* restoration, they are nevertheless restoration projects in the sense I am using the term here and worth noting because they represent the principle of faithfulness to the model in an extreme and especially clear way. Their weakness is that they downplay the dynamic features of the system being restored.

7. Practitioners often define objectives for restoration projects in terms of what they call "the historical range of variation," meaning the ways in which an ecosystem might change "naturally" over a given period of time. In this view, a restorationist might aim to guide a system back to a previous condition during a certain historic period and then allow it to move around freely within the boundaries defined by that period. Deciding on and defining those boundaries is one of the restorationist's first tasks. For a discussion of this idea see P. Morgan, G. H. Aplet, J. B. Haufler, H. C. Humphries, and W. D. Wilson, "Historical Range of Variability: A Useful Tool for Evaluating Ecosystem Change," *Journal of Sustainable Forestry* 2 (1994): 87–111. Also see Joan G. Ehrenfeld, "Defining the Limits of Restoration: The Need for Realistic Goals," *Restoration Ecology* 8, no. 1 (2000): 2–9.

8. William R. Jordan III, "Appelplatz," *Restoration & Management Notes* 12, no. 2 (1994): 115.

9. While consistent with the dictionary definition of the word "restoration," this point ignores the word's positive connotation, suggesting a return to a better or more desirable condition. Unfortunately, I know of no English word for the deliberate return of a living system to a former condition, understood dynamically and in a value-neutral way.

10. For an exchange on this point, see J. Aronson, Richard Hobbs, E. Le Floc'h, and David Tongway, "Is 'Ecological Restoration' a Journal for North American Readers Only?," and "William R. Jordan III replies," both in *Ecological Restoration* 18, no. 3 (2000): 146–49.

11. The classic argument for the clear use of language and the dangers of euphemism and related linguistic vices is George Orwell's "Politics and the English Language" (in *A Collection of Essays* [New York: Doubleday Anchor Books, 1954], 175), where Orwell insists that "What is above all needed is to let the meaning choose the word and not the other way about." In a lighter vein, consider the following remark on naming plants: "Settlers became so fond of pumpkins that when they migrated to a place where their traditional pumpkins wouldn't grow, they adopted the nearest native squash and called it a pumpkin"(Gail Damerow, *The Perfect Pumpkin: Growing, Cooking and Carving* [North Adams, Mass.: Storey Communications, 1997], 5). Such easy relativism is bad news, of course, for anything like a pumpkin or an ecosystem that depends on an accurate label to survive.

12. Daniel Janzen, "Tropical Ecological and Biocultural Restoration," *Science* 239 (January 1988): 243–44; Narayan Desai, "A Community-based Restoration/Education Program in India," *Ecological Restoration* 17, no. 3 (1999): 133.

13. The reasons for the exemplary character of the best work on the prairies are interesting. For one thing, the prairies, nearly wiped from the landscape in the eastern, "cornbelt" part of the Midwest by the end of the nineteenth century, were obvious candidates for restoration. For another, though the prairies are not necessarily easy to restore, most of the plants they harbor reach maturity quickly and are amenable to traditional horticultural and agronomic techniques. And, since prairies never had legal protection, as for example, wetlands now have, attempts to restore them usually reflect interest in the prairie itself, uncompromised by financial concerns or regulatory requirements. As a result, classic projects like Greene Prairie or the Morton Arboretum prairie have been amateur projects in the best sense, as many restoration projects are today, not only on the prairies but in other kinds of ecosystems as well. For a discussion of these ideas see my foreword to *The Tallgrass Restoration Handbook: For Prairies, Savannas and Woodlands,* ed. Stephen Packard and Cornelia F. Mutel (Washington, D.C.: Island Press, 1997), xiii–xviii.

2. The Challenge of Reinhabitation

1. For compilations of Leopold's most widely read writings, see Aldo Leopold, *A Sand County Almanac, with Essays on Conservation from Round River* (New York: Ballantine, 1966); and Curt Meine and Richard L. Knight, *The Essential Aldo Leopold: Quotations and Commentaries* (Madison: University of Wisconsin Press, 1999). Standard works on Leopold include Susan Flader, *Thinking Like a Mountain: Aldo Leopold and the Evolution of an Ecological Attitude toward Deer, Wolves and Forests* (Columbia: University of Missouri Press, 1974); Curt Meine, *Aldo Leopold: His Life and Work* (Madison: University of Wisconsin Press, 1988); and

two works by J. Baird Callicott: *In Defense of the Land Ethic: Essays in Environmental Philosophy* (Albany: State University of New York Press, 1989); and *Beyond the Land Ethic: More Essays in Environmental Philosophy* (Albany: State University of New York Press, 1999).

2. For recent accounts of the state of the natural landscape see Edward O. Wilson, *The Diversity of Life* (Cambridge, Mass.: Harvard University Press, 1992); and Reed F. Noss and Robert L. Peters, *Endangered Ecosystems: A Status Report on America's Vanishing Habitat and Wildlife* (Washington, D.C.: Defenders of Wildlife, 1995).

3. Steven Brint, "*Gemeinschaft* Revisited: A Critique and Reconstruction of the Community Concept," *Sociological Theory* 19, no. 1 (March 2001): 6–7. Brint offers a breakdown and classification of kinds of community and notes that, while some forms of community have declined in the West, other, less demanding, forms have gained importance in social life. The strengthening of the weaker forms of association is what might be expected in a society in which the strongest forms of community are losing their hold on the conscience. My concern here is with the more intense and psychologically more demanding forms of community, which I take to represent the essential core of the experience of community.

4. James G. Flanagan, "Hierarchy in Simple 'Egalitarian' Societies," *Annual Review of Anthropology* 18 (1989): 247, 261. Agreeing with J. W. Hendricks's statement that "few, if any societies are without some form of domination, whether it is based on age, gender, kinship, or some more institutionalized form of domination," Flanagan comments, "Both I and the scholars whose studies I review call into question prevailing notions about the hierarchical, the egalitarian, and the simple." He adds that the anthropologist Marshall Sahlins "recognized the fact that truly egalitarian societies simply did not exist" and that societies are "universally" stratified at least by age, sex, and personal characteristics and suggests that the notion of egalitarian societies has been "saved" in recent years by relaxing the criteria by which it is defined. "Social inequality," he notes, quoting A. Beteille (ibid., 260), "is a common condition of all human societies." Recent research apparently leaves little room for the literalized Edens some have read into archeological records such as those at Catalhöyük in southern Turkey. See, for example, Charlotte Allen's review of several recent books, "The Scholars and the Goddess," *Atlantic Monthly*, January, 2001, 18–22; and the account of blood revenge in foraging societies in Martin Daly and Margo Wilson, *Homicide* (New York: Aldine de Gruyer, 1988), 221–27. War, of course, is the extreme case. My point is not that all societies are warlike—in fact, not all are—but rather that human life, like all of creation, entails inequality and existential tensions. On the "naturalizing" of egalitarianism, see the introduction to James G. Flanagan and Steve Rayner, eds., *Rules, Decisions, and Inequality in Egalitarian Societies* (Aldershot: Avebury, 1988), 1–19.

5. Richard Lee, "Politics, Sexual and Non-Sexual, in an Egalitarian Society," in *Politics and History in Band Societies,* ed. Eleanor Leacock and Richard Lee (Cambridge: Cambridge University Press, 1982), 56.

6. Ronald L. Grimes, "Coming of Age, Joining Up," in *Deeply into the Bone:*

Re-Inventing Rites of Passage (Berkeley: University of California Press, 2000), esp. 106–7.

7. For a discussion of the influence of liberalism on the development of American environmentalism, see Roderick Frazier Nash, *The Rights of Nature: A History of Environmental Ethics* (Madison: University of Wisconsin Press, 1989), especially the prologue and ch. 2. As a case in point, consider the conventional liberal response to hazing and other ritual initiation practices, which is first to deplore and then to trivialize and marginalize them.

8. Incentive is critical, since community, though certainly an ultimate good, is, like other values and virtues, rarely an immediately attractive one. Hence in some traditional societies, adolescents who try to escape initiation are simply hunted down and subjected to the ritual—a necessity, really, since under the conditions of life in a traditional society, survival itself depends on membership in a community. Rather than thinking of community in romantic terms, perhaps we should think of initiation as rather like a military draft, conferring obligations most would prefer to avoid. As a Philippina nun commented to my son, "Oh, Americans don't have community. They have too much money"—a remark that evokes Christ's comment about the rich man and the eye of the needle.

9. Joseph Campbell, *The Masks of God: Primitive Mythology* (New York: Penguin, 1959), 181.

10. Emily Dickinson, "There's a certain slant of light," in *The Complete Poems of Emily Dickinson,* ed. Thomas H. Johnson (Boston: Little Brown, n.d.), 118–19.

11. Jonathan Z. Smith, "The Domestication of Sacrifice," in *Violent Origins: Walter Burkert, René Girard, and Jonathan Z. Smith on Ritual Killing and Cultural Formation,* ed. Robert G. Hamerton-Kelly (Stanford: Stanford University Press, 1987), 191–205.

12. Leopold uses this phrase twice in the *Almanac:* in "The Round River," 189, and "The Land Ethic," 243.

13. A. L. Herman, *Community, Violence and Peace: Aldo Leopold, Mohandas K. Gandhi, Martin Luther King, Jr., and Gautama the Buddha in the Twenty-First Century* (Albany: State University of New York Press, 1999), 70. Similarly, Mark Michael finds no secure basis for distinguishing "interference" from other forms of interaction with nature ("How to Interfere with Nature," *Environmental Ethics* 23, no. 2 [2000]: 135–54).

14. Leopold, *Almanac,* 246, xix.

15. Herman, *Community, Violence,* 66.

16. It is interesting to consider Leopold's idea of community from the perspective of the development of his thinking about human relations with the land. Early in his career, Leopold often used the metaphor of an organism, then popular among ecologists (see Callicott, *In Defense of the Land Ethic,* 87 ff.), to describe a relationship so tightly integrated that there is no question of discord among the parts, since each part is decisively subsidiary to the whole. Later, when Leopold began thinking more in terms of community, he in effect elided the two metaphors, carrying over into his idea of life in community the kind of harmony that actually is characteristic of life "in" an organism.

17. David McCloskey, "What Community Is Not: Three Myths about Community" (manuscript, Seattle University, 1997).

18. The phrase is from Brian Swimme and Thomas Berry, *The Universe Story: From the Primal Flaring Forth to the Ecozoic Era—A Celebration of the Unfolding of the Cosmos* (San Francisco: Harper San Francisco, 1992).

19. See in particular Dillard's recent essay, "This Is the Life" (*Image: A Journal of the Arts and Religion* [fall 2002]), in which she tirelessly questions the possibility of meaning in a world defined by difference and limitation.

20. Catherine L. Albanese, *Nature Religion in America: From the Algonkian Indians to the New Age* (Chicago: University of Chicago Press, 1990), 185.

21. Jean-Paul Sartre, *Being and Nothingness: An Essay in Phenomenological Ontology,* trans. Hazel E. Barnes (New York: Citadel Press, 1966), 197.

22. In his valuable discussion of the radical sense of human unworthiness (in *The Denial of Death* [New York: Free Press, 1973]), anthropologist Ernest Becker uses the term "pure guilt" to refer to what I take to be the experience of shame. This is unfortunate because the ideas of shame and guilt are hopelessly confused in our society, and because given the choice, we generally prefer the feeling of guilt, which allows us a kind of moral sovereignty, to that of shame, which arises from our awareness of radical dependency. Andrew Delbanco's account of his experience on visiting a sick friend in the hospital (*The Death of Satan: How Americans Have Lost the Sense of Evil* [New York: Farrar, Strauss and Giroux, 1995], 15–16) refers obliquely to this confusion. Talking with his friend, who was debilitated by a brain injury, he was surprised to find that his feelings were mixed with anger. He suggests that the anger reflects a primitive urge to associate suffering or misfortune with wrongdoing, to recover a world in which "some legible relation exists between justice and suffering." Our modern sensibility, he notes, denies us this satisfaction. What it denies us, I believe, are appropriate rituals of language and action to articulate and deal with shame. In fact, we often reassure others that an experience such as illness is "nothing to be ashamed of" simply because we have no way of dealing with the shame of illness or loss except by denying it, which we can do by confusing it with guilt, since in these situations guilt is usually absent.

23. William James, *The Varieties of Religious Experience: A Study in Human Nature,* (London: Collins, 1960), 148.

24. James Hans, *The Origins of the Gods* (Albany: State University of New York Press, 1991). Hans offers the experience of excrement as a case in point, quoting (pp. 84–85) Milan Kundera's comment, in *The Unbearable Lightness of Being,* that "Shit is a more onerous theological problem than is evil. Since God gave man freedom, we can, if need be, accept the idea that He is not responsible for man's crimes. The responsibility for shit, however, rests entirely with Him, the Creator of man" (246). "If kitsch," Hans suggests, "is the absolute denial of shit in both literal and figurative respects, it allows us to put out of play our shame at being human and prompts us to imagine a world in which bodies no longer exist to embarass us with their 'imperfections' and fluids" (88–89). But kitsch, Hans argues, precludes beauty precisely because it entails the denial of this existential shame.

When Archie Bunker asks "Why do they make dolls that do all the disgusting things people do?" and Edith answers, "That's not disgusting, it's natural," it is Archie, for once, who has it right.

25. Margot Astrov, ed., *American Indian Prose and Poetry: An Anthology* (New York: Capricorn Books, 1946), 3.

26. Jean-Paul Sartre, *Being and Nothingness* (New York: Citadel Press, 1966), 237.

27. Cheryl Foster, Department of Philosophy, the University of Rhode Island, personal communication.

28. E. B. White, *Charlotte's Web* (New York: Dell, 1952), 55–65.

29. Bruno Bettelheim, *The Uses of Enchantment: The Meaning and Importance of Fairy Tales* (New York: Knopf, 1977), 140–41. An interesting bit of consilience with the ideas of the political philosopher Isaiah Berlin lends support to this set of ideas in a very different context. In a classic essay, "Two Concepts of Liberty," published in 1958, Berlin questioned the idea, fostered by the Enlightenment, that all people ultimately seek the same goals — liberty, for example, and fraternity and equality — and that these are not in conflict (in *The Proper Study of Mankind: An Anthology of Essays,* ed. Henry Hardy and Roger Hansham [New York: Farrar, Strauss and Giroux, 1997], 191–242). In fact, Berlin argued, these goals, all of which are good, often do conflict, and this led him to insist on what his biographer Michael Ignatieff called "the inevitability of tragic choice in human life" ("First Loves," *New Yorker,* September 28, 1998, 60–75). Berlin reached this idea through reflection on the political events of his time and through an analysis of the idea of liberty as it was developed by philosophers such as Locke, Kant, Rousseau, and Mill. But it is also possible to reach the same conclusion in a quite different way, "deriving" it from the idea of universal shame: a polity that harmonized all the basic values would be a polity without shame, and is therefore impossible (William R. Jordan III, "Wilderness and Community, Continued," *Restoration & Management Notes* 17, nos. 1–2 [1999]: 1–2).

30. Teilhard de Chardin, "The Mass on the World," in *The Hymn of the Universe* (New York: Harper and Row, 1961), 13–37.

3. Paradigms of Community

1. Loren Eiseley, *The Invisible Pyramid* (New York: Charles Scribner's Sons, 1970), 155; he refers to the journey to the moon on 140.

2. Roderick Frazier Nash, *The Rights of Nature: A History of Environmental Ethics* (Madison: University of Wisconsin Press, 1989).

3. I draw on Mary Douglas's discussion of liberalism in her foreword to Marcel Mauss's work *The Gift: The Form and Reason for Exchange in Archaic Societies,* trans. W. D. Halls (New York: W. W. Norton, 1990). I am also indebted to Steve Davis of Edgewood College for an introduction to liberalism and its implications for environmental thought.

4. The word's etymology points directly at this central task of relationship cre-

ation. According to Eric Partridge's *Origins: A Short Etymological Dictionary of Modern English* (New York: Macmillan, 1959), s.v. "religion", the word is very closely akin to the Latin *religare*—to bind again or to bind strongly. The central idea is apparently the formation of the deepest kinds of bonds, of obligation to others, for example, to a code of ethics, or even, as suggested by the prefix *re-*, to some original or previous ideal condition. This core idea of bonds and constraints is fundamentally at odds with liberalism, with its emphasis on freedom and individual rights.

5. R. W. B. Lewis, *The American Adam: Innocence, Tragedy, and Tradition in the Nineteenth Century* (Chicago: University of Chicago Press, 1955). Any parenthetical page citations in chapter 3 text are to this work.

6. While puritanism was deeply individualistic in one sense, it did not validate subjectivity. As Andrew Delbanco (*The Real American Dream: A Meditation on Hope* [Cambridge, Mass.: Harvard University Press, 1999], 34) writes, feelings were "beside the point" for the Puritan. "Whether a feeling comes from God or from a bad meal, the only thing that matters is how it transforms one's relations with other beings—not its internal effects within the self." Clearly, the heritage of puritanism with respect to community building is complex. In one way puritanism pushed the individual outward into relationships, not as a way of achieving salvation, but as the only valid test of feelings and ideas. Delbanco finds in this the roots of the tradition of the pragmatism developed by American thinkers such as Emerson, William James, and John Dewey. Within environmentalism, it is a feature of the pragmatic, relationship-oriented thinking of Aldo Leopold, of the hard-headed conservationism of the early part of the last century, and of much of the mainstream environmental thinking of our own time. In another way, by denying the individual's role in salvation, it denies human agency at the deepest levels and proves ultimately to be a prescription for psychological and spiritual alienation.

7. Walt Whitman, "Song of Myself," in *Leaves of Grass* (Boston: Small, Maynard, 1899), 29.

8. Ralph Waldo Emerson, "Compensation," in *Emerson's Complete Works* (Boston: Houghton Mifflin, 1894), 2:118–19.

9. Irving Howe, *The American Newness: Culture and Politics in the Age of Emerson* (Cambridge, Mass.: Harvard University Press, 1986), 10–14. The "infinite compunctions" quotation is from Emerson's essay "Love." More recently, Christopher Newfield has offered a critique of Emerson's philosophy of relationship, arguing that Emerson "resolves the tension between individual liberty and democratic group life by abandoning crucial elements of both" (*The Emerson Effect: Individualism and Submission in America* [Chicago: University of Chicago Press, 1996], 6). My argument is that some such abandonment will always be necessary in the absence of adequate means of dealing in figurative terms with tensions that cannot be resolved in any other way—the notion suggested by the story of Wilbur the pig in the preceding chapter, or by the stories of Huckleberry Finn and Konrad Lorenz's geese described in chapter 6. Emerson, Newfield argues, does this by recourse to unvarying, universal principles. The result is a form of

authoritarianism he calls "corporate" or "submissive individualism" and regards as a distinctive characteristic of American culture.

10. Joseph Campbell, *The Masks of God: Primitive Mythology* (New York: Penguin, 1959), 181. Even the "Genesis" account of creation retains elements of earlier, more direful accounts in, for example, references to separation. The reading of this account as a creation out of nothing was an innovation of fourth-century exegetes, which emphasized the separation between creator and created. (See Karen Armstrong, *A History of God* [New York: Ballantine, 1993].) Restorationist Andre Clewell has explored the implications of this for restoration in "Resistance to Restoration," *Ecological Restoration* 19, no. 1 (2001): 3–4.

11. Thomas Berry, *The Dream of the Earth* (San Francisco: Sierra Club Books, 1990), 217. For similar ideas of humans as "unnatural," see, for example, Max Oelschlaeger, "On the Conflation of Humans and Nature," *Environmental Ethics* 21, no. 2 (1999): 223–24. From a more purely ecological perspective, Edward O. Wilson comments in *The Diversity of Life* (Cambridge, Mass.: Harvard University Press, 1992), 272, "By every conceivable measure, humanity is ecologically abnormal."

12. Berry, *Dream of the Earth,* 45.

13. Rosemary Reuther, *Gaia and God: An Ecofeminist Theology of Earth Healing* (San Francisco: Harper Collins, 1992), 251–53.

14. In a speech at Kenyon College in 1946, quoted in Lawrance Thompson and R. H. Winnick, *Robert Frost: A Biography,* ed. Edward Connery Lathem (New York: Holt, Rinehart and Winston, 1981), 438.

15. Quoted at the beginning of Octavio Paz's "Mexico and the United States," in *The Labyrinth of Solitude and Other Writings,* trans. Lysander Kemp, Yara Milos, and Rachel Phillips Belash (New York: Grove Weidenfeld, 1985).

16. Roy A. Rappaport, "The Obvious Aspects of Ritual," in *Ecology, Meaning, and Religion* (Berkeley: North Atlantic Books, 1979), 187–88.

17. Harold Bloom, *The American Religion: The Emergence of the Post-Christian Nation* (New York: Touchstone, 1992), 16.

18. Bloom asserts the "difference" of the American from the European religious sensibility but says little about the character of the older sensibility. Thomas Merton provides what seems to me a clear expression of this in *New Seeds of Contemplation* (New York: New Directions, 1961), 155–56: "Every one of us forms an idea of Christ that is limited and incomplete. It is cut according to our own measure. . . . We find in Him what we want to find. . . . [Hence] it is not enough merely to imitate the Christ we have in our imaginations." In contrast, the American religionist takes it for granted that his own thoughts and feelings define the value of an experience. In this view a ritual "works" only to the extent that it moves one emotionally. Examples of subjectivism in canonic American environmental thinking are not hard to find. One that is especially relevant to restoration is Aldo Leopold's reflections on his decision to cut birch trees rather than white pines ("November," in *A Sand County Almanac, with Essays on Conservation from Round River* [New York: Ballantine, 1966], 72–74). While Leopold himself characterizes his efforts as "an attempt to rebuild . . . what we are losing elsewhere," he makes

no appeal here either to ecology or to history and concludes that he favors the pines because "I love all trees, but I am in love with pines." In fact, the issue raised here is not the desirability of love, but rather the basis for it, and the troubling acts of discrimination called for by any kind of environmental management, even the most loving. Missing from Leopold's account is any hint that the decisions he confronts as a restorationist might in some way involve some radical sacrifice of the self. This again is consistent both with Bloom's "American religion" and with the "ontological individualism" that Robert Bellah and his colleagues consider a prominent feature of mainstream American society. As they note in their classic study *Habits of the Heart,* many people are uncomfortable with the idea of sacrifice as an expression of Christian love: "It was not that they were unwilling to make compromises or sacrifices for their spouses, but *they were troubled by the ideal of self-denial the term 'sacrifice' implied*" (Robert N. Bellah, Richard Madsen, William M. Sullivan, Ann Swidler, and Steven M. Tipton, *Habits of the Heart: Individualism and Commitment in American Life* [New York: Harper and Row, 1985], 109; emphasis added).

19. Bloom, *The American Religion,* 37.

20. The reference is to Whitman's "I Saw in Louisiana a Live-Oak Growing" ("Calamus," in *Leaves of Grass*).

21. Emerson's youthful optimism later gave way to a much darker and troubled uncertainty about nature's redemptive power. In this he anticipated the pessimism that Lewis notes is characteristic of twentieth-century literature and appears to me characteristic of environmentalism generally. Given Emerson's intellectual honesty, his early rejection of ritual as the pathway to grace (most explicitly in his 1832 address "The Lord's Supper," in *Emerson's Complete Works* [Boston: Houghton Mifflin, 1894], 11:9–29) led him inevitably to this prescient conclusion. On the development of Emerson's thought, see B. L. Packer, *Emerson's Fall: A New Interpretation of the Major Essays* (New York: Continuum, 1982).

22. The phrase is by Juliana of Norwich, quoted by T. S. Eliot ("Little Gidding," in *Four Quartets* [New York: Harcourt, Brace and World, 1952]).

23. Carolyn Merchant, "Reinventing Eden: Western Culture as a Recovery Narrative," in *Uncommon Ground: Toward Reinventing Nature,* ed. William Cronon (New York: W. W. Norton, 1995). See also chapter 6 note 23.

24. Little has changed in a century and a half. A recent television production of *Moby Dick* was prefaced by a disclaimer to the effect that Melville's use of the whale as an image for the inscrutability and indifference of nature reflected a prejudice of his time that has since been corrected by the realization that whales are in fact intelligent, affectionate creatures. The implication is that if whales are intelligent and affectionate, then it follows that they are also both intelligible and responsive to human concerns. In just such ways has modernism systematically expelled the monsters, not from the world, of course, but from our reflexive consciousness and awareness of the world. A touch of skepticism is called for here, as Thoreau noted. "I believe," he wrote (in *Walden* [New York: Modern Library, 1937], 118), "that men are generally still a little afraid of the dark, though the witches are all hung, and Christianity and candles have been introduced."

25. Strikingly, Brownson was led to this idea of community by the idea that thought and understanding depend neither on the objects that are perceived nor (as Emerson proposed) on the perceiver alone but rather on "the co-operation of subject and object, the perceiver and the thing perceived" (Lewis, *American Adam*, 188). This was an early version of the idea of the participatory nature of perception developed early in the twentieth century by Edmund Husserl and Maurice Merleau-Ponty, and more recently by Frederick Turner in his idea of "performed being," which I explore later—an "ecological" or relationship-based epistemology that has proved extremely congenial to environmental thinking (David Abram, *The Spell of the Sensuous: Perception and Language in a More-than-Human World* [New York: Pantheon Books, 1996]; see esp. ch. 2). Writers who apply these ideas to our relationship with the rest of nature, however, while emphasizing perception and the sensuous as a key to closeness with nature, have rarely dealt with the more problematic aspects of the awareness and experience of the other. For Brownson, on the other hand, perception and relationship with the other was most fully achieved not only through the human community, but through history.

26. I am grateful to Prof. McCloskey for drawing my attention to this etymology. He in turn credits his friend, poet Tom Jay, for the connection. I base my comments on Partridge's *Origins* and the entry for *munus* in Cassell's *Latin Dictionary*. Theologian John Leonard has pointed out to me that this entire set of ideas is explicitly contained in the "Te Igitur" at the beginning of the canon of the Mass, in which the priest entreats God to accept and bless the offerings at the altar, characterized in the old (Tridentine) Mass as *haec dona, haec munera, haec sancta sacrificia*—"these gifts, these offerings, these holy and unspotted oblations."

27. Mauss, *The Gift*. On the widespread institution of gift exchange see Frederick Turner, "Performed Being: Word Art as a Human Inheritance," in *Natural Classicism: Essays on Literature and Science* (New York: Paragon, 1985), 25–26. Turner is Founders Professor of Humanities at the University of Texas-Dallas.

28. Douglas, foreword to *The Gift*, xv.

29. Rappaport, "Obvious Aspects of Ritual," 195.

30. Gussie in Eric Bogosian's play *Griller* acknowledges the difficulty of this move when he says, "I like to buy my own presents. It makes life so much easier" (and, as the play attests, so much lonelier). Similarly in *The Taming of the Shrew* Shakespeare dramatizes the psychological trajectory from self-absorption through shame to love and also plays with the audience's perception that this is mere self-abnegation, subordination, or domestication.

31. Mauss, *The Gift*, 5.

32. Frederick Turner, *The Culture of Hope: A New Birth of the Classical Spirit* (New York: Free Press, 1995), 46.

33. Aldous Huxley, *Brave New World* (New York: Harper and Brothers, 1960), 262 ff.

34. See Lawrence Buell's account of Thoreau's companionable relationship with certain animals in *The Environmental Imagination: Thoreau, Nature Writing, and the Formation of American Culture* (Cambridge, Mass.: Harvard University

Press, 1995), 329 ff. The danger here is sentimentality or kitsch. Actual community is emotionally challenging, and it may be that most of us are driven to it only by necessity. Consider the comment of a Des Moines woman reflecting on the attacks of September 11, 2001, a year later: "People were real. . . . Not that I want another bad thing to happen, but something in me misses the kind of country we were during those weeks," *Time*, September 11, 2002, 30.

35. Frederick Turner makes this point forcefully in a short essay on abortion: "See, at some point we have to connect with the rest of nature, and it always involves death" ("She's Come for an Abortion: What Do You Say?" *Harper's Magazine*, November, 1992, 53–54).

36. Thoreau, *Walden*, 190.

4. Awareness

1. Ernest Becker, *The Denial of Death* (New York: Free Press, 1973), 3, 261. The chapter epigraph comes from Seth Zuckerman, "Pitfalls on the Way to Lasting Restoration," in *Helping Nature Heal: An Introduction to Environmental Restoration* (Berkeley: Ten Speed Press, 1991), 25.

2. Becker, *Denial of Death*, 265–66.

3. Ibid., 274.

4. Noelle Oxenhandler, "Fall from Grace," *New Yorker*, June 16, 1997, 65–68.

5. Richard White, "Are You an Environmentalist or Do You Work for a Living? Work and Nature," in *Uncommon Ground: Toward Reinventing Nature*, ed. William Cronon (New York: W. W. Norton, 1995), 171–85.

6. See the papers by Paul Gobster, Bruce Hull, Robert Ryan, Jane Buxton, and Robert Grese at a May 1998 symposium at the University of Missouri, published as Paul H. Gobster and R. Bruce Hull, eds., *Restoring Nature: Perspectives from the Social Sciences and Humanities* (Washington, D.C.: Island Press, 2000). See also William R. Jordan III, "Restoring the Restorationist," *Restoration & Management Notes* 7, no. 2 (1989) 55.

7. Carl Jung's idea that alchemy offered a repertory of techniques for transforming consciousness is discussed by Morris Berman in *The Reenchantment of the World* (Ithaca: Cornell University Press, 1981), 78 ff.

8. The epigraph is from J. T. Curtis and M. L. Partch, "Effect of Fire on the Competition between Blue Grass and Certain Prairie Species," *The American Midland Naturalist* 39, no. 2 (1948): 437–43.

9. G. Cottam, "Community Dynamics on an Artificial Prairie," in *Restoration Ecology: A Synthetic Approach to Ecological Research*, ed. William R. Jordan III, John D. Aber, and Michael E. Gilpin (Cambridge: Cambridge University Press, 1987), 257–70.

10. R. C. Anderson, O. L. Loucks, and A. M. Swain, "Herbaceous Response to Canopy Cover, Light Intensity and Throughfall in Coniferous Forests," *Ecology* 50 (1969): 255–63.

11. For reports on these projects see Brock Woods, "Ants Disperse Seed of Herb Species in a Restored Maple Forest (Wisconsin)," *Restoration & Management Notes* 2, no. 1 (1984): n. 18; J. D. Aber, "Restored Forests and the Identification of Critical Factors in Species-Site Interactions," in *Restoration Ecology: A Synthetic Approach to Ecological Research,* ed. William R. Jordan III, John D. Aber, and Michael E. Gilpin (Cambridge: Cambridge University Press, 1987), 241–50; and T. Blewett, "An Ordination Study of Plant Species Ecology in the Arboretum Prairies" (Ph.D. diss., University of Wisconsin-Madison, 1981).

12. Donald Worster, *Nature's Economy: The Roots of Ecology* (Garden City, N.Y.: Anchor Press, 1979), esp. 289 ff.

13. For an influential critique of modern science from a feminist point of view see Carolyn Merchant, *The Death of Nature: Women, Ecology and the Scientific Revolution* (San Francisco: Harper and Row, 1980). And on ecological restoration, see her article, "Restoration and Reunion with Nature," *Restoration & Management Notes* 4, no. 2 (1986): 68–70.

14. A. D. Bradshaw, "Restoration: An Acid Test for Ecology," in *Restoration Ecology: A Synthetic Approach to Ecological Research,* ed. William R. Jordan III, John D. Aber, and Michael E. Gilpin (Cambridge: Cambridge University Press, 1987), 23–30. The metaphor drawn from chemistry or metallurgy is applicable only up to a point, especially in the ecologically favorable or appropriate settings in which most restoration work is carried out. Refining on Bradshaw's metaphor, we might say that the acid test of our understanding of an ecosytem is not our ability to *restore* it on site, but rather our ability to *create* it under a wide range of novel and ecologically *inappropriate* conditions—even to create the ecological equivalent of a tallgrass prairie on Mars, or an oak forest with no oaks but with elements (perhaps mechanical) that act as ecologically exact equivalents of oaks.

15. J. L. Harper, "The Heuristic Value of Ecological Restoration," in *Restoration Ecology: A Synthetic Approach to Ecological Research,* ed. William R. Jordan III, John D. Aber, and Michael E. Gilpin (Cambridge: Cambridge University Press, 1987), 35–46. In Roy A. Rappaport's posthumously published book *Ritual and Religion in the Making of Humanity* (Cambridge: Cambridge University Press, 1999), 456–61, he describes a new "postmodern" science that includes many elements of the restoration-based relationship with nature I describe here and actually touches briefly on the idea of ritualizing environmentally oriented activities such as advocating conservation or the "amelioration of ecological . . . disorders."

16. Recent research has documented the influence of traditional peoples on their environments in many parts of the world. For accounts of developments in this area see William M. Denevan, "The Pristine Myth: The Landscape of the Americas in 1492," *The Americas Before and After 1492: Current Geographical Research,* special issue, *Annals of the Association of American Geographers* 82, no. 3 (September 1992): 369–85; Thomas C. Blackburn and Kat Anderson, eds., *Before the Wilderness: Environmental Management by Native Californians* (Menlo Park, Calif.: Ballena Press, 1993); William Cronon, *Changes in the Land: Indians, Colonists, and the Ecology of New England* (New York: Hill and Wang, 1983); and

Stephen J. Pyne, *World Fire: The Culture of Fire on Earth* (New York: Henry Holt, 1995).

17. See, for example, Constance Pierce, "The Poetics and Politics of Prairie Restoration," and Jack Temple Kirby, "Gardening with J. Crew: The Political Economy of Restoration Ecology," both in *Beyond Preservation: Restoring and Inventing Landscapes,* ed. A. Dwight Baldwin, Jr., Judith De Luce, and Carl Pletsch (Minneapolis: University of Minnesota Press, 1994).

18. In his dialogue poem "West-Running Brook," in *West-Running Brook, Complete Poems of Robert Frost* (New York: Holt, Rinehart and Winston, 1949), 327–29.

19. Dave Egan, "Historic Initiatives in Ecological Restoration," *Restoration & Management Notes* 8, no. 2 (1990): 83–90. Egan's article also includes a brief account of similar work by Frederick Law Olmsted in the Northeast.

20. Epigraph from Stephen Packard, "Just a Few Oddball Species: Restoration and the Discovery of the Tallgrass Savanna," *Restoration & Management Notes* 6, no. 1 (summer 1988): 19.

21. Joseph Campbell, *The Masks of God: Primitive Mythology* (New York: Penguin, 1970), 181, 180.

22. In this way, restorationists follow Thoreau's advice at the end of his meditation on agriculture in *Walden,* 150: "relinquishing all claim to the produce of his fields, and sacrificing in his mind not only his first but his last fruits also."

23. Cindy Goulder, "Volunteer Revegetation Saturday," *Restoration & Management Notes* 14, no. 1 (1996): 62, with revisions by the author.

24. José Ortega y Gasset, *Meditations on Hunting* (New York: Scribner's, 1972).

25. Freeman House, "To Learn the Things We Need to Know," in *Helping Nature Heal: An Introduction to Environmental Restoration,* ed. Richard Nilsen (Berkeley: Ten Speed Press, 1991), 46–58.

26. Thoreau, *Walden,* 254.

27. Michael Pollan comments on Thoreau's negative "take" on agriculture in *Second Nature: A Gardener's Education* (New York: Atlantic Monthly Press, 1991), 4.

28. Worster, *Nature's Economy,* 78.

29. Entries for April 19 and 21, 1859, in *The Journal of Henry Thoreau,* ed. Bradford Torrey and Francis H. Allen (New York: Dover, 1962), 1470.

30. The first phrase comes from *Walden* (Modern Library ed., 101), the second from "Walking" (ibid., 619). On Thoreau's use of language and its relationship to his ideas of redemption, see Leo Marx, "Henry Thoreau," in *The Pilot and the Passenger: Essays on Literature, Technology, and Culture in the United States* (New York: Oxford University Press, 1988), 76–100. Equally dubious about the power of language to connect with or communicate reality, Whitman sought what he called a language "fann'd by the wind," and Emerson wrote of a speech of nature that is "not fancied by some poet, but stands in the will of God" (Andrew Delbanco, "Melville's Sacramental Style," in *Required Reading: Why Our Classics Matter Now* [New York: Farrar, Straus and Giroux, 1997], 14 and 21, respectively).

31. I refer here to George Archibald's celebrated practice of dancing with the cranes at the International Crane Foundation near Baraboo, Wisconsin, miming their mating rituals in order to induce ovulation in cranes raised in captivity and imprinted on people. On the ability to identify with other species, so that a man can "contain more than himself," see Loren Eiseley, "How Natural Is Natural?" in *Firmament of Time* (New York: Atheneum, 1971), 169–76; and, more recently, two articles by Michael Vincent McGinnis: "Deep Ecology and the Foundations of Restoration," *Inquiry* 39, no. 2 (1996): 203–17; and "Re-wilding Imagination: Mimesis and Ecological Restoration," *Ecological Restoration* 17, no. 4 (1999): 219–26.

32. William R. Jordan III, "I, Lightning," *Restoration & Management Notes* 14, no. 1 (1996): 62.

33. Isaiah Berlin, "Vico's Concept of Knowledge," in *Against the Current: Essays in the History of Ideas* (New York: Viking, 1980), 117. The discussion here draws on this and two other essays, "The Sciences and the Humanities" and "Vico and the Enlightenment," all in *Against the Current*.

34. Ovid, *Metamorphoses* 5:129, cited in Barry Powell, *Classical Myth* (Englewood Cliffs, N.J.: Prentice Hall, 1995), 184.

5. The Exchange

1. Robin Lewis lists marine and aquatic ecosystems in order of the "probability of success" of restoration (Lewis Environmental Services, Tampa, Fla., 1995).

2. Ronald Panzer, D. Stillwaugh, Rich Gnadinger, and George Derkovitz, "Prevalence of Remnant-Dependence among the Prairie- and Savanna-Inhabiting Insects of the Chicago Region," *Natural Areas Journal* 15, no. 2 (1995): 101–16.

3. For an introduction to the literature on restoration see Stephen Packard and Cornelia F. Mutel, eds., *The Tallgrass Restoration Handbook: For Prairies, Savannas and Woodlands* (Washington, D.C.: Island Press, 1997); Susan M. Galatowitsch and Arnold G. van der Valk, *Restoring Prairie Wetlands: An Ecological Approach* (Ames: Iowa State University Press, 1994); Jon A. Kusler and Mary E. Kentula, *Wetland Creation and Restoration: The Status of the Science* (Washington, D.C.: Island Press, 1990); Donald L. Hey and Nancy S. Philippi, *A Case for Wetland Restoration* (New York: John Wiley and Sons, 1999); Ann L. Riley, *Restoring Streams in Cities: A Guide for Planners, Policy Makers, and Citizens* (Washington, D.C.: Island Press, 1998); Dennis G. Cooke et al., *Restoration and Management of Lakes and Reservoirs* (Boca Raton, Fla.: CRC/Lewis, 1993); Leslie Jones Sauer and Andropogon Associates, *The Once and Future Forest: A Guide to Forest Restoration Strategies* (Washington, D.C.: Island Press, 1998); R. Ferris-Kaan, *The Ecology of Woodland Creation* (New York: John Wiley and Sons, 1995); Mark K. Briggs, *Riparian Ecosystem Recovery in Arid Lands: Strategies and References* (Tucson: University of Arizona Press, 1996); James A. Harris, Paul Birch, and John P. Palmer, *Land Restoration and Reclamation: Principles and Practice* (Essex: Longman,

1996); Marlin L. Bowles and Christopher J. Whelan, *Restoration of Endangered Species: Conceptual Issues, Planning, and Implementation* (Cambridge: Cambridge University Press, 1994); Donald A. Falk, *Restoring Diversity: Strategies for Reintroduction of Endangered Plants* (Washington, D.C.: Island Press, 1996). For additional sources of information on technical aspects of restoration see the journals *Ecological Restoration* and *Restoration Ecology*, as well as the Society for Ecological Restoration in Tucson, Az.

4. Janet C. Morlan and Robert E. Frankel, "How Well Can We Do? The Salmon River Estuary," *Restoration & Management Notes* 10, no. 1 (1992): 21–23.

5. David A. Wedin and David Tilman, "Nitrogen Cycling, Plant Competition, and the Stability of Tallgrass Prairie," in *Proceedings of the 12th North American Prairie Conference: Capturing a Vanishing Heritage*, ed. D. D. Smith and C. A. Jacobs (Cedar Falls: University of Northern Iowa Press, 1992), 5–8.

6. Peter W. Dunwiddie, "On Setting Goals: From Snapshots to Movies and Beyond," *Restoration & Management Notes* 10, no. 2 (1992): 116–19.

7. Joy B. Zedler and René Langis, "Comparisons of Constructed and Natural Salt Marshes of San Diego Bay," *Restoration & Management Notes* 9, no. 1 (1991): 21–25.

8. John Rieger, "San Diego Bay Mitigation Study: A Response," *Restoration & Management Notes* 9, no. 2 (1991): 65–66.

9. Though ecologically extinct—no longer capable of surviving to maturity in the wild—American chestnut is not genetically extinct. The American Chestnut Society of Bennington, Vermont, is trying to return chestnut to the forests of the Northeast, either by creating blight-resistant strains, or by developing ways to "immunize" trees (see William A. Niering, "The New England Forests," *Restoration & Management Notes* 10, no. 1 [1992]: 24–28). Projects like this push the limits of restoration, raising questions about the possibility of restoring to their natural habitat other ecologically extinct species, such as American elm and perhaps even genetically extinct species, such as the passenger pigeon or mastodon, that might eventually be recovered by cloning fossil DNA.

10. For two summers in the early 1960s I worked for the Wisconsin Department of Natural Resources on a "rough fish" crew, running sein hauls to remove exotic species from Madison's lakes. We sometimes took out several hundred thousand pounds of carp in a single day, with no apparent diminution of the population. The experience left me with a lasting sense of the size, fecundity, and inaccessibility of a biological population—a testimony to the aptness of the image of Pandora's box in Greek myth. For an overview of the exotics problem, see David Quammen, "Planet of Weeds: Tallying the Losses of Earth's Animals and Plants," *Harper's Magazine*, October 1998, 57–69.

11. Francis D. Heliotis and Calvin B. DeWitt, "Rapid Water Table Responses to Rainfall in a Northern Peatland Ecosystem," *Water Resources Bulletin* 23, no. 6 (1987): 1011–16.

12. For an introduction to the assembly rule model see Evan Weiher and Paul Keddy, eds., *Ecological Assembly Rules: Perspectives, Advances, Retreats* (Cambridge: Cambridge University Press, 1999). For recent discussions of assembly-rule the-

ory and its relationship to restoration, see Julie L. Lockwood, "An Alternative to Succession: Assembly Rules Offer Guide to Restoration Efforts," *Restoration & Management Notes* 15, no. 1 (1997): 45–50; and Truman P. Young, Jonathan M. Chase, and Russell T. Huddleston, "Community Succession and Assembly: Comparing, Contrasting, and Combining Paradigms in the Context of Ecological Restoration," *Ecological Restoration* 19, no. 1 (2001): 5–18.

13. Stuart L. Pimm, *The Balance of Nature: Ecological Issues in the Conservation of Species and Communities* (Chicago: University of Chicago Press, 1991), 248–50.

14. Rich Kahl, "Aquatic Macrophyte Ecology in the Upper Winnebago Pool Lakes," *Wisconsin Department of Natural Resources Technical Bulletin* 182 (1993).

15. D. Egan et al., eds., *The Historical Ecology Handbook: A Restorationist's Guide to Historic Ecosystems* (Washington, D.C.: Island Press, 2001).

16. On the discipline of landscape ecology, which deals with questions related to the size of ecosystems and their distribution in the landscape, see Richard T. T. Forman, *Land Mosaics: The Ecology of Landscapes and Regions* (Cambridge: Cambridge University Press, 1995). And on the factor of scale in conservation reserves, see Reed F. Noss and Blair Csuti, "Habitat Fragmentation"; and Gary K. Meffe and C. Ronald Carroll, "The Design of Conservation Reserves"; both in *Principles of Conservation Biology,* ed. Gary K. Meffe and C. Ronald Carroll (Sunderland, Mass.: Sinauer, 1994).

17. Conversation with Baird Callicott in Madison, October 1998. It is worth noting, especially in connection with the idea of restoration as a way of refining ecological ideas, that ecologist John Curtis, who succeeded Leopold as a principal researcher at the Arboretum in the 1940s and 1950s, developed his more "individualistic" conception of the plant community in the context of the Arboretum's restoration efforts.

18. For an authoritative discussion of scale as a factor in the ecology of ecological systems see T. F. H. Allen and T. W. Hoekstra, *Toward a Unified Ecology* (New York: Columbia University Press, 1992); and same authors' chapter in William R. Jordan III, John D. Aber, and Michael E. Gilpin, eds., *Restoration Ecology: A Synthetic Approach to Ecological Research* (Cambridge: Cambridge University Press, 1987), 289–99. Allen and Hoekstra's remarks on restoration (in *Toward a Unified Ecology,* 271–89) in fact refer to rehabilitation, the restoration of health or perhaps some other desirable feature of an ecosystem, rather than a return to a previous condition in all its aspects, regardless of their value or even their appeal to the restorationist.

19. D. C. Hartnett, A. A. Steuter, and K. R. Hickman, "Comparative Ecology of Native and Introduced Ungulates," in *Ecology and Conservation of Great Plains Vertebrates,* ed. Fritz Knopf and F. B. Samson, Ecology Studies no. 125 (New York: Springer, 1997), 72–101. For an introduction to fire ecology see Robert J. Whelan, *The Ecology of Fire* (Cambridge: Cambridge University Press, 1995). On grazing and its role in the ecology and restoration of prairies see Andrew H. Williams, "In Praise of Grazing," *Restoration & Management Notes* 15, no. 2 (1997): 116–18; and letters in response to this article by John Harrington and Richard A. Henderson in *Restoration & Management Notes* 16, no. 1 (1998): 5–8; by

Henry F. Howe, "Dominance, Diversity and Grazing in Tallgrass Prairies," *Ecological Restoration/North America* 17, nos. 1–2 (1999): 59–66; and by Coleen Davison and Kelly Kindscher, "Tools for Diversity: Fire, Grazing and Mowing on Tallgrass Prairies," *Ecological Restoration/North America* 17, no. 3 (1999).

20. Robert F. Betz, Robert J. Lootens, and Michael K. Becker, "Two Decades of Prairie Restoration at Fermilab," in *Proceedings of the 15th North American Prairie Conference,* ed. Charles Warwick (Bend, Or.: Natural Areas Association, 1996), 20–30.

21. William R. Jordan III, "Working with the River," *Restoration & Management Notes* 2, no. 1 (1984): 4–11.

22. Harold W. Rock, *The Prairie Propagation Handbook* (Hales Corners, Wis.: Wehr Nature Center, 1977).

23. Stephen Packard, "Interseeding," in *The Tallgrass Restoration Handbook for Prairies, Savannas and Woodlands,* ed. Stephen Packard and Cornelia F. Mutel (Washington, D.C.: Island Press, 1997), 163–91.

24. For a discussion of the relationship between restoration and succession, see James A. MacMahon, "Disturbed Lands and Ecological Theory: An Essay about a Mutualistic Association," in *Restoration Ecology: A Synthetic Approach to Ecological Research,* ed. William R. Jordan III, John D. Aber, and Michael E. Gilpin (Cambridge: Cambridge University Press, 1987), 221–37.

25. Pauline M. Drobney, Walnut Creek National Wildlife Refuge, Prairie City, Iowa, personal communication. For an account of the Walnut Creek project see her "Iowa Prairie Rebirth: Rediscovering Natural Heritage at Walnut Creek National Wildlife Refuge," *Restoration & Management Notes* 12, no. 1 (1994): 16–22 (the refuge's current name is Neal Smith Wildlife Refuge).

26. There are no comprehensive figures on the size and extent of restoration projects, but the Society for Ecological Restoration is working on a database of projects that will eventually prove useful in finding projects and identifying trends. A recent survey reports restoration of 45,000 acres of prairie in Minnesota alone between the 1960s and 1997; see Ross H. Hier, "Prairie Restoration in Minnesota: What's Been Done and Plans for the Future," *Land and Water* 43, no. 6 (November–December 1999): 9–11. Though this is still only a tiny fraction of the landscape, it is an important fact. Quite possibly, this represents the first time in history that an entire ecosystem has been pushed to the verge of extinction then brought back, on a regionally significant scale, through restoration efforts.

27. J. E. Weaver and Ellen Zink, "Annual Increase of Underground Materials in Three Range Grasses," *Ecology* 27 (1946): 115–27. Interestingly, Aldo Leopold's famous essay "The Land Ethic," in *A Sand County Almanac with Essays on Conservation from Round River* (New York: Ballantine, 1966) includes a reference (on 258) to Weaver's ideas about the value of "prairie flowers" as a way of rebuilding prairie soils.

28. R. M. Miller and J. D. Jastrow, "The Role of Mycorrhizal Fungi in Soil Conservation," *Mycorrhizae in Sustainable Agriculture,* Special Publication no. 54 (Madison: Agronomy Society of America, 1992), 29–44.

29. Kevin McSweeney, Department of Soil Science, University of Wisconsin-Madison, personal communication, 1998.

30. Evan Eisenberg, "Back to Eden," *Atlantic Monthly,* November 1989, 57–89.

31. Anne Matthews, *Where the Buffalo Roam: The Storm over the Revolutionary Plan to Restore America's Great Plains* (New York: Grove Press, 1992). For a more recent comment on the Poppers' ideas from the perspective of a long-time Plains dweller see Bill Whitney, "A Mixing of Metaphors: A Plains Restorationist Reflects on the Buffalo Commons," *Restoration & Management Notes* 15, no. 1 (1997): 14–15.

32. See James Karr's keynote address to a 1994 workshop in *Salmon Ecosystem Restoration: Myth and Reality,* ed. Mary Louise Keefe (Corvallis: American Fisheries Society, 1994), 2–12. For an excellent first-person account of a community-based salmon habitat restoration project see Freeman House, *Totem Salmon: Life Lessons from Another Species* (Boston: Beacon Press, 1999).

33. Chris Maser, *Sustainable Forestry: Philosophy, Science, and Economics* (Delray, Fla.: St. Lucie Press, 1994).

34. Robert H. Cadlec and R. L. Knight, *Treatment Wetlands* (Boca Raton, Fla.: CRC/Lewis, 1996).

35. In "West-Running Brook," in *Complete Poems of Robert Frost* (New York: Holt, Rinehart and Winston, 1949), 327–29.

36. William R. Jordan III, "First Habitat Reconstruction Meeting in England," *Restoration & Management Notes* 6, no. 2 (1988): 63–64.

37. Robert Elliott, "Faking Nature," *Inquiry* 25 (1982): 81–93; and *Faking Nature: The Ethics of Environmental Restoration* (London: Routledge, 1997). See more recent comments on restored ecosystems' authenticity in the following articles, all in the journal *Environmental Ethics:* Alistair S. Gunn, "The Restoration of Species and Natural Environments," 13, no. 4 (1991): 291–301; Mark Cowell, "Ecological Restoration and Environmental Ethics," 15, no. 1 (1993): 19–33; Robert Elliott, "Extinction, Restoration, Naturalness," 16, no. 2 (1994): 135–44; Donald Scherer, "Evolution, Human Living, and the Practice of Ecological Restoration," 17, no. 4 (1995): 359–80.

38. Eric Katz, "The Big Lie: Human Restoration of Nature," *Research in Philosophy and Technology* 12 (1992): 231–41; and "Restoration and Redesign: The Ethical Significance of Human Intervention in Nature," *Restoration & Management Notes* 9, no. 2 (1991): 90–96.

39. Andrew Light, "Ecological Restoration and the Culture of Nature: a Pragmatic Perspective," in *Restoring Nature: Perspectives from the Social Sciences and Humanities,* ed. Paul H. Gobster and R. Bruce Hull (Washington, D.C.: Island Press, 2000), 49–70. Light uses Katz's idea of a relationship between humans and nature that has moral import to argue for restoration as a way of developing a morally positive relationship with nature.

40. For a brief history see Paula Hirschboeck, "Soul-Making Women: A Philosophical Exploration of Imaginal Feminisms" (Ph.D. diss., The Union Institute, Cincinnati, Ohio, 1992), esp. ch. 1. In *The Spell of the Sensuous: Perception and Language in a More-than-Human World* (NY: Pantheon, 1996), David Abram sketches the history of performance-based ontology and explores its implications for our relationship with nature. See also Max Oelschlaeger's argument about the ontological power of language in *The Idea of Wilderness: From Prehistory to the Age of*

Ecology (New Haven: Yale University Press, 1991). Orestes Brownson, the Ironist party spokesman whose ideas I discuss in chapter 3, based his ideas about communion on the idea that thought resulted from the cooperation of the perceiver and the thing perceived (R. W. B. Lewis, *The American Adam: Innocence, Tragedy, and Tradition in the Nineteenth Century* [Chicago: University of Chicago Press, 1955], 188). Brownson's idea is an early version of the idea of the participatory nature of perception developed early in the twentieth century by Edmund Husserl and Maurice Merleau-Ponty, and more recently by Frederick Turner in his idea of "performed being." On a similar ontology in the social sciences, "symbolic interactionsm," see Jodi O'Brien and Peter Kollock, *The Production of Reality: Essays and Readings on Social Interaction* (Thousand Oaks, Calif.: Pine Forge Press, 1994).

41. Mircea Eliade, *The Myth of the Eternal Return* (Princeton: Princeton University Press, 1954), 3–5. Not surprisingly, the associations embedded in the etymology of the word "cosmos" are suggestive. According to Partridge, to the Greeks *kosmos* meant "the order of harmony," hence "the world" (that part of the universe that we see as orderly). It may also be related to the Latin *censere,* to think, pointing toward the cognitive processes by which the world is ordered subjectively and chaos made cosmos.

42. For an early account of these ideas see Roy A. Rappaport, "The Obvious Aspects of Ritual," in *Ecology, Meaning, and Religion* (Berkeley: North Atlantic Books, 1979); and his more extensive *Ritual and Religion in the Making of Humanity* (Cambridge: Cambridge University Press, 1999), 210.

43. Frederick Turner, "Performed Being: Word Art as a Human Inheritance," in *Natural Classicism: Essays on Literature and Science* (New York: Paragon, 1985). On the theme of iconoclasm, the rejection of images and representations and their value, which is a version of the more general skepticism or hostility about performance, see Jonas Barish, *The Antitheatrical Prejudice* (Berkeley: University of California Press, 1981). For a poet's reflections on puritanism as the enemy of art, see William Carlos Williams, "The Voyage of the Mayflower," in *In the American Grain* (New York: New Directions, 1956), 63–68.

44. Albert Borgmann, *Crossing the Postmodern Divide* (Chicago: University of Chicago Press, 1992), 110 ff.

45. The etymologies are from Eric Partidge, *Origins: A Short Etymological Dictionary of Modern English* (NY: Macmillan, 1958).

46. William R. Jordan III, "The Ghosts in the Forest," *Restoration & Management Notes* 11, no. 1 (1993): 3–4. To gain a sense of how parochial the origin-based notion of authenticity is, see Alexander Stille, "Faking It," *New Yorker,* June 15, 1998, 36–42. (This essay also appears in Stille's recent book *The Future of the Past* [New York: Farar, Straus, and Giroux, 2002], which deals with the theme of maintenance [or restoration] in more detail and links it with questions regarding the management of natural areas in a chapter on a conservation effort in Madagascar.) The Chinese commonly regard copies, often of quite indifferent quality, as the artistic and historic equivalent of original art objects—a fact that troubles many art curators in the West. And in the Japanese Ise temple tradition (see Yasutada Watanabe, *Shinto Art: Ise and Izumo Shrines* [New York: Weatherhill,

1974]), Shinto shrines are deliberately destroyed and rebuilt at fixed intervals, commonly twenty years (this ceremony was enacted at the opening of the Winter Olympics at Nagano in 1998). Sandy Kita, an art historian at the University of Maryland who specializes in Japanese art, notes that this tearing down and rebuilding is a renewal involving the desacralization of the old shrine and a "moving of the god over" to the new one. In the same way, Navajos routinely discard items from medicine bundles, ritually replacing old items with new ones, in this way maintaining the "life"—or ontological value—of the sacred emblem (Anne Jordan, National Park Service, personal communication).

Two environmental philosophers have recently articulated similar ideas in discussions of environmental ethics and an ethical appraisal of the practice of ecological restoration. Australian philosopher Yeuk-Sze Lo has suggested that if one regards the landscape as a subject rather than an object, the act of restoration may be read as a way of enhancing our relationship with it rather than as a process by which nature is compromised by culture (Yeuk-Sze Lo, "Natural and Artifactual: Restored Nature as a Subject," *Environmental Ethics* 21, no. 3 [1999]: 247–66). This is essentially what I am proposing here. Also relevant here is a recent paper in which philosophers Jim Cheney and Anthony Weston argue for an environmental ethic based on etiquette—a form of performance—rather than the other way around—an etiquette based on abstract ethical principles. This is exactly the bottom-up idea of the formulation of values and ethics through interaction with others made reflexive through performance that I propose here in connection with the practice of restoration. Interestingly, Cheney and Weston note that their thinking on this point has been influenced by their contacts with indigenous members of the Native Philosophy Project at Lakehead University in Thunder Bay, Ontario (Jim Cheney and Anthony Weston, "Environmental Ethics as Environmental Etiquette," *Environmental Ethics* 21, no. 2 [1999]: 115–34). The assumption that the copy is inherently or ontologically inferior to the "original" is commonplace in Western thought, but it is important to keep in mind that this valuation is by no means universal. Indeed, the "making of copies" through repetition of prayers or rituals is a commonplace of religious practice.

47. Mary Douglas, *Purity and Danger: An Analysis of the Concepts of Pollution and Taboo* (London: Routledge and Kegan Paul, 1966) 170, 171. On the relation between Douglas's ideas and restoration see my essay, "The Prairie and the Pangolin," *Ecological Restoration* 17, no. 3 (1999): 105–6.

48. See also Rappaport's detailed argument that the sacred is exclusively a product of ritual in "Obvious Aspects of Ritual," and in *Ritual and Religion*.

49. Paul Radin, *The Trickster: A Study in American Indian Mythology* (New York: Schocken Books, 1972), and esp. Stanley Diamond's introduction, xii–xiii.

50. Ian Frazer, *The Great Plains* (New York: Farrar, Straus, Giroux, 1989), 90 and 91.

51. See for example Susan Power Bratton, "The Management of Historic Ecosystems and Landscapes in the National Parks," in *Vegetation Change and Historic Landscape Management,* proceedings of the Conference on Science in the National Parks, ed. S. P. Bratton (Fort Collins: Colorado State University Press, 1990), 3–43.

52. Frazer, *Great Plains,* 115.

53. John Thelen Steere, "Restoring Our Bonds with Place: Cultivating Commons and Community from an Eco-psychological Perspective" (paper presented at the conference of the Society for Ecological Restoration, Rutgers, New Jersey, 1996).

54. Derek Walcott, "The Antilles: Fragments of Epic Memory," Nobel Prize speech quoted in the *New Republic,* December 28, 1992.

55. The Nature Conservancy has listed the blacksoil savannas of the Midwestern United States as g1, indicating the highest level of rarity and the highest priority for preservation of an ecological element. The savannas share this ranking with ecosystems such as maritime tundra and sandstone glades.

56. Stephen Packard, "Rediscovering the Tallgrass Savanna," in *Seventh Northern Illinois Prairie Workshop* (College of DuPage, June 1-2, 1985), ed. Russell Kirt, Wayne Lampa, and Patricia Armstrong, n.p.

57. Stephen Packard, "Just a Few Oddball Species: Restoration and the Rediscovery of the Tallgrass Savanna," *Restoration & Management Notes* 6, no. 1 (1988): 13. Bill Stevens also describes Packard's work in his account of the work of the Chicago restorationists, *Miracle Under the Oaks: The Revival of Nature in America* (New York: Pocket Books, 1995).

58. See for example, Mark K. Leach and Thomas J. Givnish, "Gradients in the Composition, Structure, and Diversity of Remnant Oak Savannas in Southern Wisconsin," *Ecology/Ecological Monographs* 69 (1999): 353-74. For an account of a more recent project that would test ideas about the character of a "lost" ecosystem even more remote in time—the Siberian steppe of some 11,000 years ago—by attempting to restore it, see Richard Stone, "A Bold Plan to Re-create a Long-Lost Siberian Ecosystem," *Science* 282 (October 1998): 31-41.

59. For a sociologist's interpretation of restoration as a way of "realizing" an ecosystem, see Reid M. Helford, "Re-discovering the Presettlement Landscape: Making the Oak Savanna Ecosystem Real," *Science, Technology and Human Values* 24, no. 1 (winter 1999).

6. Value and Make-Believe

1. Roy A. Rappaport, "The Obvious Aspects of Ritual," in *Ecology, Meaning and Religion* (Berkeley: North Atlantic Books, 1979), 175.

2. Frederick Turner, *Beauty: The Value of Values* (Charlottesville: University of Virginia Press, 1991), 51. Barry Powell, *Classical Mythology* (Englewood Cliffs, N.J.: Prentice Hall, 1995), 182-84.

3. Philippe Descola, "Societies of Nature and the Nature of Society," in *Conceptualizing Society,* ed. Adam Kuper (London: Routledge, 1992), esp. 117-18.

4. Gerardo Reichel-Dolmatoff, *Amazonian Cosmos: The Sexual and Religious Symbolism of the Tukano Indians* (Chicago: University of Chicago Press, 1971), 67.

5. Signe Howell, "Nature in Culture or Culture in Nature?: Chewong Ideas of 'Humans' and Other Species," in *Nature and Society: Anthropological Perspectives,* ed. Philippe Descola and Gísli Pàlsson (London: Routledge, 1996).

6. Laura Rival, "Blowpipes and Spears: The Social Significance of Huaorani Technological Choices," in ibid.; Philippe Descola, "Constructing Nature: Symbolic Ecology and Social Practice," in ibid., 90; Descola, "Societies of Nature," 116.

7. J. Baird Callicott, "African Biocommunitarianism and Australian Dreamtime," in *Earth's Insights: A Multicultural Survey of Ecological Ethics from the Mediterranean Basis to the Australian Outback* (Berkeley: University of California Press, 1994).

8. Victor Turner, *Revelation and Divination in Ndembu Ritual* (Ithaca: Cornell University Press, 1975), 20. For further valuable discussion of this point, see Evan Zuesse, "Ritual Encounters between Self and Other," in *Ritual Cosmos: The Sanctification of Life in African Religions* (Athens, Ohio: Ohio University Press, 1979). Zuesse suggests that in African cultures the tensions involved in this encounter are dealt with primarily through the rituals of divination, witchcraft, and possession trance.

9. Catherine Pickstock, *After Writing: The Liturgical Consummation of Philosophy* (Oxford: Blackwell, 1998).

10. William R. Jordan III and Alex Turner, "Ecological Restoration and the Uncomfortable Middle Ground," in *Healing Nature, Repairing Relationships*, ed. Robert France (Cambridge: MIT Press, 2003).

11. Arnold Van Gennep, *The Rites of Passage* (Chicago: University of Chicago Press, 1960).

12. Mircea Eliade, *The Sacred and the Profane: The Significance of Religious Myth, Symbolism, and Ritual within Life and Culture* (San Diego: Harcourt Brace Jovanovich, 1957).

13. Frederick Turner, *The Culture of Hope: A New Birth of the Classical Spirit* (New York: Free Press, 1995), 170 ff.; Konrad Lorenz, *On Aggression,* trans. Marjorie Kerr Wilson (New York: Bantam, 1966), esp. ch. 5.

14. Lorenz, *On Aggression,* 63–64.

15. Many readers have found the ending of *Huckleberry Finn* to be disappointing, and there is a large literature about it. See for example, Jane Smiley, "Say It Ain't So, Huck," *Harper's Magazine,* January 1996, 61–70; Leo Marx, "Mr. Eliot, Mr. Trilling, and 'Huckleberry Finn,' " in *The Pilot and the Passenger: Essays on Literature, Technology, and Culture in the United States* (New York: Oxford University Press, 1988), 37–53; Forrest G. Robinson, "The Grand Evasion," in *Huck Finn,* ed. Harold Bloom (New York: Chelsea House, 1990), 164–73.

16. Dennis J. Springer develops a similar interpretation of the "evasion" episode in more detail in his "Tom Sawyer's Whoopjamboreeho: The Mixed-Up and Splendid Ending of Huckleberry Finn," A Mark Twain Journal Monograph, *Mark Twain Journal* (1990): 1–51.

17. Edward O. Wilson, "Is Humanity Suicidal?" *New York Times Magazine,* May 30, 1993, 24–29. Not surprisingly, a culture that lacks means of dealing with the untoward aspects of nature productively deals with them by denial. And Lorenz's ideas are currently unfashionable. While many have criticized Lorenz's work on aggression, few have paid attention to his arresting ideas about the relationship between aggression and love. Thus Walter Burkert ("The Problem of

Ritual Killing," in *Violent Origins: Walter Burkert, René Girard, and Jonathan Z. Smith on Ritual Killing and Cultural Formation,* ed. Robert G. Hamerton-Kelly [Stanford: Stanford University Press, 1987], 169) acknowledges weaknesses in Lorenz's ideas about aggression in humans but notes that he is not aware of "any extensive discussion of . . . 'the bond,' . . . wrought by common aggression; it seems to have been shuffled into the background, which is possibly a sign of some uneasiness."

18. Edward O. Wilson. *The Diversity of Life* (Cambridge, Mass.: Harvard University Press, 1992), 272.

19. The notion that our mere presence on the planet entails a measure of shame is neither obscure nor exotic and, though we commonly suppress it, it is an integral part of our reflexive experience of the world around us. Consider, for example, the message on a T-shirt I recently saw in a shop window: "Plants and animals disappear to make way for your fat ass."

20. For a discussion of this theme see Joseph Campbell, "The One into the Manifold," in *The Hero with a Thousand Faces* (New York: Bollingen, 1949). Interestingly, as Alex Turner pointed out to me, the word "karma" shares an Indo-European root with the word *teratoma,* or tumor, which comes into English from the Greek word for monster, reflecting the realization that the new thing is always a monster, defying the rules of nature itself, as indeed the starting point for Darwinian evolution is the radical monstrosity of the genetic mutation. We can add this to "community" and "blessing" on our list of old, shame-laden words that modernism has drained of their shame.

21. F. Turner, *Beauty,* 19.

22. L. Ferrand and L. J. Frachtenberg. 1915. "Shasta and Athapascan Myths from Oregon," *Journal of American Folklore* 28 (1915): 224–28, cited in Barbara C. Sproul, *Primal Myths: Creating the World* (New York: Harper, 1979), 232–36.

23. Some resist the idea that myth expresses a sense of horror and shame at the creation that is common to all cultures, suggesting that such myths are characteristic only of hierarchical or patriarchal cultures that exploit shame as a means of exerting authority. But this doesn't seem to be the case at all. Carolyn Merchant's discussion of the Penobscot story of the origin of corn ("Reinventing Eden: Western Culture as a Recovery Narrative," in *Uncommon Ground: Toward Reinventing Nature,* ed. William Cronon [New York: W. W. Norton, 1995], 132–59) is a good example of this misreading. In this story a woman betrays her husband through a liaison with a snake. It is only after her husband has killed her and dragged her body through the forest until the flesh is gone, then buried the bones, that corn emerges from her grave. Seeing this story as "ascensionist and progressive," and affirming in its treatment of women, in contrast to the Genesis story, Merchant overlooks both its striking similarity to the biblical story and the redemptions that story offers as well. Downplaying the betrayal with which the story begins, she makes the mistake of rescuing Woman from shame, rather than crediting her with its discovery.

24. Rappaport, "Obvious Aspects of Ritual"; and *Ritual and Religion in the Making of Humanity* (Cambridge: Cambridge University Press, 1999).

25. Catherine Pickstock, *After Writing: The Liturgical Consummation of Philosophy* (Oxford: Blackwell, 1998), 261–64.

26. Rappaport, "Obvious Aspects of Ritual," 197.

27. Victor Turner, *The Drums of Affliction: A Study of Religious Processes among the Ndembu of Zambia* (Oxford: Clarendon Press, 1968), 44.

28. Victor Turner, *The Ritual Process: Structure and Anti-Structure* (Ithaca: Cornell University Press, 1977), 131–32.

29. Some scholars have questioned Turner's idea that *communitas* exists outside and provides a way of transcending the power structures of a community. These "post-Turnerian" scholars stress that the rituals that provide access to *communitas* are themselves subject to authority and point out the extent to which values associated with *communitas,* including the sacred, are linked to political power. For a discussion of these ideas, see the introduction to David Chidester and Edward T. Linenthal, eds., *American Sacred Space* (Bloomington: University of Indiana Press, 1995), 1–42; also Lily Kong, "Mapping 'New' Geographies of Religion: Politics and Poetics in Modernity," *Progress in Human Geography* 25, no. 2 (2001): 211–33. For a critical discussion of the value of ritual with special reference to ecological restoration, see Lisa Meekison and Eric Higgs, "The Rites of Spring (and Other Seasons): The Ritualizing of Restoration," *Restoration & Management Notes* 16, no. 1 (1998): 73–81.

30. Kathleen Norris, *The Cloister Walk* (New York: Riverhead Books, 1996), 100.

31. Rappaport, "Obvious Aspects of Ritual," 197.

32. Tom F. Driver, *The Magic of Ritual: Our Need for Liberating Rites that Transform Our Lives and Our Communities* (San Francisco: Harper, 1991), 9.

33. This comment on the relationship between nationalism and ritual is based on observations by David McCloskey, professor of sociology at Seattle University.

34. Donald Worster, "John Muir and the Roots of American Environmentalism," in *The Wealth of Nature* (Oxford: Oxford University Press, 1993).

35. Donald Worster, review of *John Muir and His Legacy: The American Conservation Movement* by Stephen Fox in *Environmental Ethics* 5, no. 3 (1983): 277–81; and review of *The Pathless Way: John Muir and American Wilderness* by Michael P. Cohen, *Environmental Ethics* 10, no. 3 (1988): 267–70.

36. For a brief summary of Reformation thought in a historical context, see Richard Tarnas, "The Reformation," in *The Passion of the Western Mind: Understanding the Ideas That Have Shaped Our World View* (New York: Harmony Books, 1991).

37. Since the history of Puritan attitudes toward ritual is complicated, I use the term "puritan" in a generic sense and without the capital letter to refer to the skepticism regarding the importance and efficacy of ritual that is my primary concern here. See N. E. Brooks Holifield, *The Covenant Sealed: The Development of Puritan Sacramental Theology in Old and New England: 1570–1720* (New Haven: Yale University Press, 1974), esp. the epilogue, 225–30. According to Holifield, the New England Puritans, though sharing with Protestantism generally its re-

jection of the real presence of Christ in the Eucharist (and the ontological power of the sacraments generally) actually preserved a strong sacramental consciousness. This, Holifield argues, was an important element in Puritan thinking and religious practices for roughly the century following the founding of the colony at Plymouth in 1620. It was only after the religious revivals associated with the Great Awakening that began in New England about 1720 that an "anti-sacramental" mood began to prevail and sacramentalism went into a decline from which it never recovered. In a more general way Catherine L. Albanese deals with the development of ideas regarding matter and spirit and the relationship between them in *Nature Religion in America: From the Algonkian Indians to the New Age* (Chicago: University of Chicago Press, 1990). A principal theme of Albanese's book is that the search for adequate means of thinking about and dealing with this relationship has been a major concern of American thinkers from the beginning.

38. Michael P. Cohen, *The Pathless Way: John Muir and American Wilderness* (Madison: University of Wisconsin Press, 1984), 180. Though a weakness in his thinking, Muir's repression of awareness of the terrible in nature at least suggests a sensitivity to it that is, perhaps, the first step toward finding ways to deal with it productively—a step beyond the matter-of-fact attitude of the thoughtless consumer of nature or the utilitarian conservationist.

39. Bill McKibben, "Home," in *Hope, Human and Wild: True Stories of Living Lightly on the Earth* (Boston: Little, Brown, 1995). Also printed as "An Explosion of Green," *The Atlantic Monthly* April 1995, 61–83.

40. Henry David Thoreau, *Walden and Other Writings of Henry David Thoreau* (New York: Modern Library, 1937); Thoreau comments on the cutting of the forest near the pond on 173–74.

41. For an exploration of the value of Thoreau's thought in the development of a socially friendly environmentalism, see Daniel B. Botkin, *No Man's Garden: Thoreau and a New Vision for Civilization and Nature* (Washington, D.C.: Island Press, 2000).

42. *Walden*, 143.

43. It is interesting to compare Thoreau's formula of transubstantiation with formulas such as Coke Is It, and It's The Real Thing—slogans designed to confer transcendent value of a sort on a beverage that has, in fact, acquired a kind of sacramental value for many. Like Thoreau, the Coca-Cola advertisers are careful not to specify the result of this consecration.

44. *Walden*, 271–72.

45. Leo Marx, *The Machine in the Garden: Technology and the Pastoral Ideal in America* (London: Oxford University Press, 1964), 261 ff.

46. *Walden*, 273.

47. Marx, *Machine in the Garden*, 262.

48. Andrew Delbanco, "The Skeptical Pilgrim," *The New Republic*, July 6, 1992, 37–41.

49. Frederick Garber, *Thoreau's Redemptive Imagination* (New York: New York University Press, 1977). See also William R. Jordan III, "Renewal and Imag-

ination: Thoreau's Thought and the Restoration of Walden Pond," in *Thoreau's World and Ours: A Natural Legacy*, ed. Edmund A. Schofield and Robert C. Baron (Golden, Colo.: North American Press, 1993).

50. *Walden*, 292.

7. Sacrifice and Celebration

1. A. S. Leopold, S. A. Cain, C. M. Cottam, I. N. Gabrielson, and T. L. Kimball, "Wildlife Management in the National Parks," *Transactions, North American Wildlife and Natural Resources Conference* 28 (1963): 28–45.

2. Frederick Turner, "Cultivating the American Garden," in *Rebirth of Value: Meditations on Beauty, Ecology, Religion, and Education* (Albany: State University of New York Press, 1991), 51–64 (first published in *Harper's Magazine*, August 1985, 45–52). In the next ch., "Restoring the American Prairie," Turner extends his reflections on gardening to include restoration.

3. Victor Turner, "Are There Universals of Performance in Myth, Ritual, and Drama?" in *By Means of Performance*, ed. Richard Schechner and Willa Appel (New York: Cambridge University Press, 1990), 8–18.

4. Ibid., 18.

5. Excellent recent accounts of the practice and experience of restoration from a practitioner's perspective are Freeman House, *Totem Salmon: Life Lessons from Another Species* (Boston: Beacon Press, 1999); and Stephanie Mills, *In Service of the Wild: Restoring and Reinhabiting Damaged Land* (Boston: Beacon, 1995).

6. Susanne K. Langer, "The Great Dramatic Forms: The Comic Rythym," in *Comedy, Plays, Theory, and Criticism,* ed. Marvin Felheim (New York: Harcourt, Brace and World, 1962), 244.

7. Karen M. Holland, "Restoration Rituals: Transforming Workday Rituals into Inspirational Moments," *Restoration & Management Notes* 12, no. 2 (1994): 121–25; Dave Simpson, "A Note on Restoration Theater," *Restoration & Management Notes* 15, no. 2 (1997): 179–82. For comments on restoration as an occasion for festival, see Rory Turner, "Restoration as Festival," *Restoration & Management Notes* 10, no. 2 (1992): 177–80.

8. Joseph Meeker, *The Comedy of Survival: Literary Ecology and a Play Ethic* (Tucson: University of Arizona Press, 1997), 65 ff.

9. Joseph Campbell, *The Hero with a Thousand Faces* (New York: Bollingen, 1949), 28.

10. Ibid., 29. A sacrificial ritual such as the Mass has both elements, the festive communal meal and the killing that necessarily precedes it, though the modern shame-denying sensibility tends—mistakenly—to downplay the sacrifice. Significantly, environmentalists commonly deplore this sensibility when it takes the form of indifference or ignorance regarding our sources of food.

11. In a similar vein, several authors argue that romance provides the best literary model for a performative relationship between humans and the rest of nature (see Gísli Pálsson, "Human-Environmental Relations: Orientalism, Pater-

nalism, and Communalism," in *Nature and Society: Anthropological Perspectives,* ed. Philippe Descola and Gísli Pálsson [London: Routledge, 1996], esp. 72–76 and references cited there). Two decades ago in a small book titled *The Wooing of Earth* (New York: Scribners, 1980) René Dubos suggested the act of wooing or lovemaking—another performance genre—as a metaphor for human relations with landscapes.

12. Ihab Hassan, *Radical Innocence: Studies in The Contemporary American Novel* (Princeton: Princeton University Press, 1961), 34 ff.

13. See for example Maurice Gibbons, "Walkabout in High School," in *Crossroads,* ed. Louise Carus Mahdi et al. (Chicago: Open Court, 1996), 223–29. The failure of our society to provide efficacious rituals of passage into adulthood is widely recognized and has often been identified as a possible explanation for various psychological and social problems. The point is made very well in the film *Rebel without a Cause,* a classic tale of alienation in a society that fails to provide life-change rituals. Standing at the edge of a cliff just before participating in the game of chicken that leads to Buzz Gunderson's death, Jim Stark (played by James Dean) says to Buzz, "Why do we do this?" To which Buzz replies, "We have to do something."

14. Ronald L. Grimes, *Deeply into the Bone: Reinventing Rites of Passage* (Berkeley: University of California Press, 2000), 106–7.

15. Géza Róheim, *The Eternal Ones of the Dream: A Psychoanalytic Interpretation of Australian Myth and Ritual* (New York: International Universities Press, 1945), 231.

16. William R. Jordan III, "Loss of Innocence," *Restoration & Management Notes* 15, no. 1 (1997): 3–5.

17. Frederick Turner, *The Culture of Hope: A New Birth of the Classical Spirit* (New York: Free Press, 1995), 131–44.

18. For a valuable discussion of world-renewal traditions of the Navajo and Australian Aborigines in the context of his exploration of ritual, see Roy A. Rappaport's *Ritual and Religion in the Making of Humanity* (Cambridge: Cambridge University Press, 1999), 364–70. My son Bill suggests that the predictions of worldwide calamity for the year 2000 reflected a yearning for the descent into what Victor Turner calls anti-structure as the occasion for renewing the world at the turn of the millennium.

19. Frederick Turner, *Beauty: The Value of Values* (Charlottesville: University of Virginia Press, 1991), 22 ff.; and *Culture of Hope,* 48, 165 ff.

20. See books by Stephen J. Pyne, beginning with *Fire in America: A Cultural History of Wildland and Rural Fire* (Princeton: Princeton University Press, 1982). See also David J. Strohmaier, "The Ethics of Prescribed Fire: A Notable Silence," *Ecological Restoration* 18, no. 1 (2000): 5–9. On the public backlash against restoration, see *Restoration & Management Notes* 15, no. 1 (1997), 16–37, and 16, no. 1 (1998) 9–15.

21. William R. Jordan III, "Artistic Interpretation of a Prairie Knoll Restoration," *Restoration & Management Notes* 10, no. 1 (1992): 108. I should note that Ms. Westfall does not accept my interpretation of this piece as a form of sacrifice. When I discussed this with her, she said that she feels the shame is in the destruction of the prairie, not in the killing of trees to aid in its restoration.

22. Aldo Leopold, "The Round River," in *A Sand County Almanac, with Essays on Conservation from Round River* (New York: Ballantine, 1966), 197.

23. Turner, *Rebirth of Value,* 48; also Eric Partridge, *Origins* (New York: Macmillan, 1959), s.v. "blessing."

24. James Welch, *Winter in the Blood* (New York: Harper and Row, 1974), 5–6.

25. Christopher C. Norden, "Beyond Apocalypse: Some Reflections on Native Writers, Modern Literature—and Restoration as Ritual," *Restoration & Management Notes* 11, no. 1 (1993): 45–51.

26. Emile Durkheim, *The Elementary Forms of the Religious Life* (London: Collier Macmillan, 1915), 336.

27. Freeman House, "Restoring Relations: The Vernacular Approach to Ecological Restoration," *Restoration & Management Notes* 14, no. 1 (1996): 59.

28. Leo Marx, *The Machine in the Garden: Technology and the Pastoral Ideal in America* (London: Oxford University Press, 1964). My treatment of pastoral literature is based in large part on Marx's book and conversations I had with him during a tutorial at MIT in spring 1992.

29. Michael Gershman, *Diamonds: The Evolution of the Ballpark* (Boston: Houghton Mifflin, 1993); Scott Raphael Schiamberg, "For a Glimpse of Green: The Evolution of the American Pastoral Ideal and the Urban Ballpark" (paper for a course on the representation of nature in America, MIT, fall 1995).

30. Samuel Eliot Morison, *Admiral of the Ocean Sea: A Life of Christopher Columbus* (Boston: Little, Brown, 1942), 556.

31. A promising exception is the communally oriented bioregional movement, which includes a commitment to restoration. See, for example, Michael McGinnis, ed., *Bioregionalism* (London: Routledge, 1999). For an interesting historical exception, see J. Ronald Engel, *Sacred Sands: The Struggle for Community in the Indiana Dunes* (Middletown, Conn.: Wesleyan University Press, 1983).

32. Marx, *Machine in the Garden,* 364.

33. William R. Jordan III, "Standing with Nature," *Restoration & Management Notes* 10, no. 2 (1992): 111–12.

34. Victor Turner, *The Anthropology of Performance* (New York: PAJ Publications, 1987), esp. 21–32, 72–98.

35. Leo Marx, "Henry Thoreau: Excursions," in *The Pilot and the Passenger: Essays on Literature, Technology, and Culture in the United States* (New York: Oxford University Press, 1988), 76–82.

36. Max Oelschlaeger discusses this "hermeneutical step back" in *The Idea of Wilderness: From Prehistory to the Age of Ecology* (New Haven: Yale University Press, 1991), ch. 9. For Emerson, see B. L. Packer, *Emerson's Fall: A Reinterpretation of the Major Essays* (New York: Continuum Publishing, 1982), 178 ff.

37. Marx, *Machine in the Garden,* 364.

38. Keith Winterhalder, "Early History of Human Activities in the Sudbury Area and Ecological Damage to the Landscape," in *Restoration and Recovery of an Industrial Region,* ed. John M. Gunn (New York: Springer, 1995), 17–31.

39. Robert Frost, "The Figure a Poem Makes," in *Complete Poems of Robert Frost* (New York: Holt, Rinehart and Winston, 1949), v–viii.

40. Marx, *Machine in the Garden*, 363.

41. Catherine Pickstock, *After Writing: The Liturgical Consummation of Philosophy* (Oxford: Blackwell, 1998), 176.

42. George W. S. Trow, "The Harvard Black Rock Forest," *New Yorker,* June 11, 1984, 46. For an interesting discussion of the confusion of literal and figurative experience see Thomas de Zengotita, "The Numbing of the American Mind: Culture as Anesthetic," *Harper's,* April 2002, 33–40.

43. John Rodman, "Reflections on Tamarisk-Bashing," in *Restoration 1989: The New Management Challenge,* ed. H. Glenn Hughes and Thomas M. Bonnicksen (Madison, Wis.: Society for Ecological Restoration, 1990), 59–68.

44. Richard Garber, *Thoreau's Redemptive Imagination* (New York: New York University Press, 1977).

45. Karen M. Holland, "Restoration Rituals: Transforming Workday Tasks into Inspirational Rites," *Restoration & Management Notes* 12, no. 2 (1994): 121–25, and the accompanying "box" by Stephen F. Christy.

46. Suzi Gablik, *The Reenchantment of Art* (New York: Thames and Hudson, 1991). Gablik offers a critique of modernist art and explores the work of artists like Mierle Ukeles, artist for the New York City Department of Sanitation, as examples of a new kind of art that is accessible to non-specialists and relevant to their concerns. On links between "environmental" artists and restoration see Barbara C. Matilsky, *Fragile Ecologies: Contemporary Artists' Interpretations and Solutions* (New York: Rizzoli International, 1992).

47. Ronald L. Grimes, *Reading, Writing and Ritualizing: Ritual in Liturgical, Fictive and Public Places* (Washington, D.C.: Pastoral Press, 1993), 12 ff.

8. Conservation and Community

1. Pico Iyer, "The New Business Class," *New York Times Magazine,* March 8, 1998, 37–40.

2. For thoughtful discussions of the relationship between restoration and wilderness and the role of restoration in wilderness areas, see David N. Cole, "Ecological Manipulation in Wilderness—An Emerging Management Dilemma," *International Journal of Wilderness* 2, no. 1 (1995): 15–19; David N. Cole, "Paradox of the Primeval: Ecological Restoration in Wilderness," *Ecological Restoration* 18, no. 2 (2000): 77–86; Jean Greig and Thomas Whillans, "Restoring Wilderness Functions and the Vicarious Basis of Ecological Stewardship," *Revue d'études canadiennes* 33, no. 2 (1988): 116–25. Also relevant here is my essay "Restoration, Community and Wilderness" in *Restoring Nature: Perspectives from the Social Sciences and Humanities,* ed. Paul H. Gobster and R. Bruce Hull (Washington, D.C.: Island Press, 2000).

3. William R. Jordan III, "Two Psychologies," *Restoration & Management Notes* 8, no. 1 (1990): 2.

4. Reed F. Noss, "Wilderness Recovery and Ecological Restoration: An Example for Florida," *Earth First!* 5, no. 8 (1985): 18–19; Reed F. Noss and Allen Y.

Cooperrider, *Saving Nature's Legacy: Protecting and Restoring Biodiversity* (Washington, D.C.: Island Press, 1994), 157–59.

5. For an introduction to this debate, see William Cronon, "The Trouble with Wilderness; or, Getting Back to the Wrong Nature," in *Uncommon Ground: Toward Reinventing Nature* (New York: W. W. Norton, 1995). For a comprehensive treatment see J. Baird Callicott and Michael P. Nelson, eds., *The Great Wilderness Debate* (Athens: University of Georgia Press, 1998). Also see articles by Dave Foreman and J. Baird Callicott in the winter and spring 1995 issues of *Wild Earth*.

6. For an exception see Reid M. Helford, "Constructing Nature or Constructing Science: Expertise, Activist Science, and Public Conflict in the Chicago Wilderness," in *Restoring Nature: Perspectives from the Social Sciences and Humanities,* ed. Paul H. Gobster and R. Bruce Hull (Washington, D.C.: Island Press, 2000).

7. This formulation of Tillich's idea comes from Ernest Becker in *The Denial of Death* (New York: Free Press, 1973), 281.

8. Frederick Turner, *Genesis: An Epic Poem* (Dallas: Saybrook, 1988).

Selected Readings

Becker, Ernest. *The Denial of Death*. New York: Free Press, 1973.

Bloom, Harold. *The American Religion: The Emergence of the Post-Christian Nation*. New York: Touchstone, 1992.

Denevan, William M. "The Pristine Myth: The Landscape of the Americas in 1492." *The Americas Before and After 1492: Current Geographical Research*, special issue, *Annals of the Association of American Geographers* 82, no. 3 (September 1992): 369–85.

Descola, Philippe, and Gísli Pálsson, eds. *Nature and Society: Anthropological Perspectives*. London: Routledge and Kegan Paul, 1996.

Douglas, Mary. *Purity and Danger: An Analysis of the Concepts of Pollution and Taboo*. London: Routledge, 1966.

Eliade, Mircea. *The Myth of the Eternal Return*. Princeton: Princeton University Press, 1954.

Hamerton-Kelly, Robert G., ed. *Violent Origins: Walter Burkert, René Girard, and Jonathan Z. Smith on Ritual Killing and Cultural Formation*. Stanford: Stanford University Press, 1987.

Jordan, William R., III, John D. Aber, and Michael E. Gilpins, eds. *Restoration Ecology: A Synthetic Approach to Ecological Research*. Cambridge: Cambridge University Press, 1987.

Lewis, R. W. B. *The American Adam: Innocence, Tragedy, and Tradition in the Nineteenth Century*. Chicago: University of Chicago Press, 1955.

Lorenz, Konrad. "Habit, Ritual, and Magic." In *On Aggression*. Translated by Marjorie Kerr Wilson. New York: Bantam, 1966.

Marx, Leo. *The Machine in the Garden: Technology and the Pastoral Ideal in America*. London: Oxford University Press, 1964.

Mauss, Marcel. *The Gift: The Form and Reason for Exchange in Archaic Societies*. Translated by W. D. Halls. New York: W. W. Norton, 1990.

Paz, Octavio. "Mexico and the United States." In *The Labyrinth of Solitude*. Translated by Lysander Kemp, Yara Milos, and Rachel Phillips Belash. New York: Grove Weidenfeld, 1985.

Pickstock, Catherine. *After Writing: The Liturgical Consummation of Philosophy*. Oxford: Blackwell, 1998.

Rappaport, Roy A. "The Obvious Aspects of Ritual." In *Ecology, Meaning and Religion*. Berkeley: North Atlantic Books, 1979.

———. *Ritual and Religion in the Making of Humanity*. Cambridge: Cambridge University Press, 1999.

Thoreau, Henry David. *Walden*. New York: Modern Library, 1937.

Turner, Frederick. *Beauty: The Value of Values*. Charlottesville: University of Virginia Press, 1991.

———. "Cultivating the American Garden." In *Rebirth of Value: Meditations on Beauty, Ecology, Religion, and Education*. Albany: State University of New York Press, 1991.

———. *The Culture of Hope: A New Birth of the Classical Spirit*. New York: Free Press, 1995.

———. "Performed Being: Word Art as a Human Inheritance." In *Natural Classicism: Essays on Literature and Science*. New York: Paragon, 1985.

———. "Restoring the American Prairie." In *Rebirth of Value: Meditations on Beauty, Ecology, Religion, and Education*. Albany: State University of New York Press, 1991.

Turner, Victor. *The Drums of Affliction: A Study of Religious Processes among the Ndembu of Zambia*. Oxford: Clarendon Press, 1968.

———. *The Ritual Process: Structure and Anti-Structure*. Ithaca: Cornell University Press, 1977.

Index

Aborigines. *See* Australian Aborigines

Abraham, 138, 148

Abram, David, 223n40

Adam. *See* Fall (from Garden of Eden)

adaptive management, 206n5

Adventures of Huckleberry Finn (Twain): as pastoral, 178, 180, 181, 184; relationships and, 144–45, 148

advertising, 187, 230n43

Africa: anthropocentrism in, 141–42; category violation in, 126–27, 227n8; egalitarianism and, 35

aggressive behavior: love and, 142–44, 148, 227–28n17; nonanthropocentric cultures and, 140

agriculture: conservation movement and, 28–29; crop rotation with prairie, 114–15, 173, 197; intimacy with nature and, 87–88; invention of, and existential anxiety, 39; as paradigm of human relationship with nature, 88; restoration as form of, 87–89; sacrificial rituals and, 39, 53, 88, 139; sustainable, 115; Thoreau on, 91–92, 155–56, 218n22. *See also* monstrous principle in creation

Albanese, Catherine L., 45, 230n37

alchemy, 78

alienation, Emersonians and, 63, 214n21

Allen, T. F. H., 221n18

altruism, 37

amateurs. *See* voluntarism

Amazon natives, 140

ambiguity: creative killing and, 52–53; gift exchange and, 52, 68; human violence and, 60; metaphysics of dirt and, 127–28; and performance, restoration as, 164, 187–88; relationship with nature and, 41. *See also* economics; gift exchange; other, the; shame

American Adam, The: Innocence, Tragedy, and Tradition in the Nineteenth Century (Lewis), 56–57

American Indians. *See* Native Americans

American religion, 62–63, 213–14n18

animal-rights activists, 189

animals. *See* community of humans and nature; exotic species; reintroduction of species; species, nonhuman

anthropocentrism, 140–42

anthropology, egalitarianism and, 35, 208n4

anxiety. *See* existential anxiety

aquatic ecosystems: complexity and, 98; ecological ghosts and, 104–5; input of pollutants or nutrients in, 86, 99; marine, 11, 97, 98, 99; solar energy in restoration of, 110–11. *See also* rivers; wetland restoration

Arachne, 95

Arboretum (University of Wisconsin at Madison): defectiveness of restorations, 79–81; as idea, extension of,

Arboretum *(continued)*
    205n3; killing of trees and, 172–73, 188,
    232n21; origins of, 1–2; as research fa-
    cility, 18–19; restoration as down-
    played by, 17–18, 205n3; scale and, 113;
    seed-into-sod method, 111; time-style
    of, 106–7, 221n17; volunteers and, 133
Archibald, George, 219n31
arid ecosystems, 15, 86–87
Army Corps of Engineers, 12, 116
art: analogy of, restoration and, 119,
    125–26, 129–30, 224–25n46; existential
    shame and, 45, 48–49; modernist
    alienation of, 192, 234n46; as ritual,
    descendant of, 182; sacrificial ritual
    and, 172–73, 188, 232n21; stability vs.,
    69–70, 216n34. *See also* performance;
    reproduction of ecosystems
artifacts, facts as, 124
Armstrong, Karen, 213n10
Arunta people, 176
assembly rules, 104
As You Like It (Shakespeare), 180–81
Athena, 95
audience, 162, 164, 191, 193
Australian Aborigines: initiation rituals of,
    170; singing the world into being,
    124; world renewal rituals of, 160,
    176, 203
authenticity: creation of, 125–26, 224–25n46;
    of restored landscape, 117–26. *See also*
    ontology and restoration
authority: *communitas* and, 151, 169,
    229n29; initiation and defiance of,
    171; religion and, 140; ritual as tran-
    scending, 151
autonomy, authenticity as, 118–21, 123–24

Baby Boom (film), 177, 178
Babylonian culture, 146, 171–72
back-to-the-earth movement, community
    and, 44
Bagpipes and Bonfires festival (Lake For-
    est, IL), 190
Barnes, Chris, 117
baseball, 178
beauty: as highest value, 195; as obsolete,
    52; as product of performance, 129;
    restoration and discovery of, 86–87;
    shame and, 48–49, 50, 173; value of
    restoration and, 129–30; vs. stability,

69–70. *See also* values
Becker, Ernest: on awareness of the other,
    51, 74; on shame, 210n22; on worm-
    hood, 74; on Zen, 75–76
Bellah, Robert, 214n18
Berlin, Isaiah, 93–94, 211n29
Berry, Thomas, 60–61
Bettelheim, Bruno, 49
Betz, Bob: on gardening, 87; as maverick,
    182; and monarch butterflies, 76;
    prairie restoration, 26
Bible: ambiguity intolerance and, 128; cre-
    ation account of, 40, 60, 146; sacrifice
    in, 138, 148. *See also* Fall (from Garden
    of Eden)
Big Bang, 40, 45, 50
Billy Budd (Melville), sacrifice and, 65
biophilia, 3
bioregionalism, community and, 44
birding, 180, 192
birds: habitat restoration for, 76–77; raised
    in captivity, 219n31; seed dispersal by,
    11
bison: complexity of restoration and, 98;
    economic restoration and, 115; scale
    and quality of restoration and, 107, 110
blessing, as term, 174
Bloom, Harold, 62, 63
Bogosian, Eric, 215n30
Borgmann, Albert, 124
Botkin, Daniel, 84
boundaries: categories, violation of,
    126–27, 139–42, 148; historic range of
    variation, 206n17; territorialism,
    142–44, 145–46, 148. *See also* change;
    limitation and difference
Bradshaw, Anthony, 82, 217n14
Brave New World (Huxley), 69–70
Brint, Steven, 34, 208n3
"Brook in the City" (Frost), 84
Brownson, Orestes, 65–66, 215n25, 224n40
Brumbach, Bill, 106
brush clearing, 188–90
Buell, Lawrence, 215n34
Bunker, Archie and Edith, 211n24
Burma-reed, 11
business class, 199

CalFed, 116
California: comedy in restoration perfor-
    mance in, 165; Muir's misperception

of, 200; tamarisk clearing in, 188; volunteers and regard for landscape, 133; wetland restoration in, 101, 116

Callicott, Baird, 106–7, 141

Calvinism: environmentalism and, 58, 145, 152, 212n6; redemption and, 57–58. *See also* puritanism

Campbell, Joseph: on comedy and tragedy, 166–67; on liminal state, 184; on monstrous in mythology, 60; on sacrifice, 88

categories, violation of, 126–27, 139–42, 148

Catholicism. *See* Christianity; Mass

cattle, 98–99, 131

CCC (Civilian Conservation Corps), 176–77

cedars, 112

celebration, 165–66

Central Park (New York City), restoration and, 10

change: anguish in bringing about, 38; characterization of, 105; and community as term, 66; death, 146; as difference in dimension of time, 146; environmentalism and denial of, 38–39, 167; irreversible, quality of restoration and, 102–5; reversal of, 83–85, 185; shame and, 139, 146–48, 228n19. *See also* creation; limitation and difference

chaos, 122, 124, 131, 176

chaotic systems, 103–4

Charlotte's Web (White), 49

Cheney, Jim, 225n46

chestnut, American, 102–3, 220n9

Chewong people, 141

Chicago: rhythm of restorative work, 193; volunteers and value of restoration, 133. *See also* oak savannas

children: awareness of the other and, 74; and existential shame, 49; initiation rituals and, 126–27, 168–69, 170, 171, 232n13; limitation and, 51

Chinese culture, reproduction and, 224n46

Christianity: "American religion" and, 213–14n18; and despoliation of nature, 152; Eucharist, 201; sacrifice and, 53, 215n26, 231n10; seven sacraments of, 192. *See also* Bible; communion; Fall (from Garden of Eden); Mass; puritanism; redemption; religion

cinema metaphor, 100

"Circles" (Emerson), 59

cities, valuing of nature within, 159, 179, 199–200

Civilian Conservation Corps (CCC), 176–77

clapper rail, 101

Clewell, Andre, 213n10

Coca-Cola, 230n43

coefficient of interaction, 14

Cohen, Michael, 154–55

Collins, Ed, 12, 77, 113, 170

colonial land relationship, 28–29

Columbus, Christopher, 179

comedy and festival, 165–68, 177, 189–90

communion: act of eating and, 174; Mass and, 148–49

communion with nature: avoidance of community and, 44; companion animals and, 70, 216n34; defined, 56; difference and, 60–62; language and, 92; liturgy and, 142; John Muir and, 154–55, 158–59, 230n38; purity vs., 126, 152; purposeful engagement and, 77–78; restoration and, 72–73; Rosemary Reuther and, 61; shame and, 41; Henry Thoreau and, 154, 155–59, 182–83, 202–3, 230n43; unity and, 59–60. *See also* redemption

communitas: and authority, 151, 169, 229n29; base in community and ritual techniques, 191; as evolutionary reward, 170; function of, 149–50; nationalism and fear of, 151; ordeals of initiation and, 169–70

community: availability of in modern society, 186, 216n34; *communitas* and (*see communitas*); as cultural achievement vs. given, 35–37, 42–43; Emersonians as precluding, 63; emotional convenience vs., 69; etymology of, 66; exclusiveness of, 36; failure to progress toward, 46; future of, 52–53; hierarchy and inequality as intrinsic to, 33–35, 208n4; idealization of, 33, 72; initiation rituals as central to, 35–36, 169–70, 180; Ironists and, 66, 215n25; modern myths of, 44–45; organism

community *(continued)*
    metaphor of, 209n116; pastoral art
    and, 180–81; as positive term limiting
    debate, 33, 42; puritanism and, 212n6;
    and ritual, importance of, 149–50; so-
    cial dramas and, 163; as term, 66,
    215n26; as value, and difficulty of
    achieving, 36–37; weaker forms of, in
    the West, 208n3; withdrawal from, as
    communion with nature, 44, 58, 59,
    159. *See also* land ethic; relationships;
    ritual
community of humans and nature: basic
    questions regarding, 32–33; civiliza-
    tion as key to, 54–55; community as
    essential to, 181–82; culture of nature
    and, 120, 223n39; predator and prey
    relationships and, 36, 189; purity vs.,
    126; restoration as context for, 72–73,
    184–85, 197, 201–2; rights movements
    and, 55; ritual and *(see* performance,
    restoration as); social drama and, 163;
    and sources for text, 7; stages of entry
    into, generally, 51–53 *(see also* ambigu-
    ity; economics; gift exchange; other,
    the); success of restoration projects
    and, 174–77. *See also* communion with
    nature; human regard for landscape;
    nature/culture distinction; restoration
commutation and ritual, 148–49
compassion, 61
compensation, definition of restoration
    and, 22. *See also* mitigation, legal
complexity, quality of restoration and,
    97–98, 100, 219n1
complex pastoral, 177–78, 185
concentration camp restoration, 23
conscience, ritual as forming, 151
conservation: constituency for, as shallow,
    31–32, 41, 200–201; restoration as par-
    adigm for, 26–27, 195–96, 197; resto-
    ration as part of, 12–13
conservation movement: agriculture and,
    28–29; consumption and, 42; philoso-
    phy of, 28–29; species preservation
    and, 29
conservation policies: irreproducible eco-
    systems and, 105; national parks,
    161–62
consumption: conservationism and, 42;
    minimal, ethic of, 38, 41, 71–72; sacred

other and, 38; of wilderness, pressures
    of, 159, 179–80, 197–200
copying, restoration as, 24, 93
coral reefs, complexity of restoration and,
    98
cordgrass marshes, 97
corn, origin myth of, 228n23
cosmos, 122, 163, 176, 224n41
cranes, 219n31
Crazy Horse statue, 131
creation: biblical account of, 40, 60, 146,
    213n10; monstrousness and *(see* mon-
    strous principle in creation); in
    mythology, 40–41, 45; premodern cul-
    tures and accounts of, 47–48, 60,
    146–47; ritual as paradigm of, 163–64;
    of sacred, ritual and, 122; of social
    change, ritual and, 151. *See also* Fall
    (from Garden of Eden); world renewal
creationism, environmentalism and, 40,
    41, 167–68
creative, ritual as, 151
crisis, environmental, 6
crop rotation, prairie and, 114–15, 173, 197
"Cultivating the American Garden"
    (Turner), 160–61
cultural evolution: defiance of authority
    and, 171; redemption and, 167; resto-
    ration and, 90, 133–36
culture: knowledge and, 93–94; living gra-
    ciously on planet as task of, 6. *See also*
    community; egalitarianism; hierarchy
    and inequality; human regard for
    landscape; nature/culture distinction
Culture of Hope, The (Turner), 69
Curtis, John: individualistic ecology of,
    221n17; on oak savannas, 135; succes-
    sion trends and, 112; *The Vegetation of
    Wisconsin*, 135, 204
Curtis Prairie (UW Arboretum): beauty
    of, 129–30; fire and, 10, 80; scale and,
    108; stone fences and, 12
cycles of nature, asymmetry of, 137

Dante, 167
data, as given, 124
"Daylighting the Woods" (Westfall),
    172–73, 232n21
death: burial of dead, 198–99; ecological
    immortality, 134–36; existential shame
    and, 48, 146. *See also* killing; shame

deception: gift exchange and, 68; mating rituals and, 142–43

deep ecology: community as idealized in, 33; shame ignored by, 46

defects in restorations, research and, 79–81

definition of who we are, ecological restoration and, 85–87

Delbanco, Andrew, 158, 210n22, 212n6

Denial of Death, The (Becker), 74

dependence. *See* limitation and difference; shame

Desai, Narayan, 25

Desana people, 140

Descola, Philippe, 140

deserts, 15, 86–87

destiny, 166

destruction. *See* killing; monstrous principle in creation; sacrifice

Dewey, John, 212n6

DeWitt, Cal, 103

Diamond, Stanley, 128

Dickinson, Emily, 38

difference. *See* limitation and difference

Dillard, Annie, 45

dirt, metaphysics of, 127–28

domestication: of animals, 39, 154; initiation rituals and, 169; of natural landscape, meaning and, 119–20. *See also* agriculture

Douglas, Mary, 67, 126–28, 139

drama. *See* performance

drama, social, 163

Driver, Tom, 151

dualism. *See* nature/culture distinction

duck mating ritual, 143–44

Dunwiddie, Peter, 100

dynamics, range of variation and, 22, 206n7

Earth's Insights (Callicott), 141

Earthwatch, 197

ecofeminism, 33, 46

ecology: defects in restoration and, 79–81; definition of restoration and effect on, 23; evaluation of restoration and, 101–2; as healing art, 81–82; mechanistic vs. restorative, 82–83, 217nn14,15. *See also* ecosystems; environmentalism

economics: alienation from landscape and, 159; gift exchange in contrast to, 52; implications of, 55–56; landscapes as

obsolescent and, 24–25; quality of restoration and, 102, 113–16; restoration as solution to problem of, 52; and shallowness of conservation constituency, 31–32; shame and, 41; skepticism about restoration and, 17; utilitarian relationship to landscape and, 28–29; value of restoration and, 131–33. *See also* ambiguity; gift exchange; other, the

ecosystems: assembly rules for, 104; creation of, 217n14; ecological immortality of, 134–36; intimacy with, 164; as irreproducible, 104–5; reproduction of (*see* reproduction of ecosystems); self-sustaining restoration of, 84–85, 125; succession process of, 103–4; work done by, in restoration, 77, 110–12, 116. *See also* aquatic ecosystems; forests; nature; prairies; reproduction of ecosystems; restoration; rivers

egalitarianism: Enlightenment "naturalization" of, 34–35; as social achievement vs. natural state, 35–37, 42–43. *See also* hierarchy and inequality

ego: community and, 63; hope and, 63; Ironists and, 64; limits as scandal to, 48; restoration and stilling of, 78, 125, 126; setting aside of, 61, 75–76. *See also entries at* self

Eiseley, Loren: on human abilities acquired, 90; and monstrous in nature, 45; on reentry into world, 54, 202–3

Eliade, Mircea, 121–22, 171, 202

Elliott, Robert, 119, 120, 121, 125

Emerson, Ralph Waldo: and "American religion," 62; difference and, 59, 61; and language, 218n30; and limitation, 59; and nature, 53, 58; and Original Sin, 40; and poetry as context for redemption, 183; unity and, 59–60

Emersonians: Calvinism, reaction to, 58, 212n6; defined, 58; as Hope, party of, 58–64

endangered species, 101

Enlightenment, 34–35, 151. *See also* modernism

entropy, as correlate of shame, 49–50

Enuma Elish, 146

environmental crisis, role of, 6

environmentalism: environment as concept in, 19; negative message of, 1, 2,
28; restoration movement as contribution to, 8; sources for the text and,
6–7; utilitarianism, 28–29. *See also*
community of humans and nature;
sacred, landscape as; skepticism about
restoration
environmental justice, 46
epistemological limits, 106–7
equality. *See* egalitarianism; hierarchy and
inequality
erosion, 115, 156–58
Escher, Jerry, 172
Eskimo people, 146–47
esthetics. *See* beauty
ethics: comedy and, 166; etiquette and,
225n46; minimal consumption, 38, 41,
71–72; Protestantism and, 151–53; ritual and creation of, 186; values creation and building of, 4–5, 6. *See also*
land ethic; values
etiquette, 149, 164, 193, 198, 225n46
Euripides, 139
evaluation of restoration: ecosystem definitions and, 101–2; as performance,
193; vital signs repertory and, 102;
wetlands, 101
evolution: autonomy as authenticity and,
121; avoidance of change and, 39; *communitas* and, 170; cultural, restoration
and (*see* cultural evolution); denial of,
41; land ethic and, 30; limits and,
122–23; monstrous principle of creation and, 60, 228n20; postvalue society and, 52; restoration projects and
concern for, 22, 206n7; "restore" as
term and helix of, 84; self-awareness
and, 133–34; shame and, 147; value of
restoration and, 133–34
exceptionalism, 146
existential anxiety: agriculture and, 39;
community formation and, 43; domestication of animals and, 39; as
error vs. vital experience, 45; killing
and, 42
existential shame. *See* shame
exotic species: defective restorations and
research in, 81; ecological infiltration
and, 112; fire in control of, 80; human
self-understanding and, 86; as irre-

versible change, 103, 220n10; on Key
Biscayne, 10–11; restoration as ritual
and removal of, 172, 188–89. *See also*
killing; species, nonhuman
exploitation, use vs., 42–43
extinct species: cultural evolution and, 134;
restoration quality and, 102–3, 104,
220n9

facts, 124, 183
"Faking It" (Stille), 224n46
"Faking Nature" (Elliott), 119
Fall (from Garden of Eden): Calvinism and,
58–59; Emersonians and, 58–60, 64; environmental thinkers and, 145; fortunate, 70–71; Ironists and, 64–65, 70–71;
as metaphor in nineteenth-century literature, 57; redemption from, 172
fate, 166
Fermi National Laboratory prairie restoration project: economics of restoration
and, 114; Bob Jenkins and, 108; methods used in, 109
festival, comedy and, 165–68, 177, 189–90
fire: artificial starting of, 107, 113, 130; controversy over deliberate use of, 172;
discovery of role of, 80; human role
in ecology and, 83, 85–86; prairie and,
10, 16, 80, 85–86, 107, 189–90;
Prometheus' stealing of, 94–95; ritual
of use of, 189–91
fire suppression: ease of restoration and,
98; ponderosa forests and, 15–16, 113
fishing, 115–16
Fitzgerald, F. Scott, 184, 185
Flanagan, James, 34–35, 208n4
Florida, 12, 116, 201
food, shame-denial and, 231n10
food chain, 55–56
forestry: economics of restoration and,
115–16; roll-vortex strips in, 76–77
forests: complexity of restoration and, 98;
creation of authentic, 125–26; exotic
species in, 103; fire suppression and,
15–16, 98, 113; recreation of, 81; removal for restoration, 11, 76, 171–72,
232n21; roll-vortex strips of, 76–77;
severity of disturbance and, 98;
species reintroduction in, 15
fortune, 166
Foster, Cheryl, 48

France, Robert, 227n10
Frazer, Ian, 130–31
friendship, 143
Frost, Robert, 61, 84, 116, 184
functional attributes, quality of restoration and, 100–101
Fussell, Paul, 213n18

game, restoration as, 27
Garber, Frederick, 158
Garber, Richard, 188
gardening: distinguished from restoration, 24, 87; restoration scale as, 25. *See also* agriculture
garlic mustard, 103
Gemeinschaft, 42
Genesis. *See* Fall (from Garden of Eden)
Genesis (Turner), 203–4
Gennep, Arnold van, 142, 149
Gershman, Michael, 178
Gesellschaft, 42
ghosts, ecological, 105, 117, 125–26
gift exchange: community and, 66; ecological immortality in, 134–36; environmentalism and, 71–73; function of, 51–52, 66–69, 71–72; restoration as practice of, 52, 88–89, 120–21, 139; shame and, 69, 137–39, 149; value of restoration in, 96, 133. *See also* ambiguity; economics; other, the
Gift, The (Mauss), 66–69
glaciers, restoration to conditions left by, 12
goose mating ritual, 142–44, 148
Goulder, Cindy, 89
grace: defined, 56; restoration and, 77; sacrifice and, 174
grazing, 107, 131
Great Gatsby, The (Fitzgerald), 184, 185
Great Plains, The (Frazer), 130–31
Greece, ancient. *See* mythology
Greene, Henry: esthetics of, 129; as maverick, 182; seed-into-sod method, 111
Greene Prairie (UW Arboretum), 129–30
Griller (Bogosian), 215n30
Grimes, Ronald, 36, 162, 169, 170
guilt: shame conflated with, 60, 147, 152; shame distinguished from, 46–47, 147, 210n22

habitat creation and restoration, 115
Halcyon Commons (Berkeley, CA), 133

Hans, James, shame as universal, 47, 210n24
happiness. *See* communion with nature; redemption
Hassan, Ihab, 168
Hawthorne, Nathaniel, on monstrous in nature, 64, 65
Healing Nature, Repairing Relationships (France), 227n10
health, restoration of: ecology as, 81–82; restoration distinguished from, 23, 206n9; vital signs repertory and, 102
Heidegger, Martin, 121
Herman, A. L., 37, 43
hierarchy and inequality: environmentalism as downplaying, 72; as intrinsic to community, 33–35, 208n4. *See also* egalitarianism
hiking, 180, 192
historic range of variation, 22, 206n7
history: alchemy and redemption from, 78; embracing of, Ironists and, 66, 215n25; exploration of, via restoration, 83–84; historic range of variation, 22, 206n7; pastoral tradition and, 185; quality of restoration and, 103, 105–6; rejection of, Emersonian, 58, 65–66; rescue of landscape from, 50; return to past, attempts at, 24, 83, 185; "snapshot" objectives, 17, 21, 84, 100, 206n6; value of restoration and, 130–31
History of God, A (Armstrong), 213n10
Ho-Chunk (Winnebago) people, 128
Hoekstra, T. W., 221n18
Holifield, N. E., 229–30n37
hope: ego transcendence and, 63; Emersonians and, 63–64. *See also* redemption
Hope, party of, 58–64
horticulture. *See* agriculture; gardening
House, Freeman, 77, 90, 176
Howe, Herbert, 94
Howe, Irving, 59–60
Howell, Signe, 141
Huckleberry Finn. See *Adventures of Huckleberry Finn* (Twain)
human beings: cultural evolution and gift to nature, 133–36; as ecologically abnormal species, 145–46, 228n19; as invariably destructive, 2; as most natural, 118, 123, 134; neoteny, 171; as

human beings *(continued)*
    outside nature, 29, 41, 121; under-
        standing of role of, in ecosystem,
        85–86. *See also* communion with na-
        ture; community; human regard for
        landscape; nature/culture distinction
human regard for landscape: economics of
    restoration and, 114–16, 132–33; qual-
    ity of restoration and, 97, 176, 203;
    and restoration as new paradigm,
    203–4; survival of nature dependent
    on, 15–17; value of restoration and,
    132–33
Humpty Dumpties, 104–5, 185
hunting and gathering: restoration as type
    of, 89–90; rituals associated with, 53,
    139, 140–41, 189. *See also* killing
Husserl, Edmund, 121, 224n40
Huxley, Aldous, 69–70, 186

ideas: action preceding, 196; generation of
    values and, 24–25
Ignatieff, Michael, 211n29
"I, Lightning" (Jordan), 92–93
illness, shame and, 47, 210n22
illusion, restoration as, 161–62, 164
imagination: cycles of life and death and
    need for, 137; historic, restoration
    and, 130–31; redemptive, 154–59; and
    sympathetic identification with na-
    ture, 154. *See also* performance
immortality, ecological, 134–36
incompetence. *See* limitation and differ-
    ence
Indians. *See* Native Americans
indigenous peoples. *See* Native Americans;
    traditional and premodern cultures
individualism: Emerson and, 212n6,
    212–13n9; Emersonians and, 212n6;
    liberalism and, 55; mating rituals and,
    143; pastoral art and, 180–82, 233n31;
    puritanism and, 153, 180, 181, 212n6;
    self-sacrifice vs., 213–14n18
infants. *See* children
initiation rituals: category violation and,
    126–27; community vs. individualism
    and, 35–36, 169–70, 180; defined, 168;
    elements of, 169–70; as emotionally
    demanding, 35–36, 43, 150; incentive
    and, 36, 209n8; lack of, 168–69,
    170–71, 232n13; as mandatory, 209n8;

new paradigm of restoration and,
    199; restoration and, 168–71
innocence: environmentalism and, 71–73,
    171; idealization of, Emersonians and,
    58, 64, 71; loneliness and, 63–64; loss
    of, Ironists and, 65, 66; radical,
    168–69; and sacrifice in restoration,
    172; yearning for, 179
input of pollutants or nutrients, 86, 99
insects, 76
insincerity, 68
intelligence, 145
International Crane Foundation, 219
Intichiuma, 176, 203
intimacy, 167
invasive species. *See* exotic species
Invisible Pyramid, The (Eiseley), 54
Iphigenia, 139
Irony, party of, 64–65
Iyer, Pico, 199

Jackson, Wes, 115
James, Henry, 64–65, 70
James, William, on suffering, 47
Janzen, Dan, 25, 182
Japanese culture, reproduction and,
    224–25n46
Jastrow, Julie, 173
Jenkins, Bob, 108
Jensen, Jens, 87
Job, 128
*John Muir and the Roots of American Envi-
    ronmentalism* (Worster), 151–52, 153
Joshua people, 147
justification, 183
juventocracy, 171

kangaroo rats, 11
karma, as term, 228n20
Katz, Eric, 119, 120, 121
Key Biscayne, FL, 10–11
killing: agricultural rituals and, 39, 53, 88,
    139; conservationism and, 42; ecolo-
    gists as not addressing, 55–56; hunting
    rituals and, 53, 139, 140–41, 189; liber-
    alism as not addressing, 55, 56; resto-
    ration and, 172–74, 188–91; sacred
    other and, 38. *See also* exotic species;
    monstrous principle in creation; sacri-
    fice; shame
King Lear (Shakespeare), 71, 181

Kirtland's warbler, 76–77
Kissimmee River, FL, 12, 116
Kita, Sandy, 225n46
kitsch, existential shame and, 210–11n24, 216n34
knowledge, participatory, 93–94
Kundera, Milan, 210n24
!Kung San people, 35

Lake Forest, IL, 136, 190
lakes, ecological ghosts in, 104–5
land, living close to, 43
land community. *See* community of humans and nature
land ethic: ambivalence of community and, 42–43; four values of, 30, 32, 33; selective reading of nature in, 33, 37; use vs. exploitation and, 42–43
landscape. *See* community of humans and nature; human regard for landscape; monstrous principle in creation; nature; nature/culture distinction; sacred, landscape as
landscape architecture, 115, 205n3
Langer, Susanne, 165, 166
language: of action, ritual and, 182–83; communion through, 182–83; meaninglessness and, 33, 52; and restoration definitions, 25, 207n11; restoration and learning of, 51
leadership in ritual creation, 191
Lee, Richard, 35
legal compensation. *See* mitigation, legal
leisure. *See* recreation
Lele people, 126–27, 141
Leonard, John, 215n26
Leopold, Aldo: community and, 33, 42–43; conservation defined by, 42; and organism integration metaphor, 30, 209n16; origins of thought of, 30–31; on penalties of ecological awareness, 174; on relationship with nonhuman species, 30, 32; subjectivism and, 213–14n18; use vs. exploitation and, 43; and UW Arboretum, 1–2; values, change in, 43. *See also* land ethic
Leopold, Starker, 161–62
Lewis, R. W. B., 56–58, 63–66, 70–71
liberalism: core ideals of religion and, 211–12n4; limitations of, 52–53, 55; rights movements of, 55; ritual as re-

jected by, 36, 138, 145, 151, 209n7. *See also* modernism
liberty, 211n29
Light, Andrew, 120, 223n39
liminality, 149–50, 151, 177, 184–85
limitation and difference: category violation and, 139–42; children's literature and, 49; communion and, 60–62; Emersonian thought and, 59–60; environmental thinkers and denial of shame of, 145; existential shame and, 46–47, 48, 123, 137–46; of infants, 51; nature and, 133–34; race and social status, 144–45; shortcoming and shame of, 49; territoriality and, 142–44, 145–46, 148. *See also* boundaries; change
literature: children's, and existential shame, 49; comedy and picaresque in, 165–68; initiation rituals in, 168
Lo, Yeuk-Sze, 225n46
loneliness, as theme, 63
Lorenz, Konrad, 142–44, 146, 227–28n17
love, aggressive behavior and, 142–44, 148, 227–28n17

Machado, Antonio, 61
MacIntyre, Alasdair, 52
Madison, WI. *See* Arboretum (University of Wisconsin at Madison)
Mahler, David, 112
make-believe. *See* imagination
Malaysia, 141
management, as term, 25–26. *See also* restoration
Mann, Thomas, 166
Marble Faun, The (Hawthorne), 65
Marduk, 172
marine ecosystems, 11, 97, 98, 99. *See also* aquatic ecosystems; wetland restoration
marshes. *See* wetland restoration
Marx, Leo: on pastoral literature, 177, 178, 179, 181, 183–84, 185; on Puritans, 180; on Thoreau, 157, 158, 180, 182–83
masculine, mechanistic ecology and, 82
Mass: communion, 148–49; fortunate fall and, 70; performative elements in, 186; sacrifice and, 53, 215n26, 231n10; Thoreau's transforming ritual and, 156. *See also* Christianity

mating rituals, 142–44, 148
Mattole River, 165
Mauss, Marcel, 66–69
McCloskey, David, 44
McHenry County (IL) Conservation District, 170
McSweeney, Kevin, 114
meaning making: agriculture and, 155–56; community and the other and, 43; definition of restoration and, 23–24, 25, 207n11; nature/culture distinction and, 118–19; and performance, restoration as, 164, 189–91; preservation and, 119–20; ritual commutation and, 148–49. See also value of restoration; values
Meeker, Joseph, 166, 167
Melville, Herman: community and, 44; on monstrous principle, 64, 65, 214n24; and pastoral, 181
Memorial Ecosystems, 199
Memory, party of, 57–58
Merchant, Carolyn, 228n23
Merleau-Ponty, Maurice, 121, 224n40
Merton, Thomas, 213n18
Michael, Mark, 209n13
Michigan, 76
middle landscape, 177, 178, 179, 183–84, 197
Midsummer Night's Dream, A (Shakespeare), 180–81
Midwest. See oak savannas; prairies
milkweeds, 76, 135–36
Miller, Mike, 173
Miller, Wilhelm, 87
mimesis, 92
minimal consumption ethic, 38, 41, 71–72
mining, surface, 130–31
Minnesota, 222n26
mitigation, legal: success of projects and, 175–76; as window dressing, 99
Moby Dick (Melville): community and, 44; monstrous element and, 65, 214n24; as pastoral, 181
modernism: arts as alienated in, 192; idealization of classic landscape and, 41; monstrous and, 214n24, 228n20; mystery of human relationship with nature and, 195; ontology of, 118–21, 123–24; ritual denoted by, 36, 138, 147–48, 151–53, 186, 209n7; shame and guilt conflated in, 59; subjective re-

sults of restoration and, 174–77; as unfriendly to community, 55
modern primitive in pastoral, 185
monarch butterflies, 76
monstrous principle in creation: denial of, 37–40, 45–46; Ironists and, 64–65; karma as term and, 228n20; modernism and, 214n24, 228n20; mythology and, 60, 146–47; reality of, 37, 39, 196; Thoreau and, 214n24; traditional and premodern cultures and, 60, 146–47, 228n23. See also creation; killing; shame
morality: rights movements and, 55; ritual and, 150–51. See also ethics; values
Morrison, Darrel, 205n3
Muir, John: communion with nature of, 154–55, 158–59, 230n38; misperception of California by, 200; nature as sacred and, 29, 152; Protestantism as influence on, 151–52; withdrawal from community and, 44
Mumford, Lewis, 196
mythology: creation and origin in, 40–41, 45; discovery of ritual in, 138–39; monstrous as validated by, 60, 146–47; pride and presumption in, 94–95; tragedy and comedy and, 166–67. See also religion; traditional and premodern cultures

Nash, Roderick, and rights of nature, 55
nationalism and ritual, 151, 187
national parks policy, 161–62
Native Americans: bison and, 115; burning of prairies by, 130; community and individual among, 180; Crazy Horse statue and, 131; creation stories of, 47–48, 146–47, 228n23; flood myths of, 171; gift exchange among, 68; on good and evil, 128; innocence imputed to, 179; Muir and marginalization of, 154, 200; reproductions and, 225n46; role of, in environment, 83, 130. See also traditional and premodern cultures
nature: imitation of, by restorationists, 92–93; as irreplaceable, 2, 97, 201; mythology and, 40–41; as subject vs. object, 225n46; as term, 123; utilitarian view of, 28–29. See also commun-

ion with nature; community of humans and nature; human regard for
landscape; monstrous principle in creation; nature/culture distinction; restoration; sacred, landscape as
Nature Conservancy, 135, 226n55
nature/culture distinction: avoidance of
monstrous and, 45; category violation
and, 127–28, 140–42; cultures not
sharing the, 140–42; meaning making
and, 118–19; pastoral and, 177; restorationists as rejecting, 125; sacralization
and, 141–42. *See also* community of
humans and nature
Nature's Economy (Worster), 81–82
Navajo people, 47–48, 225n46
Ndembu people, 141
neopaganism, 45, 46, 152
neoteny, 171
New England, and American chestnut,
102–3, 220n9. *See also* puritanism
Newfield, Christopher, 212–13n6
Nippersink Creek, IL, 12
nitrogen, increasing inputs of, 99
nonanthropocentrism, 140–42
noncreativity: restoration as, 24, 93; ritual
and, 151
nonhuman species. *See* species, nonhuman
non-Western cultures. *See* Native Americans; traditional and premodern cultures
Norden, Chris, 175
Norris, Kathleen, 150
North Branch Prairie Restoration Project
(Chicago), 133
North Park Village Nature Center (Chicago), 193
nostalgia, 50, 83, 202. *See also* sentimentality
numinous, 122

oaks: fire suppression and, 107; succession
trends and, 112
oak savannas: defined, 106; as endangered
ecosystem, 135–36, 226n55; historic information on, as limited, 105–6; restoration of, 77, 87, 111–12, 135–36
obligations, acceptance of, 170, 191
observation: environmental thinkers and,
75; participation vs., 91–94; Thoreau
and, 91–92
Oelschlaeger, Max, 183

Old Torlino, 47–48
ontology and restoration: archaic, 121–22;
as issue, 117–18; modernist (autonomy), 118–21, 123–24; performative
(relationship), 121–28
Oregon, 98–99
origin. *See* creation
original sin: Emersonian thought and, 40,
57, 58; as metaphor in nineteenth-
century literature, 57. *See also* Fall
(from Garden of Eden); redemption
Ortega y Gasset, José, 90
other, the: alchemy and awareness of, 78;
achieving awareness of, 51, 74; community exclusion and, 43; consumption of, 38; landscape as, and value of
restoration, 117, 118–28; nonanthropocentric cultures and, 141; perception of, 75–76; persistence of, 61–62;
restoration and awareness of, 72,
74–75; self-realization and, 149; tragedy and, 166–67. *See also* ambiguity;
economics; gift exchange; shame
Oxenhandler, Noelle, 77–78

Pacific Northwest: creation stories of, 147;
gift exchange in, 68; salmon restoration in, 115; wetland restoration in,
98–99
Packard, Steve, 77, 87, 111–12, 135–36
paganism, 45, 46, 152
pair bond, 142–43, 148
Palmiter, George, 110–11
pangolin cult, 126–27, 141
Panzer, Ron, 77
Parker, Theodore, 65–66
Partridge, Eric, 211–12n4, 224n41
pastoral literature, 177–85
Paz, Octavio, 63, 126
peat, 103
Penobscot people, 228n23
performance: ethic based on etiquette and,
225n46; function of, 138; gift exchange
as, 68; knowledge and, 93–94; as language, 51; as necessary to creation of
values, 4, 5–6, 48–49, 145, 148–49, 186,
196; the other and, 149; personal experience vs., 150; restoration as, 19, 20,
49–50, 52, 160–64; Thoreau and Muir
and, comparison of, 154–59. *See also*
art; imagination; ritual

performance, restoration as: accessibility as concern in, 192–93; audience and, 162, 164, 191, 193; author's realization of, 19–20, 49–50, 160–65; Christian sacraments and, 192; comedy and festival and, 165–68, 177, 189–90; controversiality and, 187–88; creativity and, 185–87; criticism and evaluation of, 193; genres paralleled by, generally, 165, 192; and holidays and celebrations, traditional, 192; illusion and, 161–62, 164; initiation rituals and, 168–71; intensity, degrees of, 194, 198; and pastoral genre, 177–85; practice of restoration and, 50, 190–91; and romance genre, 231–32n11; and sacrifice, world renewal through, 171–74, 176, 188–89; silence and, 193; subjective results of, 174–77, 190; tragedy and, 166–68, 177

performative ontology, 121–28

personality, 143

Piaget, Jean, 51, 74

picaresque genre, 166–68

Pickett, Steward, 84

Pickstock, Catherine, 142, 186

Pimm, Stuart, 104

pines, 15–16, 112, 113

Plains Indians, 83, 115

plants. See exotic species; reintroduction of species; species, nonhuman

Plato, 47, 128

play, seriousness of, 190

poetry, 167, 183

politics, skepticism about restoration and, 17. See also economics; skepticism about restoration

ponderosa forests, fire suppression and, 15–16, 113

Popper, Deborah, 115

Popper, Frank, 115

postcard ("snapshot") projects, 17, 21, 84, 100, 206n6

postmodernism, performative ontology and, 124

potlatch, 68

pragmatism, Calvinism and, 212n6

prairie dogs, 98

prairies: beauty of, 86; complexity and, 97–98; defects in restoration of, 79–81; erosion control via, 115; as exemplary restoration sites, 26, 207n13; and fire, 10, 16, 80, 85–86, 107, 189–90; nitrogen inputs and, 99; "real" vs. restored as research site, 18–19; scale and, 109, 110, 112–13, 222n26; severity of disturbance and, 98; soil regeneration and, 114–15, 173; soil type and, 99; successional restoration of, 111–13; vegetation dynamics of, 81, 111–13

prayer, 77–78, 150

precipitation, 81

predator and prey relationships, 36, 189. See also hunting and gathering

premodern societies. See Native Americans; traditional and premodern cultures

preservation: as destructive, 15–16, 29; as impossible, 14, 23; management as necessary to, 14–15, 130, 161–62, 205n2; meaning making and, 119–20; new paradigm of restoration and, 201; scale and, 108, 109–10; skepticism about restoration and desire for, 2, 200–201

presumptuousness of restoration, 17, 94–95

prey and predator relationships, 36, 189. See also hunting and gathering

primitivism: biblical creation story and, 60; defined, 54; modern, pastorals and, 185; monstrous in nature and, 40, 45–46

privilege. See hierarchy and inequality

Prometheus, 94–95, 138–39

Protestantism: as influence on environmental thought, 58, 145, 151–53, 212n6, 229–30n37; redemption and, 57–58. See also puritanism

psychology: and community inclusion, 43; and shame, 41

puritanism: community and, 212n6; individualism and, 153, 180, 181, 212n6; redemption and, 57–58, 212n6; ritual and, 152–53, 154, 229–30n37; use of term, 229n37

Purity and Danger (Douglas), 126–28

quality of restoration: choice of evaluation sites and, 96–97, 101; complexity of ecosystem and, 97–98, 100, 219n1;

continued input of pollutants or nutrients and, 99; economics and, 102,
113–16; epistemological limits and,
106–7; evaluation of quality, 101–2;
functional attributes and, 100–101;
historical information and, 103, 105–6;
human regard for landscape and, 116;
irreversible changes and, 102–5; relationships as critical to, 100; scale and,
107–13; severity and nature of disturbance and, 98–99; techniques used
and, 99, 109–13; unknown factors
and, 99–100. *See also* value of restoration
Queen Salmon, 165

race and racism, 144–45, 148
radical incompetence. *See* limitation and
difference
radical innocence, 168–69
Radin, Paul, 128
Rappaport, Roy: on insincerity, 68; on
postmodern science, 217n15; on ritual,
61, 122, 138, 148, 150–51, 163–64, 191
reaggregation phase, 177
reality, construction of: category violation
and, 126–27; pre- and postmodern
understanding of, 124; values creation
and, 201–2
realness. *See* authenticity
Rebel Without a Cause, 232n13
reclamation: mining and, 130–31, 205n3; as
term, 23
reconciliation, 183–84
recreation: as consumptive activity, 180,
198, 199; restoration paradigm and,
197–200; as ritual of engagement, 192
redemption: agriculture and, 88–89;
"American religion" and, 62; Christ as
sacrifice and, 172; cultural evolution
and, 167; definition of, 57; Emersonians and, 58–64; imagination and,
154–59; Ironists and, 64–71; Mass on
the world and, 53; Prometheus and,
95; puritanism and, 57–58, 212n6; restoration as, 53, 72, 88–89, 167; wilderness in cities and, 179. *See also* communion with nature; religion
redress, stage of, 163
Reformation, 153
rehabilitation, as term, 22–23, 221n18

Rehmann, Elsa, 87
Reichel-Dolmatoff, Gerardo, 140
reintroduction of species, 11–12; complexity and, 97–98; human self-
understanding and, 86; husbandry
and, 87; successional restoration and,
111–12; vs. return of species, 97–98,
100. *See also* creation; species, nonhuman
relationships: as critical to restoration,
100; development of, 120, 202,
223n39; ritual as crucial to, 149–50,
162–63; sentimentality and, 70,
215–16n34; social dramas, 163; and
value of restoration, 132–33. *See also*
community; community of humans
and nature; human regard for landscape
religion: "American," 62–63, 213–14n18;
authority and, 140; community as
value and, 36–37; and ego, setting
aside of, 61, 75–76; environmentalism
and traditional, 62; grace, 56, 77, 174;
human impact and need for, 41;
nonanthropocentrism and, 140–41;
reproduction and, 224–25n46; the sacred in, 42; sacrifice and, 53, 56,
138–39, 231n10; shamanism, 56, 140;
task of environmentalism as one of,
55–57; as term, 56, 211–12n4; value creation and, 52; wealth and, 149. *See also*
Christianity; mythology; puritanism;
redemption; sacredness; traditional
and premodern cultures
reproduction of ecosystems: art analogy
and, 119, 125–26, 129–30, 224–25n46;
authenticity controversies and,
118–20, 123; existential shame and, 123,
187; testing of, 76
Republic (Plato), 128
research. *See* science and research
resources, nature as, 28–29
responsibility, acceptance of, 170, 191
restoration: agriculture, as form of, 87–89;
arguments for, 50; beauty of landscape discovered through, 86–87;
communal practice of, 181–82; congregations of people for, 202; definition of, 21–26, 206nn5,6,7,9; as dialogue, 77–78; evaluation of (*see*
evaluation of restoration); general

restoration (*continued*)
process of, 11–13; healing distinguished from, 23, 206n9; heuristic value of, 79–84; human self-understanding and, 85–86; hunting and gathering, as form of, 89–90; as illusion, 161–62, 164; language and, 25, 207n11; limitations of, 3; as "luxury," 24–25; mitigation, legal, 174–77; as noncreative, 24; as paradigm, 26–27, 195–204; as performing art (*see* performance, restoration as); as positive factor, 2–4; precedents for, 26, 207n13; presumptuousness of, 17, 94–95; quality of (*see* quality of restoration); questions raised by, 19–21; restorative practices distinguished from, 22–23; as ritual (*see* performance, restoration as); scale and (*see* scale); shame and (*see* shame); skepticism about (*see* skepticism about restoration); "snapshot," 17, 21, 84, 100, 206n6; subjective results of, 174–77, 190; survival of ecosystems dependent on, 13–17; techniques of (*see* techniques of restoration); as term, 84; value of (*see* value of restoration); wisdom of letting it be, 77–78. *See also* community of humans and nature; human regard for landscape; land ethic

restoration ecology, as term, 19, 206n5

restorationists: alchemy and, 78; as participants vs. observers, 91–94; perception and perspective of, 106–7, 221n17; self-abnegation of, 125; subjective results of restoration and, 174–77

restorative practices distinguished from restoration, 22–23

restore, as term, 84

resurrection. *See* redemption

Reuther, Rosemary, on compassion, 61

Rieger, John, 101

rights movements, nature and, 55

Rights of Nature, The (Nash), 55

Rilke, Rainer Maria, 50

riparian areas. *See* rivers

Rites of Passage (Gennep), 142

ritual: act of killing and, 38, 53; borrowing traditions of, 191–92; chaos ordered into cosmos through, 122, 124; *communitas* and, 150, 151, 169–70, 229n29; commutation of, 148–49; creation of, 5–6, 185–87, 191–92; desire and intention in, 138–39; discovery of, mythology and, 138–39; etiquette, 149, 164, 193, 198, 225n46; function of, 138, 186; hunting and, 53, 139, 140–41, 189; initiation (*see* initiation rituals); importance of, 174, 210n22; leadership and creation of, 191; liminality and, 149–50, 151, 177, 184–85; loss of control of, 186–87; mating, 142–44, 148; modernist demotion of, 36, 138, 147–48, 151–53, 186, 209n7; as necessary to value creation, 4, 5–6, 48–49, 145, 148–49, 186, 196; in nonhuman species, 142–44; as paradigm of creation, 163–64; Protestantism and demotion of, 151–53, 229–30n37; reproduction and, 224–25n46; responsibility and, 170, 191; sacrifice (*see* sacrifice); self-awareness and, 149–50; self-critical component of, 193; social change and, 151; social harmony achieved through, 35–36; as symbolic context, 182, 187; Victor and Edith Turner, and study of, 162; violation of categories and, 126–27. *See also* performance

rivers: complexity and, 98; meanders restored to, 12; solar energy use in restoration, 110–11; spawning habitat restoration, 115. *See also* aquatic ecosystems; wetland restoration

Robin Hood, 180

Rodman, John, 188

Rodriguez, Karen, 133

Róheim, Géza, 170

roll-vortex strips, 76–77

romance, 231–32n11

Rosen, Walter, 171

Roszak, Theodore, 20

"Round River, The" (Leopold), 174

Sacramento River, CA, 116

sacred, landscape as: Calvinist thought and, 58, 152; community idealized in, 33; humans as negative factor in, 2, 29; ritual exchange and, 139

sacred and profane, as categories, 142

sacredness: category violation and, 127–28, 139–42; discovery of vs. active creation of, 42, 56; ritual creation of, 121–22; science and, 128–29. *See also* communion

sacrifice: agricultural societies and, 39, 53, 88, 139; category violations and, 127; discovery of ritual, 138–39; function of, 36, 88, 171; grace and, 174; as reenactment of primordial murder, 40, 45, 147, 171–72; religion and, 53, 56, 138–39, 215n26, 231n10; restoration as ritual performance and, 171–74, 176, 188–89; symbolic, 148–49. *See also* monstrous principle in creation; ritual

salmon restoration, 115, 165

Salmon River, OR, 98–99

Sand County Almanac, A (Leopold): as canonic, 31; withdrawal from community and, 44

San Diego, CA, 101

Sartre, Jean-Paul, 46

scale: economy of, 110; horticultural, 25, 107; logarithmic increase of, 113; quality of restoration and, 107–13; "restoration" as term and, 25–26

Scarlet Letter, The (Hawthorne), 65

Schiamberg, Scott, 178

Schulenberg, Ray, 26

science and research: defectiveness of restorations and, 79–81; new frontiers of shame and, 168; "real" vs. restored as site of, 18–19; value of restoration to, 128–29, 136

Sedna and Anguta story, 146–47

seed-into-sod method, 111–12, 135–36

seeds, harvesting and dispersal of, 11, 76–77, 113, 193

self: hope and, 64; performative interaction with the other and, 149. *See also* ego; initiation rituals

self, relational: existential shame and, 48; gift exchange and, 67, 68; Leopold, Aldo and, 37, 43

self-awareness of evolution and nature, 133–34

self-sacrifice: American discomfort with, 214n18; initiation rituals and, 169–70

sentimentality: existential shame and, 210–11n24, 216n34; pastoral and, 177, 185; relationships and, 70, 215–16n34; restoration and, 83, 187. *See also* nostalgia

separation phase, 177

sexual reproduction, 134

Shakespeare, William, 71, 180–81, 215n30

shamanism, 56, 140

shame: avoidance of, 72; category violation and, 139–42; change and, 139, 146–48, 228n19; children and, 49; evolution and, 60; existential, 46–47, 210n22; gift exchange and, 69, 137–39, 149; guilt conflated with, 60, 147, 152; guilt distinguished from, 46–47, 147, 210n22; intensification of, 39–40; limitation and difference and, 46–47, 48, 123, 137–46; new frontiers of, 167–68; reproduction and, 123; restoration as encounter with, 50, 172, 187–88; sacrifice as addressing, 39, 172–73, 232n21; sacrifice in restoration and, 172; territorialism and, 142–44, 145–46; transcendence of, 48–49, 137–51, 156–59; as universal, 47–48, 211n29, 228n23; values conception and, 128. *See also* monstrous principle in creation; performance; ritual; shame, denial of

shame, denial of: beauty as precluded by, 210–11n24; by environmental thinkers, 40, 41, 43, 46, 145–46, 153, 154–55, 230n38; as violence, 189; as Western habit, 47; and "world of wounds," 174

Shepard, Paul, 45, 167

Shinto shrines, 224–25n46

shit, existential shame and, 210–11n24

Sierra Club, 197

silence, in restoration groups, 193

Simmons, Ossian Cole, 87

Simpson, Dave, 72

sin. *See* original sin

skepticism about restoration, 16–17, 19–21, 196; authenticity issues, 96; economics and, 17, 24–25, 131–32; exotic species problem and, 103; history problem and, 17, 24; as mistake, 17; politics and, 17; preservation issues, 2, 200–201; presumptuousness issue, 17, 94–95; and ritual, 174–75; scale and, 108; static vs. dynamic goals, 84

Smith, Jonathan Z., 39

"snapshot" restoration goals, 17, 21, 84, 100, 206n6

Snyder, Gary, 45, 167

social dramas, 163

sociology, hierarchy in communities and, 34, 44

Socrates, denial of shame and, 47

soil: erosion of, 115, 156–58; regeneration of, 114–15, 173; type of, restoration quality and, 99

solar energy in restoration, 110–11

solidarity, 66–68

Southwest (U.S.), fire suppression and, 15–16, 113

species, nonhuman: arts and communion with, 182; companion animals, communion and, 70, 216n34; conservation movement and devaluing of, 29; domestication of, 39, 154; endangered, 101; extinct, 102–3, 104, 134, 220n9; habitat creation and restoration, 115; husbandry of, restoration and, 87; intelligence of, 214n24; moral and ethical relationship with, 30, 32; return of animals, vs. reintroduction, 97–98, 100; rights activists and, 189; territorial behavior of animals, 142–44, 148. See also community of humans and nature; exotic species; human beings; reintroduction of species

Sperry, Ted, 80

spirituality: ego and, 61; human impact and need for, 41. See also religion

sports. See recreation

stability, vow of, 179

Starhawk, 45

Steere, John, 133

stewardship, as term, 25–26. See also restoration

Still, Alexander, 224n46

strip-mining, 130–31

structural issues in restoration, 103, 104

subjectivity, 212n6, 213–14n18; and restoration results, 174–77

succession, ecological, 103–4

successional restoration, 111–13

suffering, shame and, 47, 210n22

"sunflower forest" (Eiseley), 54

symbolic context: reconciliation and, 183–84; ritual as providing, 182, 187; sacrifice and, 148–49; wilderness and, 155, 158–59, 202–3

synthetic ecology, as term, 19, 206n5. See also restoration ecology

tamarisk, 188

Taming of the Shrew, The (Shakespeare), 215n30

techniques of restoration: expected improvement of, 116; prairie as intercrop, 114–15, 173, 197; quality and, 99, 109–13; ritual of restoration and, 190; seed harvesting and dispersal, 11, 113, 193; seed-into-sod methods, 111–12, 135–36; solar energy use, 110–11; successional restoration, 111–13

technology, 164; and value creation, 39

Teilhard de Chardin, Pierre, and Mass on the world, 53

television, 187

territorialism, 142–44, 145–46, 148

Texas, succession trends and, 112

theater. See performance

Thoreau, Henry David: on agriculture, 91–92, 155–56, 218n22; communion with nature of, 154, 155–59, 182–83, 202–3, 230n43; and killing, 45; and language, 92; on the monstrous, 214n24; pastoral and, 180, 181; on redemption of nature, 188; withdrawal from community and, 44, 58, 59

Tiamat, 172

tides, 97

time, 50, 84, 98. See also change

time-style, 106–7

Tönnies, Ferdinand, 42

traditional and premodern cultures: anthropocentrism and, 140–42; archaic ontology of, 121–22; community vs. individual among, 180; creation stories of, 47–48, 60, 146–47, 228n23; egalitarianism and, 34–35; flood myths of, 172; gift exchange in, 68; good and evil in, 128; initiation rituals of (see initiation rituals); innocence of, 179; Muir and marginalization of, 154, 200; performative ontology and, 124; reproductions viewed by, 225n46; role of, in ecology, 83, 130; romanticization of, 72; sacrificial rituals of (see sacrifice); shame as universal and, 47–48, 60, 228n23; totem animals, 115; world renewal rituals of (see world renewal). See also mythology; Native Americans; religion

tragedy, 166–68, 177

trampling, 10, 131

transubstantiation, 148–49, 152, 156; redemptive imagination and, 154–59. *See
also* redemption

trickster figure, 167

tropical forests, complexity and, 98

Trow, George, 187

Turner, Alex, 228n20

Turner, Edith, 5, 46, 162

Turner, Frederick, 5, 162; beauty as obsolete, 52; "blessing" as term, 174; creation myths, 146, 147; death and
nature, 216n35; gardening as performance, 160–61; *Genesis* poem of,
203–4; gift exchange, 69; juventocracy, 171; make-believe, 175; mating rituals, 143; performed being, 122–23,
224n40; ritual commutation, 148; ritual sacrifice, 138, 171; shame as universal, 46, 49, 146; stability vs. beauty,
69; transcendence of shame, 48–49,
150, 195

Turner, Victor, 46, 162; anti-structure,
232n18; *communitas,* 149–50, 229n29;
creativity of ritual, 151; expressive action, 141–42; making the obligatory
desirable, 4, 149; phases of ritual process, 177; relationship and ritual, 162,
163; self-critical component of ritual,
193; seriousness of play, 190; social
dramas, 163

Twain, Mark. *See Adventures of Huckleberry
Finn* (Twain)

"Two Kinds of Liberty" (Berlin), 211n29

Ukeles, Mierle, 234n46

Unbearable Lightness of Being, The (Kundera), 210n24

underground component of ecosystems:
irreversible change in, 103; as poorly
understood, 99, 100

unity: *communitas* as, 150; Emersonian
thought and, 59–60

University of Wisconsin at Madison. *See*
Arboretum (University of Wisconsin
at Madison)

unworthiness, radical, 46–47, 210n22. *See
also* shame

urban environments, valuing of nature
within, 159, 179, 199–200

use: exploitation vs., 41–42, 209n13; restoration as solving dilemma of, 16

utilitarian relationship to landscape, 28–29

value of restoration, 117; authenticity as
issue in, 117–28; beauty and, 129–30;
community and, 51–53; definition of
who we are, 85–87; ecological immortality, 134–36; economic value, 131–33;
evolutionary value, 133–34; ghosts
and, 105, 117, 125–26; as gift, 96, 133;
historic value, 130–31; human relationship to landscape and, 132–33;
quality and (*see* quality of restoration); scientific value, 128–29, 136;
skepticism about (*see* skepticism about
restoration)

values: advertising and, 187, 230n43;
change in, difficulty of, 38, 43; community as, difficulty of, 36–37; of land
ethic, 30, 32, 33; performance as necessary to creation of, 4, 5–6, 48–49, 145,
148–49, 186, 196; positive vs. negative
feelings and, 128; postvalue society,
52; religion and creation of, 52–53; restoration as creating, 19, 201–2; ritual
in creation of, 186; shame and creation of, 4–6, 48–49, 137–51; technology of creation of, 4–6. *See also* ethics

vegetation. *See* exotic species; reintroduction of species; species, nonhuman

Vegetation of Wisconsin, The (Curtis), 135

Vico, Giambattista, on maker's knowledge, 93–94

violence, human vs. natural, 60. *See also*
aggressive behavior; killing

voluntarism: gift exchange and, 67–68; importance of, 113; recreation and, 198,
199–200; value of restoration and,
132–33; vs. professionally run projects,
13, 207n13

"Volunteer Revegetation Saturday" (Goulder), 89

Walbiri people, 160, 170

Walcott, Derek, 133

Walden (Thoreau): agriculture and, 91–92,
155–56, 218n22; as pastoral, 180, 181;
redemptive imagination and, 155–59;
symbolic wilderness and, 155, 158–59;
withdrawal from community and, 44

water pollution, human self-understanding and, 86
wealth, 149, 187
Weaver, John, 114
weddings, 198
Weil, Simone, 77–78
Welch, James, 175, 176
Wendt, Keith, 18, 19, 206n5
Westfall, Barbara, 172–73, 188, 232n21
Weston, Anthony, 225n46
wetland restoration: breaking up drain fields, 12, 77, 86; cattle removal and, 98–99; complexity and, 97–98, 100; economics and, 116; evaluation of quality, 101; irreversible change in, 103; severity of disturbance and, 98–99; species reintroduction, 11, 97
White, E. B., 49
White, Richard, work and relationship with nature, 78
Whitman, Walt: and language, 218n30; and loneliness, 63; rejection of civilization and, 58
Wild Earth, 201
wilderness: as construct, 201–2; consumption pressures on, 159, 179–80, 197–200; literal, 154, 155, 158, 159, 179; management as required for, 14–15; new paradigm for, 200, 201–2; symbolic, 155, 158–59, 202–3
wildflowers, exotic species and, 103
Wildlands Project, 201
Wilson, E. O., 4, 145–46
Winnebago (Ho-Chunk) people, 128
Winter in the Blood (Welch), 175
Wisconsin. See Arboretum (University of Wisconsin at Madison)
Woods, Brock, 19
world renewal: apocalyptic thinking and, 232n19; Australian Aborigines and, 160, 176, 203; new paradigm of restoration and, 198–99; restoration as unconscious, 160; and sacrifice in restoration, 171–74, 176, 188–89; subjective results of, 174–75
Worster, Donald: ecology as healing art, 81–82; on Protestantism, 151–52, 153; on Thoreau as observer, 91

Zaire, 126–27
Zedler, Joy, 101
Zeus, 95, 139
Zuesse, Evan, 227n8

Indexer: Victoria Baker
Compositor: Binghamton Valley Composition, LLC
Text: 10/13 Galliard
Display: Galliard
Printer and binder: Friesens Corporation

DATE DUE

GAYLORD

PRINTED IN U.S.A.